Social work, social care and
social planning: the personal
social services since Seebohm

SOCIAL POLICY IN MODERN BRITAIN

General Editor: Jo Campling

SOCIAL WORK, SOCIAL CARE AND SOCIAL PLANNING: THE PERSONAL SOCIAL SERVICES SINCE SEEBOHM

Adrian Webb and Gerald Wistow

LONGMAN
London and New York

LONGMAN GROUP UK LIMITED
Longman House, Burnt Mill, Harlow
Essex CM20 2JE, England
Associated companies throughout the world

*Published in the United States of America
by Longman Inc., New York*

First published 1987

BRITISH LIBRARY CATALOGUING IN PUBLICATION DATA
Webb, Adrian
  Social work, social care and social planning: the personal social services
  since Seebohm. —— (Social policy in modern Britain)
  1. Public welfare —— Great Britain —— History —— 20th century
  I. Title   II. Wistow, Gerald   III. Series
  361'.941   HV245

ISBN 0-582-29601-3

LIBRARY OF CONGRESS CATALOGING IN PUBLICATION DATA
Webb, Adrian Leonard.
  Social work, social care and social planning.
  (Social policy in modern Britain)
  Bibliography: p.
  Includes index.
  1. Social service —— England.   2. Social service —— Wales.
  3. England —— Social policy.   4. Wales —— Social policy.
  I. Wistow, Gerald, 1946- .   II. Title.   III. Series.
  HV249.E89W43 1987   361.6'1'0942   86-10325
  ISBN 0-582-29601-3

Set in 10/11 pt Plantin Comp/Edit 6400
Produced by Longman Singapore Publishers (Pte) Ltd.
Printed in Singapore.

CONTENTS

EDITOR'S PREFACE

This series, written by practising teachers in universities and polytechnics, is produced for students who are required to study social policy and administration, either as social science undergraduates or on the various professional courses. The books provide studies focusing on essential topics in social policy and include new areas of discussion and research, to give students the opportunity to explore ideas and act as a basis of seminar work and further study. Each book combines an analysis of the selected theme, a critical narrative of the main developments and an assessment putting the topic into perspective as defined in the title. The supporting documents and comprehensive bibliography are an important aspect of the series.

Conventional footnotes are avoided and the following system of references is used. A superior numeral in the text refers the reader to the corresponding entry in the list of references at the end of each chapter. A select bibliography is found at the end of the book. A number in square brackets, preceded by 'doc.', e.g. [doc. 6, 8] refers the reader to the corresponding items in the section of documents which follows the main text.

The restructuring and consolidation of the personal social services in the early 1970s was one of the last confident acts of the post-war era of consensual social policy. In the late 1960s the Seebohm Committee laid down a blueprint for the development of these services, but even in doing so its approach partly prefigured the uncertainty which has subsequently surrounded state social services. Seebohm was cautious about the problem of resources and less than clear-cut about the question of objectives. The history of the personal social services since Seebohm has been a turbulent one: questions have proliferated. This textbook has therefore been specifically designed to provide a framework within which to examine current issues and unravel the complex inheritance of these services. The book is an analytical text rather than a merely factual one. The essential nature of the personal social services is highlighted by emphasising some of the key dilemmas which they pose:

1. what are, and should be, the functions, roles and tasks of the personal social services?
2. what weight should be attached to social work, to social care and to social planning; how can they be made effective – individually and in concert?
3. what is and should be the relationship of social work to the personal social services?
4. what are the respective roles of the state, voluntary, private and informal sectors and how are they changing?
5. to whom should social workers and others be responsible and accountable and what is implied for organisational structures and management processes?
6. what impact does central government have on local social services departments and other bodies – and how?
7. is there really a shortage of resources in the personal social services or are resources simply used inappropriately?
8. have there been 'real cuts' or merely 'cuts in growth'?
9. does it make sense for ministers to cast social services departments in an 'enabling role'?

In order to provide a unique introduction to the personal social services, the authors have continuously blended these questions with a historical perspective so as to locate contemporary concerns and developments within the assumptions, attitudes and constraints inherited from the formative period of the 1960s and early 1970s. Discussion of this inheritance, and its implications, is not confined to one or two 'historical' chapters, it is an integral part of the analytical approach taken to the services and their development.

The book will stimulate all who are interested in and concerned with the personal social services to ask questions: experienced practitioners, senior managers and policy-makers will benefit as much as under-graduates and social-work students. But questions demand answers. On topics where the authors are particularly well qualified by reason of their empirical research, the answers are as authoritative as is possible. For example, the unravelling of policy processes between central and local government offers a strong base from which to pursue the details of the complex field of administrative politics. The examination of trends in resources provides as definitive an illustration as is currently possible of the scale and nature of the 'cuts' which have affected the personal social services.

On many issues, however, 'answers' cannot be definitive, or based primarily on empirical evidence; they are a matter of judgement and of the view of the world adopted by the observer. The approach to such issues adopted in this book is to clarify their main dimensions and features, to identify key concepts underlying debate and to establish a framework from which the reader can explore both evidence and opinion more fully. The book is a contribution to debate as well as the most up-to-date introduction to the personal social services in England and Wales.

Jo Campling

AUTHORS' PREFACE

The personal social services as we now know them were the creation of a period of sustained concern and pressure for reform in the 1960s. They came into their own in the 1970s as Social Services Departments in England and Wales and Social Work Departments in Scotland began to pull together the previously scattered elements of statutory social work. But the personal social services are more than that implies: they involve much activity outside the state social services and they are not synonymous with social work. These are two of the principal themes of this book. Trends in policy and resources and the problematic nature of management and organisation are others. The argument which runs throughout the book is that the personal social services are faced with the difficult problem of combining social work, social care and social planning in responsive and fruitful ways. It is a problem which has not been adequately resolved; it is also a problem to which there will never be a simple or unequivocally correct answer.

Adrian Webb
Gerald Wistow

ACKNOWLEDGEMENTS

This book draws on two bodies of experience, both of which involve countless debts. One of us (Adrian Webb) has been teaching courses in various aspects of the personal social services since the late 1960s. Colleagues and students at the London School of Economics and at Loughborough University of Technology have helped sharpen and winnow ideas over these years; their contribution is incalculable. The same is true of the many people involved in the development of the Personal Social Services Council in its first years (it was created in 1973, but abolished by the first Thatcher Administration in 1979). These influences are most especially strong in the first seven chapters.

Since 1979, however, we have been jointly engaged in the difficult but rewarding task of building a research centre within the Department of Social Sciences at Loughborough during a lean period for social science research. The Centre for Research in Social Policy now consists of ten full-time researchers and a large part of the Centre's work is in the personal social services field – broadly defined. The development of this research programme has contributed enormously to the structure and content of this book. Colleagues in the Centre have shaped our joint work and thinking, but so too have the very many practitioners in the field who have assisted in and commented on our work. We gladly acknowledge our debt; we also ruefully note that the development of this research programme turned what was intended as a rapid and concentrated piece of writing into a greatly extended exercise. We have had to become expert at writing in those brief spells which can be wrested from the constant flow of demands, crises and entrepreneurial ventures which academic life has become. Our debt to Jo Campling is therefore a very large one: she has harried and cajoled within a framework of patient understanding and continual support. No author could ask more of an editor.

Although the results of our research projects are not reported in this volume, our themes and ideas do reflect the many contacts we have developed through our empirical research. Countless social workers, managers, civil servants and members of local authorities, health authorities and voluntary bodies have been interviewed in recent years and many have helped us over extended periods. It is obvious that empirical research could not survive without such willing and often enthusiastic collaboration. It is less obvious that text books of this kind can also owe much to such collaboration. For this same reason we should like to acknowledge the generous financial support of the organisations which funded those research projects which most influenced the writing of this book: the Nuffield Foundation, the Joseph Rowntree Memorial Trust and the Economic and Social Research Council.

Our families have borne the usual brunt, though – like us – they have no idea how much this book has added to the demands on our time and how much it has provided a welcome long-term goal. Secretarial staff have no doubts on this score! Our debt to all the secretaries in the Department of Social Sciences is enormous, but especially so in the case of Lorraine Jones, Lynn Payne and Joanne Hibbert. We, of course, accept responsibility for all errors and infelicities.

We must finally acknowledge the kind permission of the following to reproduce copyright material:

George Allen & Unwin Ltd (Document 2); Association of Directors of Social Services for Table 8.7; Bedford Square Press for National Council for Voluntary Organisations (Documents 13 & 19); the Brunel Institute of Organisation and Social Studies & Heinemann (Document 15); Derbyshire County Council (Document 21); The Fabian Society (Documents 8 & 10); Gower Press and the Author, P. Hall (Document 6); The Controller of Her Majesty's Stationery Office & Lord Seebohm (Documents 7 & 9); The Controller of Her Majesty's Stationery Office (Document 11) and Tables 2.1, 2.2, 5 (in Document 17), 8.2, 8.3, 8.5 & 8.6; the Rt. Hon. Patrick Jenkin M.P. (Document 14); National Institute for Social Work (Document 19); Pitman Publishing & the Author, Prof. Eric Sainsbury (Document 1); Policy Studies Institute & the Author, Prof. R. A. Parker (Document 5); Routledge & Kegan Paul Ltd and the Authors, Dr. Michael Baylery (Document 12) & Robert Holman (Document 18).

Part one
INTRODUCING THE PERSONAL SOCIAL SERVICES

Chapter one

DEFINING THE FIELD: A MIXED ECONOMY OF WELFARE

THE SCOPE OF OUR STUDY

The lepidopterist must first catch the butterfly; we must capture the essence of the personal social services. That this presents problems will soon become apparent; that the problem of identification reflects a more deep-seated ambiguity will emerge more gradually. To begin with the issue of definition is not mere pedantry, in itself it is to pose important queries about the nature and condition of the services which we seek to understand.

Sainsbury has offered an admirably positive definition: 'The personal social services are concerned with the individualisation of services, and with adjusting the use of certain resources by individuals, families or groups, according to an assessment of their differential needs.'[1] [doc. 1] The personal social services, he argues are 'concerned with needs and difficulties which inhibit the individual's maximum social functioning, his freedom to develop his personality and to achieve his aspiration through relationships with others'.[2] These definitional statements are entirely acceptable in principle; but they fail to identify the personal social services, as they presently exist, for two reasons. First, they are too broad: the same things could be said of most health or education services, or of employment and careers advisory services. Second, they do not convey the reality of a set of services which are largely involved in providing crisis help to many of the most vulnerable and poorest members of our society. Sainsbury's positive definition conveys a far too rosy picture. Can we, therefore, paint a more prosaic but more realistic picture of the personal social services to set alongside his positive definition? We will attempt to do so by concentrating on how these services are organised and on what they actually do. In doing so we will also indicate the range of this book and those elements of the personal social services which we will be considering.

Whereas the National Health Service and the income maintenance system are underpinned by a relatively uniform system of organisation and set of national policies, the same is not true of the personal social services. This is partly because the statutory components of the personal social services are largely the responsibility of local government and are therefore characterised by local variation, but it is also because policies and legislation governing them vary by country within the United Kingdom. In England and Wales the personal social services are most clearly identified with the work of the Social Services Committees which must be appointed under the terms of the Local Authority Social Services Act 1970. Since the re-organisation of local government in 1974, these committees have had to be appointed in each of 116 local authorities [doc. 2]. They, in turn, appoint a Director of Social Services and preside over the work of what is usually called the Social Services Department (SSD). In Northern Ireland, however, the personal social services are united with the health services and are organised by area boards.[3] In Scotland the personal social services revolve around the Social Work Department of the regional (local) authorities, under the terms of the Social Work (Scotland) Act of 1968. These departments incorporate the probation and after-care service, which the SSDs in England and Wales do not, and have a wider remit in which social work is more clearly dominant [doc. 3].

This degree of variation cannot be covered adequately in a basic text and we will therefore confine ourselves to a discussion of the position in England and Wales. However, this does not mean that the issues raised have relevance only in England and Wales; far from it. Indeed, many of them are as important in a large number of other industrial countries as they are throughout the United Kingdom.[4] Although we begin with a circumscribed and essentially arbitrary focus on England and Wales, the questions generated will, nonetheless, enable us to move beyond these limitations.

However, to narrow our focus geographically does not resolve the problem of outlining the essence of the personal social services. The problem which we face can be characterised quite sharply by a question: are the personal social services necessarily synonymous with social work and the organisation of social work? If this were so, we could simply argue that they are the form taken, in policy and organisation, by social work. We would then be able to by-pass the fact of different patterns of organisation in the United Kingdom. But to take this line would make either one of the terms, social work, or personal social services, redundant. Such a state of affairs might be convenient, it might be desired by many, but it certainly does not describe the present state of policy or terminology. We would assert, with Sainsbury, that 'it is inappropriate to link personal service and social work too closely'.[5] Indeed, in England and Wales the remit of the SSDs seems to reflect a decision to treat them as neither synonymous with social work (Probation remains a separate service) nor as an integral part of health care (they are structurally separate from the NHS).

Whether this decision was wise or inappropriate is not immediately at issue, although it has been debated elsewhere.[6] The fact is that there are somewhat different ways of proceeding in the United Kingdom and in the case of England and Wales the approach has been to create Social Services Committees and SSDs in order to handle a range of activities and not simply to provide an organisational setting for social work. Social Services Departments do not embrace the whole of social work, but they do deploy the skills of a variety of workers – home-helps, occupational therapists, residential care staff – who are not field social workers. One possible response to this diversity within SSDs would be to argue that everything done in SSDs is really social work regardless of the label attached to the worker; another would be to see a traditional and narrow idea of social work as in the process of expanding to embrace all the activities of SSDs. Rather than resolve the issue of the relationship between social work and the personal social services in these ways, however, we ought to keep it open as a question and examine it more fully. To do so we must adopt a working definition of the personal social services which is independent of social work, even if it is a rather unsatisfactory one.

The approach we will adopt therefore is to equate the personal social services with the kinds of work done by SSDs and the client groups served by them. To adopt such a circumscribed view of our field and to base it so securely upon a set of public policy decisions might seem inappropriate. Nevertheless, there are very good reasons for beginning at this point and only raising wider questions later. The first reason is that, linguistically, the personal social services were virtually the creation of the last few years of the 1960s when the idea of SSDs was taking shape. Before then the term was hardly needed, nor was it very widely used. It was sufficient to talk, for example, of child care, medical social work, and the welfare services; for each had its separate existence. The second reason flows from the first: bringing these separate services together under one organisational roof was itself a major development and as such it is worthy of re-appraisal in its own right.

One corollary of identifying the SSDs as the statutory core of the personal social services in England and Wales is that we exclude Probation and After-Care from our remit. This is certainly to ignore one important service which should be seen as part of the personal social services – broadly defined. However, this exclusion provides us with the room to explore more fully another corollary of our working definition: statutory services are only part of the story – beyond them is a whole array of voluntary, private and informal provision which is of great significance and which cannot be ignored. Indeed, it is the changing character of this 'mixed economy of welfare' which forms a large part of the recent history of the personal social services [doc. 4].

A BELATED ENTRY ONTO THE WELFARE STAGE

The classical conception of the Welfare State as it developed in Britain during and after the Second World War centred on a set of state social services in the following fields: income maintenance; health; education; and housing. The personal social services were added as the 'Fifth Social Service'[7] only at the beginning of the 1970s. That they were coherently organised some twenty-five years after the first four state social services might be expected to have had an effect on their nature and development; their lengthy gestation also might be taken as a sign that they were not so straightforward a case as the classical quartet.

The Local Authority Social Services Act became law in 1970. This was the 'slim, dry technical document'[8] which gave life to the personal social services in their contemporary form. The most formative single document which preceded it was the Seebohm Report of 1968.[9] The story of these years of debate, discussion and policy-making have been told elsewhere[10] and some of the issues involved will be reviewed in Chapter 3. What matters for the moment is that the Seebohm Report advocated, and the Local Authority Social Services Act decreed, the creation in England and Wales of a uniform and unified pattern of administration for a range of previously dispersed services. With very few exceptions, this meant the creation in the local authorities of entirely new SSDs.

These SSDs had two rather different inheritances. The most prestigious and best developed was the strong social-work tradition of child care, medical social work and psychiatric social work. In each of these a considerable degree of professional organisation, training and expertise had been established. In the case of child care, professional social work had grown out of the early post-war drive to develop

5

'boarding out' (fostering) as a clear alternative to caring for children in the children's homes. It was an early example of what later came to be called 'community care' (see Ch. 4). Historically, medical and psychiatric social work had deeper professional roots, but they were much more closely linked to the work and work places of medical doctors – as they still are.

Compared with each of these, the other inheritance was far less strongly professionalised. It embraced the work of welfare officers – and home helps and residential care staff – working with the elderly in particular and the younger physically handicapped to a much smaller degree. It also included mental-welfare officers who worked – in close contact with doctors – with the mentally ill and mentally handicapped. This inheritance was firmly shaped by a substantial dependence on care in residential homes and hospitals – institutions which were under the long shadow of the Poor Law. Many of the local authority homes for old people, and a majority of hospitals for the mentally disordered, had been Poor Law institutions. It was hardly surprising, therefore, that the Seebohm Report was in part a crusade finally to wrest these services from the grip of this inheritance. This is not to deny that much progress had been made, but community care and the development of the social-work contribution to these services had a long way to go in theory and practice. The statutory core of the personal social services – the SSDs – therefore began life as a distinctly mixed bag. But the personal social services have to be seen as an even more diverse universe: the statutory core is only the beginning of the story.

A MIXED ECONOMY OF WELFARE

People in need of help, guidance and care have four basic choices. They can:

1. seek the support of their kin within the nuclear, or the wider, family or turn to neighbours and friends in their local area or workplace;
2. attempt to buy the help they need for cash payments in the 'market place';
3. look to voluntary organisations and/or volunteer workers;
4. turn to statutory social services.

One or more of these possibilities may not be a realistic option in practice, but where more than one of them does exist as a real possibility we may speak of a 'mixed economy of welfare'. In particular, this term points to the fact that statutory social services are not necessarily the sole, or even the primary, means of help. In this sense all the five major social services are in fact areas in which a mixed economy of welfare exists. Informal help and care (that provided through the 'fine structure of society' – family, friends and neighbours) remains a dominant means of meeting a wide variety of social needs – not for every needy individual but for a large proportion of people.[11] Moreover, the 'market place' is also widely used to satisfy needs even in those fields where state services seem to be dominant. The purchase of proprietary medicines and aids is a major form of 'market place' health care, for example. Indeed, private sector provision is probably least important in scale in precisely that field in which it has been most controversial in principle, namely the education of school-age children.

Despite the ubiquity of the 'mixed economy' in meeting social need, however, in 1970 the newly recognised and reorganised personal social services held an almost unique claim to be seen as the leading example of a mixed economy of welfare. The state services were still poorly financed and under-developed and they existed alongside the informal care system. It was not then known just how extensive voluntary and informal provision was, though it was certainly considerable. In addition, private provision was quite extensive in some fields. It ranged from the 'unobserved' purchase of care from hotels and boarding houses by some elderly people and their families, through the widespread use of the private child-care services provided by child minders, to the officially registered existence of private nursing and residential homes. That this diversity of care and help outside the state services did not make the personal social services the pre-eminent example of a mixed economy of welfare was due only to the fact that owner-occupation and private renting made the field of housing the outstanding case of non-state sectors operating alongside state social provision.

Nevertheless, we have said enough for it to be clear that the personal social services can only be understood if the whole mixed economy of informal, private, voluntary and statutory help and provision is taken into account. However, this makes it impossible to draw a rigid and unambiguous boundary around the personal social services. Families which consist of caring individuals do not divide that care into health, education and personal social services care. These labels are essentially the arbitrary products of the scale, complexity and legal foundations of state services. Similarly, many voluntary organisations are of particular value precisely because they sprawl across the organisational and professional boundaries created by the growth of state social services.[12] Age Concern, to take just one example, provides a crucial service to elderly people because it can offer integrated advice and policy proposals on matters which the state would begin to parcel out and label as income maintenance, housing, health and personal social services. It makes no sense to try and divide off the 'personal social services part' of Age Concern from its other activities.

Consequently, we consider that it is essential to accept and live with a broad, loose and ambiguous delineation of our field as consisting of all the work undertaken by SSDs with the addition of all the activities within the informal, voluntary and private sectors which correspond broadly to the remit of the SSDs. It may be objected that this 'definition' hinges wholly upon the essentially arbitrary scope of the SSDs as laid down in legislation. That is true. But as we have indicated, the need to define the personal social services is itself merely a result of the presence of the state as one actor in a field of social need and responses; we might just as well, therefore, accept the role of the state as the defining factor.

THE SCOPE OF THE PERSONAL SOCIAL SERVICES

The next chapter outlines in some detail the work and functions of the personal social services and the balance between different activities to be expected in the typical SSD. Let us, at this point, merely reiterate that the creation of the SSDs brought together a range of client groups which had hitherto been catered for separately across a variety of agencies. The key client groups are: the elderly, especially the frail and otherwise dependent elderly; children at risk of receiving inappropriate parenting and care, or at risk of committing offences; the mentally handicapped; the mentally ill; younger chronically sick and disabled people (many old people are also chronically sick and disabled); and other people in need of support, advice, financial assistance, care or protection. In each case, but to greatly varying degrees and in different senses, the concern is also with the whole family of which the person is a member.

The duties and powers placed upon the SSDs in respect of these client groups sprang initially from three separate post-war sources: the National Health Services Act 1946; the National Assistance Act 1948; and the Children's Act 1948. The legislative base of the services has become much wider in scope over the years, but the immediate post-war legislative origins of these services reflects the complex and ambiguous role of the personal social services in relation to other state services.

The history and present status of policy and legislation in each of the client groups cannot be outlined in this book; appropriate texts are available.[13] What we will have continually to note, however, is that the personal social services exist in a close but often uneasy web of intersections between the health and income maintenance services; they are also strongly related to education and housing services. By their very nature – historically and in the work they do – they are beset therefore with problems of interaction, collaboration and conflict across the organisational and professional boundaries which litter the social-policy landscape. They cannot readily exist in self-sufficient isolation. They cater for needs experienced by a wide variety of clients who typically are, or need to be, in contact with other social services. Consequently, they are frequently cast in the role of 'services of last resort' in relation to the rest of the welfare system, while also pursuing goals and objectives which are distinctive to the fields of social work and social care.

THE STRUCTURE OF THE PERSONAL SOCIAL SERVICES

The minister responsible for exercising policy and managerial oversight is the Secretary of State for Social Services, and the Department of Health and Social Security (DHSS) is the responsible central government department in England – operating with and through the Welsh Office in Wales. The DHSS is a very large and curious department of state. Its remit embraces three fields of social-service provision: social security, health, and personal social services – in descending order of financial importance. In principle, each of these fields of social policy needs to be closely related to the others. To a considerable extent in its organisational structure, however, the DHSS is effectively two departments working in parallel: social security; and health and personal social services.

The personal social services are not the preserve of a special division or section of the DHSS. A central organisational feature of the department is the multi-disciplinary client groups (elderly, children etc.), each of which spans the interests of both the health and personal social services – which are therefore seen as closely interrelated. However, beyond these client groups there are inevitable organisational differences. The National Health Service (NHS) is directly managed by the DHSS and specialist divisions are necessary for this purpose. The personal social services, of course, are the preserve of local government and the voluntary and private sectors and are not directly managed by DHSS. There used to be a Local Authority Social

Services Division (it is now a section of a larger division) which took responsibility in general terms for links between the DHSS and the SSDs, but local authorities were not directly accountable to it in a managerial sense. The minister's managerial responsibility is similar to that in other areas of local government service: he has to be satisfied that a local authority is complying in a reasonably satisfactory way with the duties placed upon it in legislation. Beyond that, the minister's role, and therefore that of the DHSS as a whole, is to amplify the policy framework laid down in legislation and to advise and monitor SSDs.

The relationship between DHSS and the SSDs which this description omits to mention is that of the 'inspectorate'. The inspection of the quality of work undertaken has been an important means of giving life to the minister's overall managerial responsibility in several spheres of local authority activity (e.g., education). It is an important means by which the minister may gain and transmit a judgement about a local authority's compliance with legislative duties. Inspection is also, by its existence and status, a potentially important source of leverage on local policy and professional practice. This has been amply demonstrated in the case of education[14] and was also clear in the days of the Children's Service which was the responsibility of the Home Office. The Seebohm reorganisation brought the Home Office inspectorate into the DHSS and transformed it. It was subsumed within a newly created Social Work Service (now the Social Work Inspectorate) which discharges its various roles through a network of regionally based officers who relate to the centrally based staff located within the DHSS heartland. They in turn relate to each of the client groups and present the social work viewpoint in policy discussions, just as doctors and nursing staff present the medical viewpoints. The knowledge of local conditions, developments and issues gained by the regionally based officers is intended to be a key element in policy-making.

Throughout the 1970s the Social Work Service consistently emphasised its advisory role at the national and local levels, rather than its inspectorial role – which it nonetheless retained. From the beginning it was also able to exercise at least some influence on local policy formation within SSDs, if only by virtue of the fact that it directly exercised the control which the DHSS possessed over local authority capital expenditure. This was, until the mid-1970s, the primary area of SSD activity under direct DHSS control and it was an important means of trying to shape what local authorities planned to do.[15] However, this channel of influence was greatly curtailed from the mid-1970s onwards: first by substantial cuts in the level of capital expenditure; and, second, by changes – during the early 1980s – in the overall pattern of central government control of local government expenditure. But during the early 1980s inspection came back into vogue and the newly renamed Social Work Inspectorate may strengthen the centre's influence over SSDs in the coming years. Nevertheless, there is room within the framework set by national legislation for local policy-making by Social Services Committees and by staff. The major direct constraint is financial, in which field the Treasury and the Department of the Environment are powerful in their role as decision-makers on the levels of central government financial support made available to local authorities. But the more diffuse constraints set by policy advice, guidance and ideas about what constitutes good practice are certainly not to be discounted. For English SSDs, the policy advice and guidance is that of the DHSS; in the case of the eight SSDs in Wales the influence is that of both the DHSS filtered through the Welsh Office and, increasingly, of the Welsh Office acting on its own account.

It is impossible to say precisely how influential DHSS is, or how much room for manoeuvre SSDs have within the overall framework set by central government. The answer varies over time and by topic. The impact of other central government policies on SSDs and on the voluntary and private sectors is also indeterminate but important, as is that of the local health authorities. What is clear, however, is that local variation between SSDs is not so great as to make a nonsense of the broad description of national features and trends which we will provide in subsequent chapters.

The same cannot be said for the 'voluntary sector'. Non-statutory help and provision has only recently begun to attract serious attention and our understanding is limited. Nevertheless, what is quite apparent is that the work of voluntary organisations is very important in its scale[16] and extremely diverse in form. A national summary of what is involved is not available and would be practically meaningless if it existed. The same is largely true of informal care. It is possible, for example, to summarize what families do by way of caring for and supporting their members,[17] but the variation is so great as to make the use of such summaries extremely difficult. These reservations also apply to the statutory sector, but the caution needed when making interpretations is of a different order – not least because the data available do allow us to map much of the variation in the statutory services. The kind of descriptions which can be made, nationally, of the statutory and non-statutory forms of help and service are therefore very different.

In the next chapter we will begin to describe the field of work of the personal social services in more detail, but the data used – as opposed to the broad categories – will relate to the statutory services provided by the Social Services Departments. A fuller discussion of non-statutory provision of help and care will be reserved for Chapter 5. The private sector, which has been expanding and changing in recent years, will also be discussed in Chapter 5. The major growth, to date, has been in the field of residential care and for the moment it is sufficient to note that it is primarily in the case of residential provision that the data on local authority services have to be viewed with increasing caution and analysed alongside data on the private sector.

REFERENCES

1. SAINSBURY, E., 1977 *The Personal Social Services*. Pitman, p. 3
2. Ibid.
3. Ibid.
4. THURZ, D. and VIGILANTE, J. L., 1975 and 1976 *Meeting Human Needs*, Vols 1 and 2. Sage; WILLIAMSON, A. and ROOM G., 1983 *Health and Welfare States of Britain*. Heinemann
5. SAINSBURY, E., op.cit.
6. ROYAL COMMISSION ON THE NHS 1979 (Chairman, Sir Alec Merrison), Cmnd 7615. HMSO
7. TOWNSEND, P., 1970 *The Fifth Social Service*. Fabian Society
8. HALLET, C., 1982 *The Personal Social Services in Local Government*. George Allen & Unwin
9. *Report of the Committee on Local Authority and Allied Personal Social Services*, 1968 (Chairman: Lord Seebohm), Cmnd 3703. HMSO
10. HALL, P., 1976 *Reforming the Welfare*. Heinemann
11. MORONEY, R., 1976 *The Family and the State: Considerations for Social Policy*. Longman; see also: LAND, H., 1978 'Who cares for the family', *Journal of Social Policy*, 7 (3) pp. 257–8; GRAYCAR, A., 1983 'Informal voluntary and statutory services: the complex relationship', *British Journal of Social Work*, vol. 13, no. 2, 379–93
12. For examples see: TINKER, A., 1981 *The Elderly in Modern Society*. Longman; MITTLER, P., 1979 *People Not Patients*. Methuen; MALIN, N., RACE, D., JONES, G., 1980 *Services for the Mentally Handicapped in Britain*. Croom Helm; TOPLISS, E., 1982 *Social Responses to Handicap*. Longman; PACKMAN, J., 1981 *The Child's Generation: Child Care Policy in Britain* (2nd edn). Basil Blackwell

13. GRIFFITH, J. A. G., 1966 *Central Departments and Local Authorities*. George Allen & Unwin; REGAN, D. E., 1977 *Local Government and Education*. George Allen & Unwin

14. JUDGE, K., 1978 *Rationing Social Services*. Heinemann; BOOTH, T. A., 1979 *Planning for Welfare: Social Policy and the Expenditure Process*. Basil Blackwell and Martin Robertson

15. WEBB, A. L., DAY, L., WELLER, D., 1976 *Voluntary Social Service Manpower Resources*. Personal Social Services Council; REPORT OF THE COMMITTEE ON THE FUTURE OF VOLUNTARY ORGANI-SATIONS, 1978 (Chairman: Lord Wolfenden), *The Future of Voluntary Organisations*. Croom Helm; HATCH, S., 1980 *Outside the State*. Croom Helm; HADLEY, R., HATCH, S., 1981 *Social Welfare and the Failure of the State*. George Allen & Unwin

16. MORONEY, R., *op.cit.* (ref. 11); HUNT, A., 1978 *The Elderly at Home*. HMSO

17. Ibid.

BY THEIR DEEDS YOU SHALL KNOW THEM

One of the difficulties which we touched upon in the last chapter was that of the apparent lack of focus in the personal social services. The National Health Service is focused on health or, rather, on curing sickness and to a lesser extent on preventing it. The edges of the health field may be fuzzy, but the heart of the matter is clear enough. The same can be said of housing, income maintenance and education. It may not be easy to explain or defend the *objectives* of education, for example, but we all have a rough idea of what to expect if we become a consumer of an educational service.

In general, social services tend to be organised by reference to one or more of three bases for drawing boundaries: by the type of problem addressed; by the major skill involved; by the client group involved. The problem in health care has clearly been labelled as that of sickness and ill health. The skill in education services is that of pedagogy, whether it be exercised in the reception class of an infants school or the postgraduate class in a university. The client group in the youth service is apparently unambiguous. Beneath these simple facades there are great uncertainties and difficulties, but there are at least readily recognisable facades to present to the public.

The case of the personal social services is different from that of the other main social services. As evidence of this, very many people, perhaps most, would not readily know what the personal social services entail, do, or stand to achieve. It is like the infamous case of blindfolded people confronting an elephant for the very first time, each part of the beast may produce some shaft of recognition in those who bump into it, but the whole remains indefinable. For example, the problem which the personal social services address is not merely that of social deviance, though it is a large component of much of the work undertaken, nor yet is it personal – and group – deterioration and incapacity, though they too are important. The single skill of social work cannot be said to be the defining characteristic unless it is seen to include not only all residential work and day care, but also all the social care and maintenance activities of the domiciliary services. Even if social work were to be so broadly defined, however, social work is not a dominant skill in the sense that medical doctoring is. For example, the pattern of referral of clients to day care, home helps and meals on wheels varies from locality to locality and case to case. Social workers are important gatekeepers, but they are not the sole gatekeepers of the personal social services; doctors are the sole gatekeepers of the health services.

This state of affairs may be a reflection of the recent genesis of the personal social services, but it may equally reveal a more fundamental truth about them: that they are a slightly amorphous collection of activities brought together for convenience but lacking a single *raison d'être*. This is certainly a point of view and it is by no means a condemnation. One of the major weaknesses of the NHS is that medical doctors have all too successfully galvanised nearly every part of it into action as a sickness service. But a somewhat loosely integrated body of activities many be as effective in the long run as a highly coordinated and single-minded ensemble. The Moscow State Circus is not necessarily less entertaining than the Bolshoi Ballet; it is simply based on a different concept of unity.

Let us proceed, therefore, by identifying what the personal social services do and let us begin by noting the groups of people with whom they work. The core client groups are readily identified: the elderly; the physically handicapped; the mentally ill; the mentally handicapped; and families with children. Whether, in each case, the personal social services potentially exist to help all people in these groups or only particular clusters of people who cannot cope, or whose problems are more than usually great, is a point to which we will return. It is a somewhat unresolved issue in principle (though scarcity of resources resolves it, in the more selective direction, in practice). For the moment, however, let us add that while these client groups are dominant in that their needs run away with the vast majority of the resources available, the personal social services are certainly not less important to the more 'marginal' client groups: the homeless; alcoholics and people with drug dependency problems; and the array of people needing advice and guidance in negotiating their way through the complexities of society – especially the complexities of the state and its relationships with its citizens.

THE TASKS

To name the client groups does not tell us what the personal social services do for and with them. One way of proceeding is to identify the broad groupings of activities recognised in administrative and professional practice: residential, day and domiciliary care, and field social work. Beyond these labels, however, we can more closely specify some of the tasks undertaken. They are many and varied, but any listing must include the following key types. (It must be noted that they are *not* necessarily all undertaken by professional staff or even paid staff – some may be taken on by volunteers.)

Hotel functions. The provision of accommodation and catering services (e.g., in residential homes, hostels and meals services in people's own homes and in day centres).

Domestic care. The carrying out of a great range of domestic work from laundry and cleaning services, to shopping and gardening (e.g., in residential homes, hostels, and in people's own homes).

Personal care. The undertaking of basic tasks necessary for personal well-being and bodily maintenance on behalf of people unable to perform these tasks by themselves (e.g., bathing, dressing, manicuring, hairdressing and toileting the frail elderly and the physically or mentally handicapped).

Nursing care. Personal care may and does overlap with the 'medical' field so as to include basic nursing functions (e.g., tending the bedbound and supervising the taking of medicines).

Extending personal capacities. The provision of aids, adaptations and special equipment to enable people with impairments to undertake tasks they could not otherwise manage (e.g., housing adaptations, mobility aids, braille typewriting facilities).

Social integration. Combating social isolation and the promotion of involvement in social life (e.g., friendly visiting, day centres, social clubs, subsidising telephones).

Surveillance and monitoring risk. The surveillance – an ugly term – of people who are at risk of deterioration, of confronting undue dangers and stress, or of causing the same to others (e.g., alarm systems, street wardens, 'policing' interpersonal relationships in residential homes, containing people liable to cause or come to harm).

Life enhancement. The enrichment of the lives of people with limited or narrow opportunities for gaining personal satisfaction (e.g., occupational therapy, the development of creative pursuits through Intermediate Treatment).

Work and employment. The provision of work environments or the maximisation of capacities for paid work among the impaired (e.g., sheltered workshops, industrial enclaves, adult training centres).

Advice, guidance and advocacy. The provision of general and specialist advisory and advocacy skills (e.g., much casework activity for all groups, welfare rights work, community organisation and support).

Social therapy. The limiting and repairing of damage to social relationships, self image, personal adjustment etc. (e.g., bereavement counselling, the renegotiation of family relationships and patterns of interaction).

The stimulation of community. The mobilisation of problems and needs and of the capacity to resolve or respond to them (e.g., community organisation, the fostering of self-help groups, the advocacy of community interests).

Enforcing norms, rules and procedures. The exercise of social control in relation to individuals or groups.

These tasks and activities are not intended as an exhaustive list. For example, they neglect the assessment and diagnosis of problems, the coordination of multiple services and agencies, and many other activities. What the list is intended to do, however, is to indicate the sheer variety of the work undertaken in the personal social services and the way in which the tasks defy any neat classification by the principal labels under which the workers themselves can be categorised. Many of the activities – such as enriching people's lives – may equally fall to residential or day-care staff, volunteers, or field social workers. Both the variety of tasks and the absence of exclusive 'ownership' of most of them by groups of workers have been factors in the problem of defining social work as well as in pinning down the essence of the personal social services.

THE FUNCTIONS

Let us move on from the identification of tasks to the delineation of broad functions. Most of the work of the personal social services can be seen to contribute to one or more of three basic functions:

1. social control;
2. the promotion of change – in individuals, in social relationships, and in the social environment;
3. social maintenance.

Social control

The importance of social control in social work and the personal social services surfaced most sharply as a major source of controversy in the 1960s and early 1970s.[1] The implication was that social control was ostensibly exercised over individuals and groups in the interests of the wider society, but that the defence of social order and of established norms and modes of conduct was ultimately undertaken in the interests of particular elites: men, as opposed to women; the middle classes; a ruling class; the capitalist system and those who benefit from it.[2] That social control is notionally exercised on behalf of 'the society', but that not all citizens may gain equally from the defence of the social order, is undeniable. However, it is worth distinguishing more clearly three senses in which this function can be seen to be controversial.

First, it may be that any and all social control is seen to be inappropriate and the involvement of social services in it is unacceptable. There has certainly been a strand of such libertarianism in the debate about social workers as agents of social control. Nevertheless, substantial elements of social control do seem to be inevitable in complex societies and it may be helpful to be more specific in our criticisms of it as a major function of the personal social services.

The second approach, therefore, is to argue that particular categories and forms of social control are inappropriate and unacceptable. For example, the Children and Young Persons Act 1969 embodied the view that an approach to juvenile delinquency which overtly emphasised punitive social control was likely to penalise children who were not fully responsible for the ways in which they had learned to behave and who were unlikely to change their behaviour unless given personal help and more supportive social environments. An undue emphasis on punitive responses was therefore seen to be both an unacceptable and an inefficient way of defending codes of behaviour (the criminal law) which were seen to be crucial to society. The need for social control was not disputed, but the *mode and tenor* of it was. An expanded role for social workers in this field of social control was seen to be a desirable change by those who shaped the Act.

By way of contrast, the reduced reliance on compulsory admissions to mental hospitals during the post-war years was the product of widespread agreement that far less social control need be exercised over the mentally ill and the mentally handicapped than in the past. To a certain extent it would be more accurate to say that the increased ability to control the behaviour of mentally disordered people through drugs reduced the need for other forms of control, but there was also a real belief in the need for more toleration within the community so as to make possible defensible treatment of the mentally ill and the mentally handicapped.[3] What this example also illustrates is that it may be the adequacy of the safeguards built into the exercise of social control which is at issue, rather than the necessity, form and mode of social control itself.[4]

A third possibility is that criticism of social control is really criticism of the nature of the society in which it occurs, rather than of the specific instances. In other words, the argument may be that social control is defensible in a just society, but is wholly indefensible in an unjust society because it systematically reinforces injustice. The judgement is one of the social order and system, not of individual acts of social control. Moreover, it may be further argued that for social services to be a major means of exercising social control is to conceal the real nature of that control and that society by lending a cloak of caring respectability. This viewpoint is most clearly associated with the marxist perspective in which social control is rejected because of its central role in maintaining capitalism in being, not because it is inherently unacceptable or unnecessary. However, to associate this concern with the justice of the whole social order exclusively with marxism is to risk distortion. For example, it is perfectly possible to argue that social controls directed at maintaining the work ethic are of dubious legitimacy in a society characterised by the injustice of mass unemployment, without rejecting capitalist society *per se* or implying that a socialist society would automatically avoid this moral dilemma.

By returning this discussion of social control full circle to the question of who are the real beneficiaries of social-control mechanisms, we have highlighted the need to add a final point. Much social control exercised through the personal social services is indeed primarily to be understood as a defence of the social order first and foremost, but much is also a defence of the rights and well-being of particular individuals – especially vulnerable individuals. The prime example is that body of child-care legislation which clearly places the protection and well-being of the child to the fore. Social control is not necessarily a process of subjecting the individual to the dictates of a state bent on protecting a particular social system, it may also be the means by which the state regulates interpersonal relationships in situations where some individuals are weaker than others. The criticism of the leniency shown to men who abuse and assault women is precisely a cry for more effective social control of this kind – and therefore for a more just society through social control.

The promotion of change

The promotion of change is the bedrock of social work. One type of change, in unacceptable behaviour, has already been discussed in referring to social control. However, there are many other types of change sought in individuals and in the social relationships between individuals. They include the development of greater self awareness and understanding and the improvement of self image. They also include improvements in the quality of parenting and in relationships where children might suffer from particular levels and types of conflict between the adults who care for them. Another major area of problems is that of the guilt, bereavement and despair experienced by people who suffer the death of a very close companion, the birth of a handicapped child, or the admission to a residential institution of a person for whom adequate care can no longer be provided. These are the classical stock in trade of social casework, and they will remain so.

A second type of change has been seen, especially in recent years, to be even more important than the first. It is the promotion of social change in the environment – most often the immediate social environment – of people who are inherently vulnerable or are oppressed by that environment.[5] Such social change can also take many forms. A prominent approach is embodied in the term 'welfare rights'. The object is to make available to individuals financial and other forms of help which are potentially on offer from social and other services but which are unused or are being withheld. The object is also the improvement – by pressure – of social rights. Another approach is the mobilisation of community awareness and political pressure in an attempt to improve the provisions made for whole groups of people – typically residents of a locality – or to modify the social environment in more fundamental ways. The object may also be to release the capacity for mutual aid and support within the group or community. These kinds of approach have often received critical attention because the target of the activity is frequently an authority: local government, central government, a particular service. However, it must be noted that the target of social change may also be synonymous with the 'clients', as in mutual aid, or it may be that amorphous entity 'public opinion'. The latter is the case in attempts through public education to increase the acceptability of the mentally ill, the mentally handicapped, or the discharged prisoner.

What each of these social change approaches has in common is an orientation to more than one individual or family. The object is to benefit whole groups, and change is typically sought in the behaviour of whole groups, in administrative systems, or in the socio-economic system itself. It may seem obvious that this orientation complements that of the social-casework tendency to focus on individuals and families and the group-work orientation towards small groups and their dynamics.[6] In practice, in-fighting between these approaches has often tended to overshadow their complementarity. The reasons are complex and need not be entered into in detail here. However, it must be noted that these different approaches do rest on divergent philosophies and diagnoses of what the problem really is and where it resides. Social casework was long dominated by an individualistic model which underplayed other causes of, and solutions to, problems. To admit the other approaches, therefore, required a change in understanding and orientation among the 'employers' of social workers – politicians and administrators – as well as among trainers, recruits and old hands. However, the need for a change in orientation towards group work and community work was also underpinned by a need for a switch in resources away from the individualistic orientation of traditional social casework. Resources can be every bit as difficult to shift as attitudes and philosophies. During the 1970s the focus on promoting change did shift from a primarily individualistic one to include a group and community dimension, but the rate and degree of change was not what had been called for by many critics of the post-war tradition of social casework.[7] The tendency in official policy during the early 1980s has been to return towards a closer focus on individuals and families.

Social work, social care, and social planning

Social maintenance

While social control and the promotion of change are readily recognisable functions of the personal social services, the term social maintenance is our own and is therefore unfamiliar. The reasons for introducing our own term is that we want to distinguish firmly between social maintenance as a *function* of the personal social services and the idea of social care – which is a term that is now applied to whole areas of work with socially dependent people such as the frail elderly and the mentally handicapped. The function which we wish to identify is simply that of helping to *maintain* a reasonably acceptable way of life for those who are at risk of not being able to do so for themselves.

A crucial feature of social maintenance is that, unlike the change-oriented activities noted above, it is essentially about preserving an individual's status quo, or even the management of deterioration with decency. The activities typically grouped under this title are what Parker has called 'tending activities'[8] [doc. 5]. They are the provision of domestic, personal, and some basic 'nursing' help and care for people who are incapacitated by frailty, physical disability, acute or chronic illness or mental handicap. As such they are not necessarily oriented towards the promotion of change in the individual or the wider social environment. Although change may be implicated, the first object is to ensure that people's level of physical, domestic or social functioning is maintained or allowed to deteriorate in a controlled way. This is important. The professionalisation of work has typically centred around the promotion of change because that is what requires, or justifies, the esoteric knowledge, specialisation and mystique essential to 'a profession'. But the essence of social maintenance is its ordinariness; it is an attempt to sustain an ordinary way of life where this is under threat. As such, it is not an obvious candidate for professionalisation. Indeed, its value to the consumer may depend on it remaining a 'sub-professional' and 'ordinary' activity – albeit organised and planned. Herein lies one source of the uncertain relationship between social work as a profession and the personal social services as a heterodox set of services.

A second feature of social maintenance is that it is a crucial function which could nonetheless be denied a fair share of attention, support and resources precisely because it is 'sub-professional'. It could be ignored or undervalued by professionals. The third feature of social maintenance which we need to note is that it is central to what has become a major policy issue: social care. The demands for domestic and personal help have grown considerably over past decades, particularly as a result of the growth in the elderly population but also as a result of a long-standing policy commitment to shift responsibility for the non-medical care of the elderly, mentally ill and mentally handicapped away from hospitals and the NHS and towards the personal social services. As demand has risen there has been increasing pressure systematically to plan and organise basic caring services so that demand and supply will balance. The need to develop social care and to recognise it as one of the principal components of the work of the personal social services has come to the fore.

The term social care is a comparatively recent addition to the lexicon of the personal social services: the activities are not new, but the identification of them as an entity is.[9] One reason for grouping activities together under a new banner is to call attention to what they have in common; another is to gain support for them; a third is to create a convenient label for things which are being transformed in similar ways and which need therefore to be discussed as a single phenomenon. There is an element of all three in the way in which social care has emerged as an issue in recent years. Put simply, the ability of families to care for their most dependent members – the old, sick and impaired – is changing in puzzling ways at the same time as the policy thrust towards community care is placing far greater demands on families and communities to provide such care.[10] The immediate need is for more organised support through home helps, day centres, meal services, etc.; the underlying need is for more analysis of the policy problems and for sound planning based on this analysis.

Implicit in the need to plan is the need to distinguish the roles and contributions of different types of workers and to establish the most productive way of staffing services. This is where the relationship between social care and social maintenance becomes a crucial one and it explains the need to identify social maintenance as a central but problematic function of the personal social services. The upsurge of interest in social care is a response to the increased pressure to do something for large numbers of frail and socially dependent people. But do what? The answer, to a considerable extent, is to help them – and their existing carers – to cope. A large part of what is needed is unglamorous domestic and personal tending and support. The key function is that of social maintenance; and the key care givers are likely to be non-professionals: kin, friends, neighbours and volunteers. But this picture can be very misleading. To provide such care may demand considerable skill as well as other qualities, such as patience and fortitude.

The problem – though not the solution – is obvious. The demand for social care involves a subtle, unpredictable and changing mixture of the social maintenance and social change functions. To maintain a person's level of coping may often require simple support, but it may also depend on the engineering of change in social relationships, in attitudes and levels of personal adjustment, and in the wider social environment which influences the roles which people play and the resources to which they have access. In practice, therefore, what is termed social care involves a great variety of tasks and skills from the most humble to the most scarce and sophisticated. Its success depends upon matching tasks and skills effectively. The question which immediately arises, therefore, is: what role, if any, should field social workers play in the promotion of social care and how should their role relate to that of home-helps, residential-care staff, day-care staff, volunteers, kin and all the other people who have something to contribute? However, this is not only an issue in relation to social care. It permeates the personal social services because the whole endeavour is characterised by similar problems of matching diverse skills to diverse tasks. This can best be illustrated by looking more closely at the type of work done in the personal social services and the types of workers who do the work.

TYPES OF WORK AND TYPES OF WORKER

The simplest way to give some indication of the relative importance of different types of work undertaken in the personal social services is to note the way in which resources are allocated between different activities. Table 2.1 summarises the position in 1982/3. The figures shown are for England only, but the pattern of expenditure is broadly similar in Wales. What the table clearly indicates is the overwhelming importance of residential care which, in total, accounted for 44 per cent of the gross expenditure (including charges) of SSDs. Residential care of the elderly alone accounted for nearly a quarter of the expenditure (residential child care accounted for approximately 13%). Community care, which includes home help, meals on wheels, fostering and the provision of aids and adaptations for the handicapped and telephones for the isolated absorbed about 18.5 per cent. Administrative costs were the next most important item, followed by day-care services of all kinds. Field social work was the smallest of the major expenditure categories; the 12 per cent allocated to this activity included the costs of senior social workers and team leaders but not those incurred on managerial and specialist advisory staff with a social-work background who were deployed in the upper reaches of departmental hierarchies.

This broad pattern of expenditure has been stable over time. For example, figures for 1972/3, in the early post-reorganisation days, were not greatly dissimilar. The main change over the decade was a reduction – which is continuing – in the share of the budget commanded by residential care (down from 48.5% in 1972/3 to the 44% of 1982/3) and an increase in the shares commanded by field social work and, to a lesser extent, by day care.[11] It would, of course, be surprising if this broad pattern had changed dramatically because it would indicate a very substantial and quite rapid change in the work and role of the personal social services. Change should more reasonably be sought in the more detailed activities. The most noticeable change is the reduction over the decade in the share of expenditure allocated to residential care for the elderly (down from 29% to 24%) and the recent reduction in residential child care. Some of the minor areas of expenditure, such as preventive and supportive services to families, adaptations to homes and contributions to wardens' salaries also suffered a decline in their share. The significance of these changes over time will be considered in Chapter 8. For the moment, the basic structure of expenditure serves as a rough guide to the pattern of activities in the SSDs.

An alternative way of reflecting the balance of work in SSDs is to examine the proportions of the total labour force engaged in each sphere of activity. These proportions, as for 1983, are shown in Table 2.2. The categories are broadly similar to those in Table 2.1, as are the figures. Residential care again emerges as the major area of activity, followed by community care – especially the home-help service. These figures are for whole-time equivalent staff; the actual numbers of home helps employed would distort the picture somewhat because the service depends so heavily upon employing large numbers of part-time workers.

The obvious conclusion to be drawn from these tables is that the largest single set of tasks performed in the SSDs is that which can best be called the 'hotel', domestic and personal care activities. These activities are at the heart of residential care, community care and much day care and they centre around domestic cleaning, meals provision, domestic management and basic personal caring tasks. Their significance does vary somewhat from one setting to another, however. In the residential care of children, for example, they tend to be a necessary adjunct to the real purpose, which is that of promoting the development of well-adjusted children. By way of contrast, in the

Table 2.1   Local authority Personal Social Services: Current expenditure in England in 1982/3 (continued on p. 27)

	£000	Percentage of total	Sub-totals as rounded percentages
Field work			
Social-work staff	270,372	12.0	12
Residential care			
Children	292,324	13.0	
Elderly	538,166	23.9	
Younger physically handicapped	42,299	1.88	
Mentally handicapped – children	25,853	1.15	
Mentally handicapped – adults	66,048	2.94	
Mentally ill	16,311	0.72	
Other	3,007	0.13	
Sub-total	984,008	43.8	44
Day care			
Children	5,239	0.23	
Intermediate treatment	10,746	0.48	
Day nurseries	76,079	3.38	
Pre-school playgroups	5,884	0.26	
Elderly (excluding meals in clubs, and day centres)	24,063	1.07	
Meals	11,046	0.49	
Adult training centres	78,851	3.5	
Other	45,218	2.0	
Miscellaneous support services	18,277	0.81	
Sub-total	275,403	12.25	12

long-term residential care of old people they tend to be dominant and the primary function of residential homes in relation to long-term residents – even in the most enlightened examples – tends to be that which we have called social maintenance. People's physical, mental and social functioning is maintained where possible or allowed to deteriorate as gradually as possible.

This is not a criticism. It is merely a reminder that modest objectives are entirely appropriate in some cases and that the very environment in a residential home for old people may, in turn, limit the objectives which can be realistically entertained. It must also be emphasised that the limited objectives implied in the social maintenance function

Table 2.1 *continued*

	£000	Percentage of total	Sub-totals as rounded percentages
Community care			
Home helps	245,413	10.9	
Laundry	774	0.034	
Boarding out (fostering)	69,246	3.08	
Preventive services (in families)	7,449	0.33	
Meals on wheels	31,588	1.4	
Adaptations to homes	5,442	0.24	
Aids	7,803	0.35	
Telephones	5,610	0.25	
Contributions to Warden's salaries (sheltered housing)	7,539	0.335	
Holidays	7,476	0.333	
Other	28,205	1.25	
Sub-total	416,545	18.5	19
Administration			
Field work	76,668	3.4	
Residential care	110,698	4.9	
Day care, domiciliary and other	92,212	4.1	
Sub-total	279,578	12.4	12
Training	14,131	0.63	
Research and development	8,493	0.38	
Sub-total	22,624	1.0	1
Total	2,248,530		

Source: Adapted from: DHSS, *Health and Personal Social Services Statistics for England, 1985*. The figures shown include receipts from charges made for services. We are grateful to DHSS for giving us access to the figures in advance of their publication.

nevertheless demand skilled and dedicated staff precisely because the constraints are severe. The danger is that the absence of a strong base on which to build a claim to unequivocal professional status will result in the neglect of the training and support needs of such staff. Unfortunately, training for residential workers has indeed been relatively neglected, despite the steady growth in the representation of residential and day-care workers' interests.

Social work, social care, and social planning

Table 2.2   Staff of local authority Social Services Departments in England in 1983

	Whole-time equivalents	Percentage of total	Sub-total as rounded percentages
Social work			
Management and supervisory	4,253	2.0	
Senior social workers and social workers	19,581	9.3	
Other	4,133	2.0	
Sub-total	27,967	13.3	13
Residential care			
Children	19,910	9.5	
Elderly and physically handicapped	55,959	26.6	
Mentally ill and mentally handicapped	8,388	4.0	
Sub-total	84,257	40.1	40
Day care			
Children	9,143	4.4	
Elderly and physically handicapped and mentally ill	6,381	3.0	
Adult training centres	8,087	3.8	
Sub-total	23,611	11.2	11
Community care			
Home helps	51,745	24.6	25
Other			
Headquarters and area office staff	19,117	9.1	
Miscellaneous	3,296	1.6	
Sub-total	22,413	10.6	11
Total staff	209,993		

Source: Adapted from DHSS, *Health and Personal Social Services Statistics for England, 1985*. We are grateful to DHSS for giving us access to the figures in advance of their publication.

Not all places in residential homes are filled by long-term residents. In the case of child care, residential homes have always been used for short-stay and diagnostic purposes. Some progress has also been made in recent years in using residential care for short-stay purposes in the case of other client groups. This may contribute to a different and more recently emphasised form of social maintenance – that of supporting families who care for their own dependents but who need periods of respite and recuperation. This, however, also illustrates another reason why even the humblest of objectives may need to involve skilled and sensitive people. For example, taking an old person into care temporarily to give the family carers a 'holiday' can itself be a delicate task, but it can also reveal potential stresses, or opportunities for development, in the relationship between the family carers and the old person. Simply helping to maintain a caring relationship may therefore result in the identification of opportunities for modifying that relationship which could benefit the old person, reduce the strain on carers, or increase the rewards experienced by them. Here is the essential dilemma of so much work in the personal social services: it does involve comparatively unambitious social maintenance objectives, but fulfilling those objectives may involve identifying opportunities for change and progress – or signs of rapid decline and potential collapse. This is true of individuals, of the social relationships within which they live and of the wider social environment. The need is to perform mundane and routine work, which might be seen to be inappropriate to, or beneath the dignity of, a 'professional' worker, without allowing it to become wholly routine and without losing the opportunity to diagnose potential changes for better or for worse so that appropriate action can be considered. It is a mixture of activities and functions which in differing proportions characterises much residential care, day care, domiciliary provision and neighbourhood work. Whether the solution to the staffing issues posed is to give improved training to care staff to ensure that supervisory and managerial staff are well trained and skilled, or to bring all these different groups of workers into close working contact with social workers, is a very debatable issue to which we will return.

We have placed special emphasis on social maintenance as a primary function of the personal social services in order clearly to demonstrate the crucial but problematic relationship between humble and mundane activities on the one hand and opportunities to effect, or forestall, change on the other. In practice it is always debatable whether the objective should be simply to shore up and maintain a person's way of life or whether to attempt to affect changes or anticipate those – such as the final collapse of a relationship or of family care for an old or mentally handicapped person – which may spontaneously occur. Our argument is that because professionalisation concentrates on the management of change as a high-status activity demanding scarce skills, it can easily downgrade the humbler objectives while creating an artificially sharp distinction between maintenance activities and change-oriented activities. This distinction is reinforced by giving the professional and non-professional staff substantially – perhaps disproportionately – different amounts of training, status and income. That these issues are of great importance in the personal social services is underlined by the sheer numbers of staff who are not field social workers. That their contribution is maximised and well used is essential.

Whether these problems of matching tasks, roles, functions and skills have been satisfactorily resolved in the personal social services is a question to which we will return at various points in the book. The importance of the question, however, explains the need to avoid defining the personal social services in terms of social work. The question also points to another way in which the role and tasks of the personal social services can be categorised and understood. Services must be made available to clients, but if they are to be appropriate and adequate and if resources are to be well used there also needs to be planning and management. These activities need to be distinguished and their inter-relationship needs to be examined.

SERVICE DELIVERY, PLANNING AND MANAGEMENT

The nature of service delivery is readily understood. It involves the traditional, active skills which we have been discussing. However, the meaning of planning is much less clear. For a period in the 1970s it became synonymous with the preparation of statistical forecasts of how services would develop over a ten-year or three-year period: these forward plans were required of each SSD by DHSS. They were often produced by administrative and managerial staff with little involvement by staff at the field level. Forward planning of this kind has ceased to be fashionable, but it has left an image of planning as a remote and technical process. Yet our argument is that the most appropriate use of resources – especially staff – and the provision of appropriate services and help depends upon intelligent and informed appraisal and re-appraisal of the work to be done, the needs to be met and the skills and resources to hand. Ideally, planning is just one element of the management task; it is the forward-thinking part.

Ideally, also, the management task is an integral part of running good services: it is not something remote from and superior to service delivery.

Unfortunately, just as planning came to be seen as remote and technical, so management tends to be seen as the function of administrative and managerial staff who sit at the top of the staff pyramid and who are seen to be out of touch with field level reality. To distinguish the planning and management functions from the specialist staff who are seen to dominate them is, therefore, important. Once again we are emphasising the need for a flexible use of skills and contributions if vital functions are to be performed appropriately.

If planning can be seen in simple terms as a process of organised thinking about the future, management can be broken down into three basic components. The first is husbanding resources so as to meet need and fulfil objectives. What this entails is promoting effectiveness and efficiency. Resources must be used to create help of a kind which is valid and appropriate and resources must be made to go as far as possible. This is a part of the management function which could and should be built into the roles of all staff. Anyone can waste resources or use them well – even if the resources are only their own time. The allocation of resources to meet needs is not something which can or should be left solely to staff called 'managers'.

For example, one feature of social work which has gradually been recognised to be endemic is that of 'gatekeeping', or the rationing of services between clients. The Barclay Committee identified it as a central feature of the social work task[12]; some critics of Barclay denounced it as the indeed endemic but illegitimate result of cuts and government tight-fistedness. The truth is that resource allocation is in fact totally inescapable. Even abundant resources can always be used in different ways and rationing resources between different uses can never be avoided. However, there is a world of difference between allocating resources continually to the most pressing demands, or on the first come first served principle, and developing a strategy designed to use resources to a particular purpose. There is also a world of difference between accepting the need to allocate a given stock of resources between an overwhelming number of needs and demands and developing a consistent strategy designed to alter that imbalance between need and demand. Both involve a move towards planning as we define it; both involve and affect fieldworkers, as well as administrators, and will do so to an even greater extent in the future.

The second component of the management task, therefore, is planning. It is the husbanding role projected into the future. It too is a function which need not and should not be the exclusive preserve of a small specialist staff.

The third component of the management function is somewhat different. It concerns accountability. One way of implementing policies is to make everyone responsible for putting them into practice through a hierarchy of accountability. Managers are then necessarily people in special roles; they are people who have others responsible to them. But it must be emphasised that even staff at the field level may therefore by managers: everyone who is responsible for a subordinate is a manager in respect of that subordinate. Management in the sense of exercising accountability is just one part of many people's roles. It involves home-help organisers, meals on wheels organisers and every social worker who is responsible for the work of a social work assistant or a group of volunteers. To equate the functions of management – including planning – with a comparatively small group of administrative and managerial staff is inaccurate, misleading and potentially wasteful of skills and contributions. What this attitude reflects is the scale and remoteness which characterise many SSDs. These are issues on which we will elaborate in later chapters.

THE NON-STATUTORY 'SECTOR'

Beyond the SSDs, as we have indicated, is a vast array of non-statutory provision and help. The easy way of referring to it is to lump it together and call it the non-statutory 'sector'. However, this convenient shorthand can be profoundly misleading if it suggests a coherent and coordinated set of services. What exists beyond the state is a large, fundamentally important, but highly varied world of activity ranging from the care provided within the confines of the family to that formally delivered by well-established and securely based voluntary organisations.[13] However, even the most organised of these fields of action – that involving voluntary organisations with national reputations and remits – is very far from being as homogeneous and coordinated as the state services. This is not to say that the work done is inferior in any way, merely that it is much more difficult to describe and summarise. Moreover, it is also difficult to predict what will be available to any particular town, village, neighbourhood or street.[14] To describe an average picture is to create an even more dangerous myth than is the case in the statutory services. Our description must therefore be sketchy and tentative.

We can best proceed by identifying the main categories of activity

which constitute the non-statutory 'sector'. The now traditional approach is to distinguish:
(a) private services;
(b) informal care;
(c) voluntary organisations.
To these we will add:
(d) volunteering;
(e) mutual aid, or self help.

By private services is meant the provision of help or care through the price/market mechanism, usually with a view to making a profit. People who are disabled but who can afford to buy in help, and families who can avoid some of the pitfalls of child rearing by hiring nannies or mothers' helps, may satisfy all their 'welfare needs' through the market place. Similarly, frail old people, or their relatives, may be able to afford to choose the services offered by private residential hotels, or nursing homes, or they too may buy in domestic help – or even companionship. The private 'sector' therefore mirrors much, if not all, of the activities of the statutory and voluntary services. However, it tends only to be recognised as falling within the sphere of the personal social services when it is linked into the statutory services by virtue, for example, of licensing arrangements, or the likelihood that people buying care for themselves will exhaust their means and thereby generate a demand on state services. The acknowledged 'private sector' therefore consists largely of such activities as residential care and child minding. However, the relationship between statutory and private provision is becoming increasingly important.

Until recently, informal care also tended not to be seen as an integral part of the personal social services. The care and support provided by informal networks – families, friends and neighbours – was largely taken for granted and, not infrequently, it was taken for granted that it was in decline. A sharp change in viewpoint has occurred in recent years. While early advocates of community care[15] were precisely concerned to commit public policy to the support and maintenance of informal care, the real upsurge of interest in informal care did not begin until the mid-1970s. Two issues have been the focus of attention. The first, the range and capacity of informal care, was highlighted, for example, by Moroney's work on the family[16] and subsequently there has been much concern over the implications for state services of any decline in this capacity. The second issue is that of the relationship between the formal services and informal care. One strand in this thinking, epitomised by Bayley,[17] emphasised the lack of 'fit' between formal and informal care: services provided did not readily and

33

conveniently complement the patterns of coping developed by people in their informal networks.[18] A second strand, emerging from this, has concentrated on the ways in which formal services could be redirected and refocused so as to support informal care more fully. This second strand has been characterised both by doubts as to whether formal services can successfully relate to informal care[19] and by more confident assertions that this could and should be achieved.[20] A third strand of thinking has drawn on the observation that most, though not all, of the informal carers are women. The costs borne by these carers in terms of financial, physical and psychological strain have begun to be explored.[21] The 'costs to carers' viewpoint has implications both for estimates of likely future levels of informal care and for the role of formal services in relation to informal care.

What is undeniable in the case of informal care is that, while it has always been with us, it has only lately become a subject of intensive study and debate. The same is true of voluntary organisations. They remained as a major feature in the personal-social-service field during the post-war years, despite the growth of state welfare, precisely because the personal social services were an ill-organised and poorly financed area of state provision. But the Seebohm changes did not herald their demise. This might have happened had the 1970s followed the path of the earlier post-war decades; but, in practice, there were important differences. One was the failure of the SSDs to develop as a universal and comprehensive state service in the mould of the NHS or education, the second was the set of changes which had already begun to effect a demise in the dominant position of the state even in these areas of universal service. By the 1970s the heavily professionalised, and bureaucratised, state social services were being seen not to be sufficient. Alternatives, not least those provided by voluntary organisations, were viewed as inherently attractive and not merely as evidence of gaps in the cover provided by the state. Voluntary provision was showing strong signs of expanding and taking new forms. This was nowhere more obvious than in the broad field of health and welfare. Hence the need to be aware that the personal social services are best characterised as a shifting pattern of pieces in a kaleidoscope, rather than as a neatly integrated 'system'.

The main blocks or 'sectors' are clear enough: statutory; private; informal and voluntary. However, there is a need to identify two other forms of provision which are not additional and separate sectors, but which cut across two or more of these sectors. The first is volunteering, by which is meant the provision of help or support without significant payment (expenses may be paid and 'paid volunteers' are an increasingly important and complicating factor). Volunteers differ from the friends, relatives or neighbours who may help a person in the sense that their contribution is to some degree organised and formalised. The essential difference in principle is that volunteers are an organised means of providing – to 'strangers' who need help – that which informal networks provide 'naturally'. These distinctions do not necessarily stand up to close scrutiny in practice, especially now that more attempts are being made to use street wardens, social workers, etc. to 'organise' informal care. Nevertheless, the basic distinction between formalised volunteering and informal care does continue to have much validity and is useful in principle when describing the scope of the personal social services.

One of the important features of volunteering is that it is by no means confined to voluntary organisations. Many voluntary organisations do depend on volunteers for fund-raising or for the provision of direct services, but many are also staffed wholly or very largely by paid staff. Conversely, while statutory services depend upon paid staff in the main, the use of volunteers has grown very considerably and is a major aspect of many of them. In particular, many SSDs employ volunteer organisers specifically to deploy the time and skills of volunteers. Private services, such as private residential homes, may also use volunteers. Both because it involves a substantial resource (approximately 15% of the population are probably acting as 'volunteers' at any one time)[22] and because it cuts across the main 'sectors', volunteering needs to be identified as important in its own right.

Mutual aid, or self help, is the final and most recently recognised area of activity which we need to identify. It could be argued that mutual-aid groups comprising people with similar problems who have come together to support and help each other are essentially a sub-group of voluntary organisations. In part this is true and the expansion of mutual aid is certainly one of the forces which has begun to transform the voluntary sector. Mutual aid has helped shift the emphasis from a preoccupation solely with delivering help and care to those in need, to one of helping those in need to organise and act for themselves. In the process a critical cutting edge has often emerged. Mutual aid groups exist, in part, because formal services are either inherently insufficient or are neglectful of problems to which people themselves give greater priority than do professionals.

Nevertheless, it is important to treat mutual aid as of intrinsic interest and not to subsume it wholly within the voluntary sector. Most mutual aid groups of any size would be classified as voluntary organisations, but what is essential is not their organisational form but their operating principles.[23] Mutual aid, in theory, is a commitment to blurring, or eliminating totally, the distinction between the helper and the helped. It dispenses with the client–provider relationship which is at the heart of formal services: statutory, voluntary and private alike. Its essence is the reciprocity of giving and receiving which is possible among a group of 'fellow-sufferers'. As such, mutual aid is not confined, in principle, to the voluntary sector. Any reasonable supportive environment could harbour a mutual aid group: a local authority day centre; a private residential home; or a voluntary organisation which primarily exists to provide direct services of a traditional kind. Mutual aid is essentially a philosophy of helping which could be widely transplanted and as such it merits separate recognition as a key and developing component of the personal social services.

REFERENCES

1. HIGGINS, J., 1980 'Social control theories of social policy', *Journal of Social Policy*, vol. 17, pt. 1, Jan.; BALDOCK, P., 1980 'The origins of community work in the UK', in Henderson, P., Jones, D., Thomas, D. N. (eds) *The Boundaries of Change in Community Work*. Allen & Unwin, pp. 23–5

2. LEONARD, P., 1983 'Marxism, the individual and the welfare state', in Bean, P., Macpherson, S. (eds) *Approaches to Welfare*. Routledge and Kegan Paul; CORRIGAN, P., LEONARD, P., 1978 *Social Work Practice Under Capitalism: A Marxist Approach*. Macmillan

3. BEAN, P., (ed.), 1983 *Mental Illness, Changes and Trends*. John Wiley

4. JONES, K., 1972 *A History of the Mental Health Services*. Routledge and Kegan Paul

5. TOWNSEND, P., *et al.* (May 1970) *The Fifth Social Service: Nine Fabian Essays*. Fabian Society; BAILEY, R. and BRAKE, M. (eds), 1975 *Radical Social Work?* Edward Arnold; CORRIGAN, P. and LEONARD, P., 1978 *Critical Texts in Social Work and the Welfare State*. Macmillan Press

6. VICKERY, A. and SPECHT, H. (eds), 1977 *Integrating Social Work Methods*. Allen & Unwin; PINCUS, A. and MINAHAN, A., 1973 *Social Work Practice: Model and Method*. Peacock, Illinois

7. SINFIELD, A., 1970 'Which way for social work?', in Townsend, P. (ed.), 1970 *The Fifth Social Service*. Fabian Society; BALDOCK, P., op.cit. (ref. 1)

8. PARKER, R., 1981 'Tending and social policy', in Goldberg, E. M. and Hatch, S. (eds) *A New Look at the Personal Social Services*. Policy Studies Institute

9. GOLDBERG, E. M. and CONNELLY, N. (eds), 1981 *Evaluative Research in Social Care*. Heinemann, p. 2; GOLDBERG, E. M. and HATCH, S. (eds), 1981 op.cit. (ref. 8)

10. Ibid.; WEBB, A. L. and WISTOW, G., 1982 *Whither State Welfare? Policy and Implementation in the Personal Social Services, 1979–80*. Royal Institute of Public Administration

11. WEBB, A. L. and WISTOW, G., March 1983 'Public expenditure and policy implementation: the case of community care', *Public Administration*, vol. 63, pp. 21–44

12. BARCLAY, P., 1982 *Social Workers: Their Role and Tasks*, Report of a Working Party. Bedford Square Press

13. HATCH, S. and MORCROFT, I., 1977 'Factors affecting the location of voluntary organisation branches', *Policy and Politics*, vol. 6, no. 2

14. HATCH, S., 1980 *Outside the State*. Croom Helm

15. TOWNSEND, P., 1962 *The Last Refuge*. Routledge and Kegan Paul

16. MORONEY, R., 1976 *The Family and the State: Considerations for Social Policy*. Longman

17. BAYLEY, M., 1973 *Mental Handicap and Community Care*. Routledge and Kegan Paul

18. ROBINSON, T., 1978 *In Worlds Apart*. Bedford Square Press

19. ABRAMS, P., December 1977 'Community care: some research problems and policies', *Policy and Politics*, vol. 6, no. 2

20. HADLEY, R. and McGRATH, M. (eds), 1980 *Going Local: Neighbourhood Social Services*. Bedford Square Press; BARCLAY, P., op.cit. (ref. 12)

21. EQUAL OPPORTUNITIES COMMISSION, 1980 *The Experience of Caring for Elderly and Handicapped Dependents*, Survey Report; FINCH, J. and GROVES, D., 1980 'Community care and care in the family: a case for equal opportunities?', *Journal of Social Policy*, vol. 9, no. 4, pp. 487–511; NISSEL, M. and BONNERJEA, L., 1982 *Family Care of the Handicapped Elderly*. Policy Studies Institute

22. BARCLAY, P., op.cit. (ref. 12); HADLEY R. and HATCH, S., 1981 *Social Welfare and the Failure of the State*. George Allen & Unwin; HUMBLE, S., 1982 *Voluntary Action in the 1980s*. The Volunteer Centre

23. ROBINSON, D. and HENRY, S., 1977 *Self Help and Health*. Martin Robertson; RICHARDSON, A. and GOODMAN, M., 1982 *Self Help and Social Care: Mutual Aid Organisations in Practice*. Policy Studies Institute; BRIMELOW, M. and WILSON, J., 1982 'A Problem Shared', *Social Work Today*, vol. 13, no. 19, 19 Jan.

Chapter three

ORIGINS AND OBJECTIVES

The Seebohm Committee was appointed in December 1965 'to review the organisation and responsibilities of the local authority personal social services in England and Wales, and to consider what changes are desirable to secure an effective family service'.[1] Few committees, it might seem, have been told so clearly that their task is to promote a particular type of change to which an initial commitment has already been made. It was therefore no surprise that the second paragraph of the Report, published in July 1968, unhesitatingly stated

> We recommend a new local authority department, providing a community based and family oriented service, which will be available to all. This new department will, we believe, reach far beyond the discovery and rescue of casualties, it will enable the greatest possible number of individuals to act reciprocally, giving and receiving service for the well-being of the whole community.[2]

A report containing so few surprises might seem to have been unnecessary. Indeed, Richard Crossman's diaries suggest that the Report was poorly received in Cabinet and was something of a barrier, rather than a facilitator, of the kinds of changes which had been discussed for some years.[3] Similarly, much academic criticism of it centred on its failure to prescribe a clear philosophy for the personal social services and on its inadequate information and research base.[4] Yet, taking the opposite view, Donnison felt able to describe it as a 'great state paper' and to hail it as a more than adequate basis for action.[5] Moreover, as we shall see in the next chapter, even the short introductory statement quoted above marked a real philosophical break with the past and foreshadowed issues which would surge to prominence in the late 1970s.

The key to the paradox is that the Seebohm Report itself was in essence a lens which refracted, and in some cases focused, the real changes which were already well underway. The Report, to change the metaphor, provided a sounding board for ideas which had already been articulated; it legitimated a particular direction of change at a time when some kind of change was almost inevitable and many of the possibilities had already been more or less ruled out of court. For our purposes, therefore, the real interest lies in the years before and immediately after the deliberations of the Seebohm Committee, rather than in the deliberations themselves.

THE PRE-SEEBOHM YEARS: ISSUES AND PROBLEMS

The pressures which eventually led to the creation of the Seebohm Committee can be viewed in two ways. The first is to note two essentially separate and unrelated services – Child Care, and Health and Welfare – each dominated by its own set of problems and issues.[6] Child care was practised in local authority Children's Departments under the watchful eye and close scrutiny of the Home Office. The welfare services were provided by local authorities either through Welfare Departments which were separate from environmental health, or through combined Health and Welfare Departments. Either way, the welfare services needed by the elderly, sick and impaired were related to or closely involved in the world of medicine and health-care provision and were delivered locally under the less watchful gaze of the Ministry of Health.[7] That these distinct services and policy worlds of child care and health and welfare touched one another was due in part to the fact that both involved the use of social workers. But there was also an undoubted degree of overlap in that some families were clients of both services.

Another way of understanding the move towards the organisation of the personal social services as we now know them is to identify specific issues and problems, many of which spanned the service boundaries. That this is the more useful approach is suggested by the fact that the boundaries were eventually swept aside and the separate development of the two services gave way to the creation of a single service. Of the many issues which might be identified, four are particularly outstanding:
1. the problem of coordination;
2. the problem of delinquency and of policy towards the family;
3. the rise of community care as a key statement of policy intent; and
4. the consolidation of social work as a profession.

The problem of coordination

The long and halting process of breaking up the Poor Law led directly to an unavoidable problem of coordination.[8] The Poor Law had been a multi-purpose service dealing with all manner of problems presented by poor people. The services which gradually came to replace it were more specialised and had over time to be regrouped and reorganised in the search for a modicum of coordination across professional and organisational divisions. One such regrouping created the NHS in 1946 and another the Children's Service in 1948. But this pattern of post-war change did not remove the problem of coordination, it merely modified it and set a new stage on which the time-worn script could be rehearsed yet again.

The Children's Act of 1948 was the product of a review of provision for children 'deprived of a normal home'. It expressed the first post-war burst of enthusiasm for 'community care'. Properly organised and supported boarding-out of children was seen to be more in their interests than life in residential homes; though such homes were also seen to be capable of improvement by reductions in size and improvement in staff quality. The newly promoted role for field social work in child care was shaped by these demands for good fostering (and adoption) practice and effective liaison. However, the issue which later came to dominate child care – the neglect of children in their own homes – took a back seat at the inauguration of the new service.

The problem of coordination was sharply revealed throughout the 1950s in work with children living at home who were at risk. Whether this risk was manifest as a problem of school non-attendance, delinquency, ill treatment, or neglect of the child, other agencies were almost inevitably involved. The result, as the Majority Report of the Royal Commission on the Poor Law had predicted of specialisation, was a 'multiplication of enquiries and visitations, causing annoyance and waste of time and money'.[9] It was not denied that duplication and overlap was a reality, but whether it could readily be solved was less certain. The response during the 1950s was the encouragement, by joint circulars of the ministries involved, of structured case-conferences. It was not until the 1960s that a more radical restructuring of service boundaries became a serious possibility. By then, however, the child-care debate had taken a new turn and was dominated by the problem of delinquency. What linked the two decades of discussion was a perception that, whether child neglect or delinquent behaviour was the problem to the fore, the most appropriate solution involved early preventative action – which in turn required a clear allocation of responsibilities and powers.

If coordination in the case of child care involved an emerging profession working together with more established services, such as education and health, the problem in the welfare field lay in the incomplete nature of the reorganisation involved in creating the NHS and abolishing the Poor Law. The National Health Service Act of 1946 had created the infamous tripartite structure in which health services were provided by a centrally controlled hospital system, a local-government-based set of community and public health services, and a network of independently contracting family practitioners. The problem of coordination was ready-made and institutionalised in the one, optimistically named, National Health Service. However, the 'welfare' part of the package involved further complications. Social work – medical and psychiatric – was also based firmly in the health, especially the hospital, system. In addition, some of what we have already called the social care role was allocated to the NHS: home-helps were part of the local medical services. On the other hand, the remainder of the social care role was separately removed from the shadow of the Poor Law by the National Assistance Act of 1948. This act placed a mish-mash of duties and powers in the hands of local authorities; the core was the provision of residential care. The same desire for smaller and more humane institutions surfaced in the case of the elderly as in the case of children, but the interest in community care was much less apparent in the early years.

The fact that some local authorities chose to combine their health and welfare activities in a single department while others kept the two separate merely underlined the lack of a coherent approach to the 'welfare' services in theory and in legislation. But the fundamental problem of coordination lay in the fact that health and welfare services needed to exist as a well developed set of substitutes and complements, while the organisational base was an untidy reflection of a series of compromises. As with child care, the basic problem of coordination was increasingly overshadowed by the emergence of a single, dominant policy issue – community care. Unlike child care, however, it was an issue which emphasised the need for coordination at the planning level even more than at the field level.

Delinquency, child care and the judicial system

The great 1960s debate on child care and delinquency was the product of two forces. The first and the most direct was that of rising trends in crime statistics. The second was a fundamental recasting of the problem of delinquency: the theory of the problem changed and with it the theory of the solution. The shift in the theory of the problem was towards a greater belief in the social causes of criminal behaviour. At its more radical this shift located causes firmly in malfunctioning social institutions, such as schools; in the reinforcement of delinquency by institutions, such as courts of law, which hung labels around children which they then lived up to; and in social situations, such as relative deprivation amid affluence or enhanced opportunities for low-risk crime. At its less radical, this process of re-interpretation focused on the family and the pressures which distort and stunt family life.

The theory of the solution embraced a mixture of leads from these new ideas about cause, but fixed especially on the family and on preventative social work. Preventative social work meant a central place for social workers. It also meant more flexibility and discretion for them, and that in turn implied changes in the role of the courts – which had in any case come in for criticism as a fount of stigma and labelling. The response in England and Wales was to expand the role of the social worker by reducing the powers of the courts while retaining the latter in their essentials. The Scottish answer was to highlight more fully the importance of a broad social education of children away from crime, in collaboration with their families.[10] Under the Scottish system the role of the court was effectively dispensed with where the facts of a case were agreed and Children's Panels were established as bodies which would make decisions about, and supervise, work with families.

Despite the differences, the central thrust was the same in both cases: it was towards an expansion of social work with children and a modification of relationships between this expanded service and the courts on one hand and education and probation services on the other. In the case of Scotland the outcome, as we noted earlier, was the creation of Social Work Departments embracing the child-care and probation functions as well as the 'welfare' services for the elderly, chronically sick, mentally ill and handicapped. In England and Wales there was the possibility that a much narrower 'family' service would result which would essentially be a 'super child care service'. This at least was the direction in which Home Office ministers seemed to be moving.[11] For, unlike Scotland, there was no single department in Whitehall which could take an overview of the different, but not unrelated, developments taking place in the various 'welfare' services.

The search for community care

Many apparently self-explanatory policies dissolve into complexity on closer inspection, but few can be more complex and uncertain than the idea of community care. For this reason we will discuss its meaning in more detail in Chapter 4. For the moment, however, we can identify a few of the definitive strands which emerged in the post-war years. Two related concerns of the early years have already been noted: the creation of alternatives to institutional care and the humanisation and improvement of the institutions which remained. Of these, the former at least is clearly within the compass of community care. We have also noted the uneven post-war development of ideas in the child-care and welfare services. The health and welfare legislation permitted the development of a home-help service and some other domiciliary and personal care services, but in a half-hearted fashion. No requirement positively to promote community-based services was laid upon these services by Parliament. The same must be said of child-care legislation in that the basic Act of 1948 had to be amended in 1963 and 1969 in order to allow the growth of the range of community-based preventative approaches which now exists. Nevertheless, the spirit of the early child-care policies was certainly more distinctly favourable to the community-care approach. While the opportunity of providing financial support to families as a preventative measure was built into legislation in the Children's Act 1963, the years of debate about delinquency added a search for community alternatives to penal institutions.

Change in child care was a comparatively continuous process of learning and consolidation compared with the more episodic reorientation which took place in the health and welfare field. Several forces were at work in the 1950s and 1960s. The first was a steady and strong reaction against the unnecessary containment of the elderly, mentally ill and handicapped in institutions, many of which were grossly inappropriate. The second was a medical drive to practice 'real medicine' in hospitals and to avoid the use of hospitals for 'social warehousing' – especially of the mentally ill and handicapped. Advances in the control of symptoms triggered this move, but it depended on increased public acceptance. The third was a concern with the high costs of hospital care and the perception of community-based care as a lower cost alternative. Although all three motivations were intermingled over a long period of time, the first and second were most characteristically represented in the debate which led up to the Mental Health Act 1959 and the third in the ten-year plans for hospital-bed reductions introduced in the 1960s.

Social work, social care, and social planning

The implications, as well as the course, of these moves towards community care differed in the child-care and welfare fields. The pressure to improve coordination was a case in point. The development of community care generally enhanced the need for good working relations between field workers from different professions and different agencies. In the health and welfare field, however, the need to *plan* the whole set of services for the long-stay, chronic client groups was inescapable. Community care not only implied the need to add new services to the repertoire of the local authority welfare services, it also meant that patient care had steadily to be moved from the hospitals to these services. This required long-term planning of a reasonably high order. In principle it was planning which could be stage-managed from the centre by the Ministry of Health.

By way of contrast, the planning implied in developing community care for children was at one level much simpler and at another was virtually impossible. The comparatively simple planning was that needed within Children's Departments in order to expand options. The more unrealistic was that necessary across a very wide range of agencies – housing, health, income maintenance, education and employment – if vulnerable families were to be given the best possible chance of rearing children in an environment conducive to law-abiding behaviour and personal fulfilment. It was a task that was essentially beyond a local authority department, and perhaps beyond central government too.

Social work professionalisation

In the years before Seebohm at least eight groups of field social workers, or potential social workers, could be identified: psychiatric social workers; medical social workers (almoners); probation officers; child-care officers; mental-welfare officers; welfare officers; housing-welfare officers; and education-welfare officers. Of these, only the first four were well along the road towards something like full professional standing. The types of training offered to each group had traditionally varied, as had the proportions of practitioners with professional qualifications. Moreover, each group of social workers was located within a different organisational setting and the extent of discretion, of managerial control, and of independence of other – 'superior' – professions, also differed greatly. The story of the push for greater coherence, organisation and unity across this plethora of divisions has been told elsewhere.[12] What can be noted here is that the search for a common professional identity rested on two basic pillars, that of organisational change to bring the professional sub-groups together and that of a common training structure able to produce the set of generic skills necessary for the performance of all types of social work. Without the belief that social work had a common core which could be embodied in a generic training, structural reorganisation would have seemed much less necessary; with it, the case for change was a powerful one. The first moves towards a generic training were taken in the 1950s and bore fruit in the form of the first generic training course in 1954.[13] Moves towards creating a united professional front followed, culminating in the formation in 1963 of the Standing Conference of Organisations of Social Workers. Together these developments not only made change more necessary, they began to tip the balance firmly in favour of a form of reorganisation which brought most types of social work together in a single service. A degree of political, as well as professional, organisation had been achieved.

A FAMILY SERVICE?

Of the developments we have noted, the most powerful during the early 1960s was the concern to adopt a more preventative approach towards delinquency and child care. This attracted a considerable body of academic and pressure-group support and a fair head of steam was generated behind the idea of using the well-founded child-care services as a basis on which to build a more extensive service to deal with families and their problems. The focus was essentially that of families with children. Much of the concern was voiced in and around the Labour Party and it was no surprise when the process of developing policy in Opposition turned the spotlight on this issue in 1963/4. It happened in a study group on crime. As Hall notes,[14] seven members of the Labour Party study group chaired by Lord Longford subsequently became key members of the incoming Labour Government in 1964 and several of them were supporters of the Longford idea of a Family Service.[15] The Longford scrutiny of crime and responses to it was therefore a formative influence on future thinking. However, its remit touched on the personal social services only in relation to issues of child care and preventative social work with families; the welfare services figured much lower on the Labour Party's pre-election agenda.

There were arguments for a wider process of reform which would create a new service encapsulating provisions for the elderly, mentally ill and disabled, as well as children, but the focus of political and policy-making interest had centred around crime and not around alternative topics such as community care or the future of social work. In the event, the Longford Report translated these existing priorities into a suggested order of governmental action for the future; victory for Labour in the 1964 General Election transformed this rough timetable into an agenda for each of two government departments. For the Home Office the task was rapidly to develop and implement the proposals for a Family Service which would support a Family Court. For the Ministry of Health there was the vague consensus that something had to be done about the welfare services – presumably through the creation of a committee of some kind which could examine needs and options.

The Home Office began to run with its proposals for change almost before the Ministry of Health had realised that play had begun: a draft white paper was ready for discussion early in 1965. Nevertheless, the possibility of a quick reform which would produce a Family Service was soon halted. Whether inter-departmental rivalries or external pressures for a wider policy review were the more important is not clear. However, this does appear to be one of those occasions when an influential group of outsiders – mainly academics and professional social workers active in or sympathetic to the Labour Party – was a key factor. The case put by the group hinged around two points: that the future development of the welfare services ought to be considered in conjunction with that of the child-care services and that any proposals for reform ought at least to consider the possibility of bringing the scattered subsections of the social-work profession together. The first was politically astute, the creation of a Family Service could have drained away reforming zeal and left the lower priority welfare services with little hope of making up ground. The second was professionally astute and it was no accident that the majority of the experts in the group were closely involved in the newly created National Institute for Social Work.

Whatever the balance of ministerial, departmental and external pressures, the Home Office plans for a Family Service were stalled and the creation of what was to become the Seebohm Committee was announced in 1965. Nevertheless, this itself represented a partial accommodation with Home Office interests. The Committee was instructed to consider, as we have noted, how best to create an effective family service. It was also intended to act quickly and not to allow the opportunity for rapid reform to pass by. However, the membership of the Seebohm Committee reflected the fact that the central question had become much broader than that of child care and delinquency; it had in fact become a general review of the future of social work and the need for an effective organisational structure for the growth of the health and welfare, as well as child-care, traditions in social work. The Committee's specified task was easily reconciled with this broader perspective by defining the family very loosely to embrace households including elderly and impaired people as well as children – even one-person households. In short, the family was not to be equated with child rearing. The priorities and the definition of the problem made concrete by Longford in Opposition had therefore been unscrambled in the course of policy-making in office. The stage was set for the Seebohm Committee's move towards the establishment of a unified departmental structure for the personal social services.

THE SEEBOHM PROPOSALS

As Hall has persuasively argued, the Seebohm Committee pre-determined its choice of recommendations in the very way that it defined the problem to be tacked[16] [doc. 6]. A major component of the problem was that of coordination. Because the Home Office was allowed to proceed with reforms of the juvenile justice system independently of the deliberations of the Committee, the opportunity for more preventative and discretionary work in child care was already being dealt with and the Seebohm discussions could therefore take up the threads of the coordination debate undisturbed. This choice of problem was the first decisive move towards a unified department as the likely recommendation. The second was the attention given to the confusion caused to the public by organisational and professional 'Balkanisation'. The need from the public's point of view, it was argued, was for a 'single door on which to knock'.

The third, however, was less readily predicted from the history of the previous public debates and in retrospect it can be seen as very important. A major difficulty facing the divided services, it was asserted, was that they provided only limited career prospects and were politically weak and therefore starved of resources [doc. 7]. From this definition of a problem it was but a short step to the conclusion that only a single, united department, large enough to compete with the big spenders of local government, could hope to gain and retain more resources for the personal social services. Such a conclusion contained the assumption, of course, that the newly reorganised personal social services would be located within a new local government department and would not be developed as an adjunct to the health services. But that decision had effectively been made when the membership of the Committee was chosen with such obvious, if not exaggerated, regard for the interests of social work. Given the identification of these problems, therefore, it was a less than startling outcome when the Committee recommended that a new, unified Social Service Department should be the model on which to develop the personal social services within local government. The more interesting point was that the solution was conceived in terms of a resource as well as a coordination problem. Despite the subsequent criticism that the report was a far from convincing statement of the scale and nature of the needs and demands against which the shortage of resources could be measured, the expectations of a newly invigorated social-work profession had been enunciated quite clearly: they included more resources as well as more professional unity.

The organisational changes recommended by Seebohm and those enacted in 1971 were the same in principle, but they differed in detail. The Probation Service and hospital social work had been excluded from consideration by the initial terms of reference and were not, therefore, included in the Seebohm model of a Social Services Department. Probation has remained a separate service, but hospital social work was transferred to the SSDs at the time of the simultaneous reorganisation, in 1974, of the NHS and local government. However, the 1970 Act itself produced a narrower reform than Seebohm had envisaged: the welfare activities of education and housing departments were not transferred to the new SSDs. At the outset (in 1971), therefore, the new departments consisted largely of the old child-care and welfare services plus the important transfer from local-authority health services of the home-help service.

Even if the Seebohm Report, like the 1970 Act, had limited itself to initiating this structural reorganisation, it would have been important. It is easy in retrospect to minimise the nature of this change. It is when confronted with the organisationally fragmented nature of the personal social services in many other countries that one realises that the structural core of the Seebohm vision had much to recommend it in its own right. In principle, the SSDs are multi-purpose departments which can act with real flexibility in moving resources from one use to another. The very diversity which makes the SSDs difficult to describe in simple terms ensures an ability to put together different packages of help for different client groups. This merit is not to be underestimated, nor is the political strength of a department which commands a large share of a local authority's budget and whose chief officer is accepted as a full member of the team of chief officers. However, the resultant size of SSDs has been something of a millstone in operational terms, even if it has been a source of political muscle within local government.

Once one moves beyond organisational restructuring, however, the merits of the Seebohm Report are far less self-evident and uncontroversial. The Report was seen as both too radical and non-radical, as a 'great state paper' and as unconvincing and pusillanimous. In particular it was criticised for failing to articulate the consumer's viewpoint, for minimising the extent and range of unmet need and for neglecting to develop a clear and distinctive philosophy for the personal social services[17] [doc. 8]. The mixed reception accorded to the report is partly explained by the fact that the critics were comparing it with the classic investigative committees of enquiry which, especially in the late 1950s and early 1960s, had done so much to improve the level of understanding on a topic by in-depth analysis and data collection. But this was not to compare like with like. Seebohm had been specifically required to act quickly in a field where a general direction of change had been outlined in advance. It was not the same kind of Committee as some of those which had immediately preceded it; a substantial body of data collection and research was not envisaged.

Nevertheless, the assembled expertise ought to have been capable of producing a coherent philosophy. Did Seebohm really fail on this count? The first answer must be that the fiercest critic – Townsend – was really condemning Seebohm for not advancing his own particular philosophy, that of the personal social services as an instrument in the pursuit of equality.[18] It can be reasonably argued that this is not necessarily everyone's vision and that Seebohm may simply have articulated a philosophy which was not to Townsend's liking. However, it may also be that the report was so overwhelmed by concern with machinery as to be inattentive to more fundamental problems. Let us critically examine the report from this point of view.

The first striking feature of the Committee's approach is that the analysis of the deficiencies of the existing services did not include a critique of their philosophy or of their lack of a clear philosophy. The factors identified – the inadequate range and level of service, poor coordination, problems of access for clients and insufficient adaptability – implied that all that was needed was a better version of what existed. They were all problems which could be tackled by the mere fact of reorganisation. In short, not only had the definition of the problem pointed to organisational change as the solution, but that solution had apparently influenced the definition of the problem. The investigation revolved in a rather narrow compass.

That other ideas were abroad in the Committee is first suggested in the short chapters devoted to each of the client groups. They variously identified the need to create comprehensive systems of service characterised by a commitment to care in the community, a preventative approach, and an extension of service beyond crisis-oriented provision. These were isolated ideas rather than a concerted credo; but they did come together more completely in the subsequent chapters which concentrated on prevention, the community and consumer involvement [doc. 9], and the role of social work and of training. Did they amount to a coherent philosophy?

One of the most rapidly developed features of the new SSDs in the early 1970s was that of generic social-work practice. About this the report was decisive, but not detailed. The clear aim was to move beyond the mere treatment of symptoms and in order to do so, it was argued, each client, or family, should be the responsibility of a single worker who could take a broad overview and guide the client to and through the specific forms of help which they needed. Each field social worker therefore needed to gain a wide range of experience and skills so that they could perform their role adequately. Specialist knowledge and experience were seen as appropriate and necessary, but as a resource to be tapped by field workers rather than as a means of limiting the kinds of work to be undertaken by each worker. The clear role for specialists which was identified in the report was as consultants, either at headquarters or at area-team level. Beyond this the future was but vaguely outlined; the need was to make a break with the past and to allow SSDs to adapt as they learned from experience.

The general enthusiasm for generic social work was not an isolated phenomenon, it was congruent with a broader view of the role of the personal social services. Let us call it the search for a continuum of service. That this theme was not readily identified as a coherent philosophy by later critics can best be explained by the fact that it too was dominated by the need to break with the past. It was essentially a reactive identification of a key need, but it was not obviously less valid or radical for that. For example, the existing state of the children's and welfare services was one of a developing but incomplete move from the Poor Law emphasis on institutional provision towards a continuum of provision, extending from minimal support of people in their own homes to the complete assumption of responsibility for the personal, domestic and social care of them in residential settings. The hope was that a comprehensive continuum of service could be achieved in practice – and for every client group. This creation of a genuinely comprehensive range of services was at the heart of the Seebohm view of community-based care.

In addition, however, a clear change in philosophy was espoused. The Poor Law dependence on residential care had not been accidental, it had sprung from the conception of state services as 'residual'. Provision by the state had been seen as appropriate and necessary only when individual independence and family care had proved to be irretrievably lost or wanting. The residential role for the state therefore involved total care in institutions for people who could not, or should not, continue to live in the community. It was this philosophy of state care which Seebohm wished to see discontinued and replaced by a range of flexible and infinitely variable services designed to *complement*, not displace, the capacity for independent coping. Hence, the appropriate philosophy of service was seen to be summarised by three terms: comprehensive; community based; and preventative.

One further element must be added to this vision of the SSDs' future role. There were indications throughout the report that the personal social services ought to move towards that ideal of a universal service which had been firmly entrenched in other state social services. These indications are to be found most obviously in two perceptions. The first was that a comprehensive, as opposed to a residual, service would necessarily embrace many people who had not traditionally looked to the personal social services for help and who were not yet at the point of breakdown in independent coping (for example, families who were successfully caring for their children – or their handicapped members – but who needed advice or minimal support). The second was that the existing services were overwhelmed by problems which had reached crisis point, such that a more preventative approach was impossible to achieve. To move beyond crisis work and to tackle problems of less severity and at an earlier stage would also imply working with new sets of clients. These perceptions reinforced each other and suggested that the services ought in the future to be available to a wider population than in the past. To them was added a third perception which ensured that the ideal of a universal service was never far from the surface of the Committee's thinking. This was the belief that, far from actively encouraging people to seek help, the Poor Law inheritance was one of deterrence and stigmatisation. This was a barrier which had to be overcome.

The treatment of this theme was uneven and disjointed, however. In clearly identifying it – and some of the other strands of thinking noted above – we run the real risk of inventing for Seebohm a philosophy which did not directly leap from the pages at the time. The report was written around arguments about administrative change and the broader vision was allowed to trickle through these administrative concerns as best it might. The idea of a universal set of personal social services based on the new SSDs was a clear case in point; it emerged by implication rather than by declaration. Consequently, the central problems and issues were not well debated.

The essence of universal services is that they are available to the whole population in respect of problems which are not respecters of class, creed or social standing. Some such problems were noted by the Committee. Bereavement was one; the uncertainties and stresses of child rearing another. Preventative work in these fields inevitably implies a universal approach, yet the tradition had been to concentrate on the poor – if not the poorest – members of society. To move beyond a fragmentary discussion of such issues would have demanded careful consideration of the range and scale of those universal problems which were to be tackled and of the resource implications of doing so. But the estimation of resource needs was precisely one of the tasks which the Committee chose not to undertake in view of the difficult economic climate in which they deliberated.

To conclude that the Seebohm Committee had no philosophy would be wrong. We have noted strands of a philosophy which indicated the need for a clear break with the past. Nevertheless, we must conclude, as did Townsend, that a coherent philosophy was not stated unambiguously. More was implied than was made explicit and the resource implications of – and therefore constraints upon – change in the desired direction were carefully neglected. To say this, however, is to return to a point which we made much earlier. The personal social services were only belatedly restructured as the fifth social service. They broke free of the past in an incomplete way in the 1940s when a new legislative base was being laid and it took time to achieve the momentum for a second phase of change. By the time that momentum had been achieved the great heyday of the 'welfare state' had already begun to show signs of waning. The Seebohm Report can best be understood and appreciated as the product of a watershed: as the beginning of an era of doubt and austerity to be followed by outright disbelief in the enlarged role for the state to which the post-war years had given effect. To see, and to judge, Seebohm as one of the great architectural blue prints of the brave new 'welfare state' is therefore to misplace it historically. This is not to exonerate the architects for some rather limp prose and weakly developed themes, but it is to remember that in the optimism of the 1960s there were the seeds of a less rosy, even despairing period for social policy.

REFERENCES

1. REPORT OF THE COMMITTEE ON LOCAL AUTHORITY AND ALLIED PERSONAL SOCIAL SERVICES (SEEBOHM COMMITTEE), 1968 Cmnd 3703, July, para. 1

2. Ibid.

3. CROSSMAN, R. H. S., 1977 *The Diaries of a Cabinet Minister*. Hamilton, vol. 3; HALL, P., 1976 *Reforming the Welfare*. Heinemann

4. TOWNSEND, P. (ed), 1970 *The Fifth Social Service*. Fabian Society

5. DONNISON, D. V., Oct. 1968 'Seebohm – the report and its implications', *Social Work*, vol. 25 no. 4

6. HALL, P., 1976 *Reforming the Welfare*. Heinemann

7. GRIFFITH, J. A. G., 1966 *Central Departments and Local Authorities*. George Allen & Unwin

8. HALL, P. op.cit. (ref. 6) ch. 1; THOMAS, N. in Chapman, R. A. (ed.), 1973 *The Role of Commissions in Policy Making*. George Allen & Unwin

9. Quoted in HALL, P. op.cit. (ref. 6) p. 2

10. REPORT OF THE KILBRANDON COMMITTEE, 1964 *Children and Young Persons in Scotland*. Scottish Home and Health Department and Scottish Education Department, Cmnd 2306

11. HALL, P. op.cit. (ref. 6); COOPER, J. 1983 *The Creation of the British Personal Social Services 1962–74*. Heinemann

12. DONNISON, D. *et al.*, 1975 *Social Policy and Administration Revisited*. George Allen & Unwin, ch. 11

13. HALL, P., op.cit. (ref. 6)

14. Ibid.

15. REPORT OF A LABOUR PARTY STUDY GROUP, 1964 *Crime, a Challenge to us All*, (Chairman: Lord Longford)

16. HALL, P. op.cit. (ref. 6)

17. TOWNSEND, P. op.cit. (ref. 4)

18. Ibid.

Chapter four

TRENDS AND DEVELOPMENTS

POST-SEEBOHM ISSUES AND TRENDS

The Personal Social Services Act 1970 was among the last outputs of a dying Parliament: implementation became the responsibility of the new Conservative administration led by Mr Heath. That the Seebohm proposals were successfully plucked from oblivion and enacted at the eleventh hour was due in part to the energetic campaigning of social-work interests and indicated their enthusiasm for change.[1] But there were doubts and pockets of resistance too. In particular, the medical interests in local government had been outflanked by the new strength and cohesion of the momentum for a change which solely benefited the social-work profession. All Medical Officers of Health stood to lose some part of their department – for example, control of the home-help service – and those who were responsible for combined health and welfare departments stood to lose a considerable slice of their empire. This was a change in their fortunes only surpassed by their complete removal from local government in the reorganisation of the NHS in 1974.

Despite the doubts, however, the implementation of the structural changes proceeded largely without incident. The government had accepted the Seebohm argument that the appointment of a Social Service Committee and a Director of Social Services should be a legislative requirement and that the Minister should have some control over the kinds of people shortlisted for the new (Director) posts. A social-work hegemony was underwritten by law and subsequent practice. Very few of the new directors came from backgrounds other than social-work – broadly defined. Medical doctors did not retain their considerable grip on the welfare services.

The new Social Services Departments were not merely the product of a tinkering with administrative machinery, however. They leapt into life with far more vigour than the Seebohm parentage might have suggested was likely. This was because their early years of existence were characterised by the confluence of a number of inheritances, trends and issues. At least six can be identified:

1. the philosophy of change implied in the Seebohm Report itself;
2. the scale and complexity of the new departments;
3. the reformative legislation of the late 1960s;
4. the momentum of change in social work;
5. the rate of increase experienced in personal social services expenditure;
6. the movement towards comprehensive rational planning and corporate management in local government.

Philosophy and implementation

The first of these has been dealt with. The Seebohm inheritance at the level of objectives and philosophy can be summarised as consisting of an ideal model of the personal social services based on a comprehensive system of services permitting a continuum of responses appropriate to varying degrees and types of need; preventive as well as 'casualty', or crisis, work; a universal rather than a residual approach such that stigmatisation would be minimised and access maximised; a community orientation which embraced the decentralisation of work and much decision-making to area teams and also a commitment to working with communities and to encouraging consumer participation; a generic base for social-work practice which broke free from mere symptom-oriented specialisation and treatment.

As we have argued, some of these strands of the philosophy were more clearly presented than others and the impact of the whole was greatly blunted by the preoccupation with organisational change. Nevertheless, some of the message found its way into each of the new Social Services Departments and a relatively coherent version of the whole was articulated by some of the directors and departments. This was hardly surprising: Seebohm had reflected and focused some of the key issues confronting the leaders of the social work profession. For some, at least, thinking had moved beyond the formulations actually presented in the Seebohm Report. It was as well that at least some philosophical inheritance was available because the Act of 1970 provided none, and the policy base was slender indeed for what was to become an important, though comparatively small, social service. We will return to this issue later in the chapter.

Social work, social care, and social planning

Scale and complexity

The increased scale and complexity of the new SSDs need not detain us at this point. It was an issue which resulted in a burst of organisational theorising, dispute and some innovation.[2] This theorising partly reflected the fact that most new directors lacked experience of organisations as large as the ones over which they now presided. It was also the product of the Seebohm enthusiasm for area-based teamwork, and it echoed a much wider debate about the appropriateness of hierarchical forms of organisation – especially in community-oriented, professionally manned services. What needs to be noted for the moment, however, is that these organisational preoccupations were real and energy-consuming for directors and their departments in the early days of implementation.

Legislative change

The reformative legislation of the late 1960s was a far more potent and lasting preoccupation, however, in that it embraced the dominant idea of the time: moves towards community-based and preventative provision rather than dependence on residential institutions; an emphasis on previously neglected client groups; and a shift from an individualistic to a social model of causation in explaining and responding to problems. The symbolic importance of the legislation was even greater than its undoubted practical significance – and much greater than the actual results achieved during the early 1970s. Three pieces of legislation can be identified as clearly influential: the Health Services and Public Health Act 1968; the Children and Young Persons Act 1969; and the Chronically Sick and Disabled Persons Act 1970.

The first was primarily a corrective to the narrow range of powers and duties allotted to the welfare services in 1948. It enabled local authorities directly to do much, especially for old people, which previously they had done indirectly through voluntary organisations. Examples were the provision of meals on wheels services, warden services and adaptations; the provision of home help on an adequate scale became mandatory. The Act, therefore, reflected the concern to develop a continuum of welfare services in the community.

The second of these Acts had the most radical origins of the three, but was most obviously and quickly compromised by partial implementation.[3] Nevertheless, it greatly altered the role of social work in relation to children, especially delinquent children. As we have already noted, it was the product of a fundamental recasting of views of delinquent behaviour and of the response to such behaviour. It gave greater discretion to social-services departments in dealing with children, at the expense of the courts and magistracy, and it developed the idea of preventative and community-based work in the form, especially, of Intermediate Treatment. It embodied the spirit of a period of social and professional change.

The third of these Acts introduced the chronically sick and disabled – a much neglected group in the past – into the same service philosophy. Moreover, it placed local authorities under a duty *to seek out* need in this field and to develop their provision in an informed way. Symbolically, the Act summarised and focused the expanded role of research and planning which the Seebohm changes had inserted into the decision-making processes of the SSDs. The early thrust of research and analytical work was universally concentrated on exploring problems of need identification and measurement. The Act legitimated this role for research and analysis, albeit in a watered-down version in practice. The legislation was honoured in partial local-government observance, in the face of a central government breach, of the requirement to seek out need. The simple fact was that the Conservative government, and DHSS Ministers in particular, lacked enthusiasm for a thorough-going accountancy of need. They permitted, even encouraged, local authorities to make token gestures in the direction of seeking out need. Nevertheless, many authorities made real efforts and the Act had an undeniable impact on thinking about disability.

Change in social work

We earlier took pains not to define the personal social services in terms of social work, but it would be foolish to deny that the social-services departments were most immediately and fully absorbed in the preoccupations of social work. Three main topics of contemporary debate therefore had a strong impact on the new departments: the merits of different concepts of generic social-work practice; the implications of a new model of problem causation; and the nature, meaning and desirability of professionalisation. Needless to say, the perennial debate about the meaning of social work echoed through these concerns, but precisely because it is perennial it need not be pursued as a separate issue at this point.

The first of these topics posed questions about the organisation of fieldwork practice, the allocation of caseloads, and the role of traditional specialisations. Social-service departments varied in their interpretation of genericism from those in which each worker was expected to carry a caseload which reflected the full range and composition of the demand falling on the department, to those which permitted the traditional specialisms in childcare, welfare and mental welfare work to flourish almost unchanged. Indeed, practice often varied considerably between area teams in a department. There was plenty of room for discussion, not least because a new form of division of labour gained ground and overlaid the basic debate: intake teams specialising in short-term work began to gain in popularity and to create room for longer-term work for other social workers.

The reinterpretation of the social problems confronting social workers posed additional questions about the division of labour in social work. The social casework tradition of the post-war years had been predicated upon individual and small-group, especially family, pathology. The approach was psychological and psycho-therapeutic in orientation. The shift towards a model of social causation was partly born in the movement surrounding the rediscovery of poverty and partly in the reinterpretation of criminality. It posed a problem. If the causes of social problems were located in social institutions and the very structure of society, how could social workers be expected to respond? Answers took many forms; but they all raised doubts about the need for, or the centrality of, traditional social casework.

In its most radical manifestations, the reinterpretation of social problems made social casework an irrelevance. The only appropriate responses were to work for fundamental change in the social system locally, and on a national or international canvas. The perception of the need for change could also take a somewhat less radical form in which the problem was to modify the impact of social institutions – education, the social-security system, the job market – on people. This, too, consigned traditional social casework to limbo, but created a new division of tasks. The key tasks were advocacy and welfare rights work at the case level and social planning at the strategic level.[4] For what this perspective revealed above all else was that the success of the personal social services depended upon the attitudes and policies of other organisations over which the personal social services had no direct control and only limited indirect influence through planning and political activities. Whether case advocacy and planning were to become the new divisions of labour based on fieldworkers and planners/managers respectively, or whether both tasks were to be welded together in a new conception of the fieldwork task, was a moot point.

At a still lower level of radical purity, the new perspective underlined the need for a bevy of ways of working which would incorporate community work, group work and other methods of intervention, as well as the more traditional forms of social casework. This approach implied that not all problems could be laid at the door of malfunctioning social institutions. Grieving for a newly dead loved one might, for example, remain a painful experience even in utopia and a traditional casework inter-personal response might seem appropriate. Indeed, the concern with social causation which sprang to life in the 1960s was rapidly accompanied by a more introspective search for meaning and fulfillment in the highly personalised spheres of life; by the 1970s it had promoted a great diversity of approaches to counselling, therapy and personal development. The highway of change had rapidly to accommodate more than one stream of traffic. Even such apparently alien perspectives as behaviour therapy came to influence a social-work profession which had originally been marked down for change because of the rediscovery of social causality and the defects of social structure and of social institutions. Social workers had become polymaths – in theory.

Just as the Children and Young Persons Act 1969 moved from a more radical recasting of the theory of the problem to a rather tame recasting of the solutions on offer, so social work practice responded slowly and somewhat undramatically to the theoretical and philosophical challenge laid before it. The SSDs experienced more tumult in debate than in methods of working. Community work was established as a token rather than as a mainstream activity in the early years and the impact of SSDs and social workers on other social institutions proved to be mildly stimulating at best, rather than revolutionary.[5] The biggest single change at the fieldwork level was probably the growth of advisory, advocacy and welfare-rights work – both as a specialist field of activity and as an integral part of the social-work role. Social casework survived in a new or modified form, it did not give way to a completely new way of working. But to say that is neither to deny the extent and depth of the questioning and debate, nor to underestimate the energy which was absorbed in creating a limited degree of change.

Issues of professionalisation revolved in particular around three main questions: how far was it legitimate for social work to pursue professionalisation as a goal and which activities – other than fieldwork – should be included in such a movement; how quickly and thoroughly could a fully trained profession be achieved; and what relationships with superordinate decision-makers were to be seen as appropriate to social work? The first of these split social work along several 'fracture planes'. Many community-minded social workers, in particular, saw professionalisation as an inappropriate aspiration. Nevertheless, the general direction of change has been that of a slow movement towards a fully accredited profession. It has embraced the second issue: professional training. A fully trained body of workers has come to be the primary criterion of full professional status and this has been approached in field social work both by the expansion of training and the slowing down of the rate of growth in the numbers of social workers. In addition, unqualified social workers and aides have been more systematically distinguished from their qualified colleagues in administrative principle, even if their roles have not always been as clearly distinguished in day-to-day practice. One of the side effects of this push towards professional status has been to focus attention on the relationship between field social workers on the one hand and residential and day-care workers on the other at the very time that the professional component in these latter areas of work has been more fully recognised in theory.

The third issue of professionalisation, that of the discretion and autonomy appropriate to social workers, is discussed at greater length in Chapter 6. The fact that it is closely connected with professionalisation, however, arises from the single model of the professional which has been so influential in contemporary thinking and writing. Autonomy in the work role and a large area of independent decision-making has been a distinctive characteristic of the 'classical' professions (especially medicine and the law). It came to be seen as a 'right', or precondition, of professional work and this view was emphasised by the streams of radical thinking about the social-work role which saw virtue in the freedom of the individual worker. For many, too, the acquisition of professional status became a necessary step in the achievement of autonomy, independence and respect. That it could also be seen by some as a *sufficient* step in the gaining of these desired benefits, points to a blind spot concerning the classical professions. They have enjoyed more than a mere status as professions, they have captured power and also built up an ability to command awe in the recipients and consumers of their skills.

A period of growth

Despite the multi-faceted nature of change in the early 1970s, these years were less a time of philosophical discourse for the average director than one of deciding how best to spend money in a comparatively rapidly growing field. Expenditure growth on the personal social services had begun to take off in the mid-1960s and continued quietly to effect change throughout the Seebohm era. Although the economy gave cause for concern and produced occasional hiccups in the upward trend of expenditure, the trend was very clear, especially in retrospect. The early period of Conservative government beginning in 1970 appeared to threaten this forward march of personal social-services expenditure, but the subsequent boom was fully reflected in further growth – not least in capital expenditures on such items as residential homes, day centres and hostels. The capital expenditure spree was to prove a mixed blessing in later years, but during the early years of the new SSDs it made for a hectic round of planning and of implementing new developments.

To put this in context, one must add that the personal social services had started from very low expenditure levels and had a long way to go to even begin to compare with longer established services; but the immediate experience and assumption was nonetheless of growth. This was most clearly underlined in the 1972 ten-year planning exercise inaugurated by the DHSS, in which it was assumed that the SSDs could expect to experience growth in real expenditure in the order of 10 per cent per annum. This was a profound and formative, albeit short-lived, influence in the new departments. The nature and impact of expenditure trends is considered in detail in Chapter 8; for the moment it is sufficient to note that the growth which Seebohm had cautiously not asked for seemed to be falling unbidden into the laps of the Social Services Committees and Directors. Growth created room for change and for an explicit approach to identifying and meeting new needs and unmet needs.

An approach to planning

The final trend which we have identified fitted into this picture of growth. The move towards rational, comprehensive forward planning was not explicitly based on expenditure growth, but the two went well together. To plan for the future is so much more manageable, and rationality is so much more attractive as a concept, in conditions of steady growth. The rate of growth experienced by many SSDs in the early days was such that there was little time for consulting with other departments, let alone negotiating priorities and strategies. But as the SSDs settled down it became clear that the idea of forward planning, especially corporate planning across the full range of local authority services and departments, had come to the fore at an opportune moment. It fitted well with some of the mildly progressive, as opposed to sharply radical, views of the role of the personal social services.

As we have noted, one version of the social-causation model of problems emphasised the importance of a variety of social institutions in initiating and shaping the difficulties faced by individuals and families. Alone, the personal social services could hope to do little about this problem. But the ideal of corporate planning provided for the authority as a whole to survey its locality, identify problems which cut across the responsibilities of different departments, and initiate concerted action to produce change and improvement. In short, corporate planning seemed to provide an arena in which the SSD could hope to begin to influence the wider environment in which it had to work and which had such a profound effect on its role and effectiveness. For some directors at least, involvement in corporate planning epitomised the social planning function of the SSDs and identified a way in which senior officers could develop a strategic role in the locality and not merely in their own department.

To discharge a strategic role, however, implies a clear view of where one is heading; it suggests a perception of broad objectives. How far were these readily available and well developed? Was there a consensus about the route which should be taken?

OBJECTIVES AND GOALS

Few of the newly appointed Directors of Social Services could have entirely failed to ask themselves: what are we trying to achieve? But their answers were more likely to be practical than philosophical because the pressure of known and suspected need, and the many issues which we have already noted, demanded immediate responses. Their problem was essentially that of establishing some sense of priorities in a hectic period of change. Academics were not so beset by the needs of the moment and could more readily choose to spend time asking the larger questions.

If we summarise the burden of the Seebohm message, we can see that it has two parts to it. The first was to meet existing unmet need and to move towards a full recognition of new needs, many of them concerned with a more preventative – rather than a 'casualty' dominated – role. The second strand was that of changing the type of service offered and developing along already established lines towards a comprehensive range of provisions, most of them firmly based in the community. Stated thus, it was a laudable approach. The problem, as we have seen, was that it was never stated forcibly and was overshadowed by less strategic matters. This was well illustrated by an essay on the philosophy of the new SSDs, written by a leading practitioner, which dwelt upon the ethical issues facing social workers but left unexamined the fundamental role of the personal social services.[6]

Nevertheless, even stated thus, the Seebohm message would not have satisfied the critics whose work was orchestrated and edited by Peter Townsend.[7] The argument advanced by Townsend himself well illustrated the level to which the debate was being raised. What Townsend wanted to establish – and to assert – was the rationale which should underpin the urge to meet social need. For him there was a simple answer: that of pursuing equality. The development of the personal social services should, he suggested, serve the purpose of reducing inequalities of both a material and social kind [doc. 10]. At the time, the general argument for equality was widely accepted as a keystone of social policy, but – even so – it needed to be examined carefully. The problem with this formulation of the objective of the personal social services, as with the more radical models of promoting social change through social work, was that the goal was so much larger and wider than the means available for its achievement. Was the pursuit of equality really an appropriate over-arching objective for services which commanded so few of the key sources and generators of inequality? The income maintenance services might be seen as a suitable vehicle, as might employment policy and education. The personal social services, on the other hand, had traditionally dealt with problems at a more individualistic level. Could they reasonably be expected to have a major impact on the structurally rooted inequalities of the society?

EQUALITY: AN APPROPRIATE AND FEASIBLE GOAL?

Equality has been a central concept of social policy, but it is not a simple one.[8] It has three broad dimensions, each of which implies different kinds of policies and not all of which are compatible one with another. We therefore need to be clear that we know what it is we are talking about before we consider it as a possible goal of the personal social services.

The first and most stringent sense of equality is that the distribution of resources in society should be brought as near to complete equality as is compatible with any notions of just reward and merit which are accepted as legitimate. One might argue, for example, that resources should be distributed equally except in so far as some people work markedly harder, longer, or in more trying circumstances than others. These people might be given rewards for their contribution to the common good, thus creating some, limited, inequality.

This inequality raises a second issue, however. People may reasonably call for equal access to the opportunities to gain such rewards – the opportunities to become unequal. If harder and longer work is the sole source of the rewards, access to such work is all that is implied. Insofar, however, as the skill component of work is rewarded, it is equal access to the opportunity to acquire rewarded skills which matters. Access to education and training may therefore be crucial. The focus shifts to include a concern with equality of opportunity.

The third idea of equality does not refer to the distribution of resources for its own sake, but to its power to compensate for, ameliorate or remove social need. From this perspective, absolute equality would not be satisfactory because people with greater needs than others would be unjustly treated by such a policy. Whatever basic distribution of resources is seen to be just, therefore, a subsequent redistribution has to be applied in order to give more resources to those in greatest need. A combination of these three approaches might be seen to yield a just society – always assuming that equality is seen as the hallmark of justice.

Our society, however, does not even begin to approximate this vision and therefore the task is not to distribute resources according to a notion of equality, but to reduce inequalities. This can be seen to involve four basic kinds of action: to reduce the *generation of* inequalities; to promote *equality of opportunity*, or access, to the better paid jobs which underpin much inequality; *to redistribute* resources from the over-rewarded *to the under-rewarded* so as to reduce unacceptable inequalities remaining in the society; and to *redistribute* resources *towards need* so as to allow for the unequal distribution of needs. It will be immediately seen that redistribution occurs twice: once as a means of effecting a movement from the richer to the poorer; and a second time as a means of effecting movement from the less needy to the more needy. They can be distinguished by calling them *vertical redistribution* (to the poor) and *contingency redistribution* (to the needy).[9]

It must be emphasised that these two forms of redistribution are only the same in so far as the poor are the only people in need. In particular, universal services (e.g., the NHS) designed to meet universal needs (e.g., sickness) will only make a limited impact on vertical inequalities in relation to the money spent on them. This is because a major part of the expenditure will be benefiting people above poverty levels who nevertheless experience the need in question. In short, a universal service is a comparatively inefficient instrument for affecting vertical redistribution; its primary purpose is contingency redistribution.

To this basic picture we must add one further perspective. The above discussion relates essentially to the distribution of material resources. It does not refer to Townsend's notion of equality of social integration. This is an important refinement of the idea of equality and has to be included in our consideration. Most people require and seek at least some degree of social involvement with others. This may most typically take the form of close relationships with significant others: spouses, offspring, other relatives, friends. To be cut off from such relationships by reason of infirmity, death (of the significant other), stigma and social rejection, lack of transport, or an inability to handle such relationships, may usually be accounted a real deprivation. It may equally be a deprivation to be isolated from the wider society in the form of groups, clubs, places of entertainment. Social integration may also be about having and performing satisfactorily in well regarded roles such as work or child rearing. *Inequalities of social integration* may therefore take the form of deprivations of at least three major kinds: of primary relationships; of involvement in wider social groups and activities; and of valued and rewarding social roles. In so far as it is possible to compensate for, remedy, or mitigate such deprivation, a goal of equality of social integration may be both valid and desirable. It may also be more readily agreed to than equality of a material kind, though it has been less readily specified and articulated in social policy.

What we must now ask is how, if at all, these ideas could apply to the personal social services, taking for granted for the time being the notion that equality is desired in all these various senses. This task has been attempted by one of us elsewhere, but the conclusions can be briefly summarised here.[10]

The least appropriate task for the personal social services is that of forestalling the generation of material inequality. The personal social services do not command the wealth or income creating processes of society and can do little to modify the structure of rewards even in their own small area of employment. However, equality of access to some kind of living income is a different matter. Impaired, sick and socially handicapped people all suffer disadvantage in job markets, or are excluded from them altogether. Both the improvement of access to work opportunities and pressure for income maintenance (e.g., through welfare rights works) are appropriate roles for the personal social services, albeit within a context which is dominated by employment markets, income maintenance services and the educational system.

The redistribution of resources to those in need is quite clearly a primary function of the personal social services, but it raises questions. The traditional concentration of poor people in the clientele of the personal social services could be seen as a guarantee that directing resources towards the needy also redistributes resources vertically to the poor (depending upon who pays for the services). However, in so far as the needs addressed are universal ones which beset middle and upper income holders as well as the poor, the personal social services have not met need very adequately in the past. Whether the services are really needed or desired by the better-off is one question to be answered. If they are, however, a move towards a universal service would reduce the degree of vertical redistribution but effect a greater equality according to need. It might also benefit the poorer sufferers of need if universal services proved to be less stigmatising and more fully utilised. Either way, redistribution and the fostering of equality seems to be an inevitable function of the personal social services, providing services are not paid for primarily by those who use them.

Equality of social integration is even more central to the work of the personal social services. It can be pursued in five distinct ways: the avoidance of the unnecessary and inappropriate use of socially isolating services (e.g., large, impersonal residential institutions); the avoidance of institutionalisation, social isolation and an impoverished social life among people who have necessarily to live in some form of institutional care; the prevention and reduction of social isolation among people living 'in the community'; the compensation of people suffering unavoidable isolation; and the removal of the stigma attached to the use of services. Each of these has a somewhat different implication for service development and they are not necessarily compatible – especially in the face of resource shortages. The action equivalents of each might be briefly characterised, too simplistically, as: expansion of community-care services; the improvement of the quality of residential care of all kinds; the improvement of the quality of community-care services and the expansion of their preventative functions; the use of community-based services to substitute for 'normal' social networks and patterns of integration; and the 'delabelling' of stigmatising conditions, types of intervention and services (not least by moving towards the provision of universal services which acquire status from their middle-class clients).

Taken together, therefore, it can be seen that the personal social services have a real role to play in reducing inequalities in resource distribution and social integration. But this does not exhaust the possibilities. A further dimension of inequality can be summarised as that of power. The opportunity to control or influence events which affect one closely and the environment in which one lives is no more equally distributed than are material resources. In so far as the object of a search for greater equality of power is that of giving people some say in issues of a predominantly local nature, the personal social services can be seen to be an appropriate vehicle. The Seebohm Report gave credence to this view by discussing work with communities and consumer involvement. Both may be seen as extending the opportunities available to the comparatively powerless. For example, increased opportunities could be generated for the elderly and impaired to exercise some influence over a social environment which is substantially shaped by the interests and needs of able-bodied people of working age with access to a reasonable income. The generation of awareness, of demands for better services in communities, and the involvement of the consumer in decision-making do not exhaust the possibilities, however. The very development of services, providing they are desired and appropriate, also reduces powerlessness by extending choices to people who would otherwise be prevented from gaining help with their particular needs.

The personal social services can be seen to have a role in relation to inequalities in material resources, social integration and power, therefore. The extent to which they can make a significant impact on each depends, however, on the way in which the services are developed.

A UNIVERSALIST SERVICE: A LATENT GOAL?

We have at several points referred to the fact that, systematically or otherwise, during the Seebohm years the personal social services were edged towards that model of a universal service developed in the post-war period. This needs closer examination before it can be said to have been a goal, however. The first question to be asked is whether there really are needs of a universal kind to which a universal service would be an appropriate response. Alternatively, are the personal social services dominated by forms of deviance of one kind or another which are narrowly located among the poor, or in other identifiable groups of people such as the inhabitants of inner city areas? The appropriate response would be to take each of the client groups and consider them in detail in order to identify the importance of needs of a universal kind and to decide whether they only become a problem for social policy when linked with poverty. Space does not permit such an exercise, but illustrative examples are worth considering.

Some of the problems brought to the personal social services are obvious and direct correlates of poverty, or are likely to be resolved rapidly if money is not tight. Homelessness is one example and debts resulting in the potential loss of the basic necessities of life – shelter heating, domestic facilities – is another. This is not to say that these problems never beset people with middle or higher incomes – especially in periods of high unemployment – merely that they are concentrated among poorer families. They typify a very large part of the problem facing the personal social services: many of the needs encountered are manifestations and by-products of poverty and could conceivably be resolved in other ways than by massaging them with the scarce liniments of social work and social care. This was a large part of what Seebohm meant by the need to move away from a casualty and crisis-oriented service. Without action elsewhere, however, the problems remain to be picked up by the personal social services and more universal needs may therefore be forced into the background.

By way of comparison, there certainly are problems which do beset people of all income groups. One obvious example is that of the dilemmas and crises of child rearing. That the issue is a universal one is reflected in the sales of childrearing manuals. Interestingly, the early formulations of the famous attempt by Sir Keith Joseph to place the notion of a 'cycle of deprivation' on the policy agenda did refer to the idea that defects in family relationships and in child rearing could ripple through the generations in well-heeled families, as much as in poor families. The point was not surprisingly lost in the uproar which surrounded the tendency of the 'cycle of deprivation' to blame the poor for their condition and problem. Nonetheless, the point remains that parenting is a problematic human endeavour and support in it may be needed across class and other social categories. The cultivation and management of successful long-term relations between couples living together is another obvious area of universal need. Coping with bereavement, caring for dependent elderly and handicapped adults, and negotiating family relationships are other clear examples of issues which give rise to problems and to a need for help across social boundaries.

To justify a move towards a range of universal provisions in the personal social services is not difficult, therefore; to pay for such provision is a different matter. To meet the kinds of universal needs noted above would require a very large social-work and counselling capacity capable of effecting a complete break with the tradition of working primarily with problems that have reached crisis proportions. Although the personal social services were characterised by growth until the mid-1970s, there was no realistic chance of that growth being sufficient to create even that form of universal service available in the health and educational fields. The personal social services were therefore destined to continue with an often crisis-oriented pattern of work and with a clientele drawn disproportionately from the poorer sections of society.

COMMUNITY CARE: A GOAL WITHOUT MEANING?

If the personal social services can be most closely associated with any one overarching policy objective, it is that of community care. This is the most widely applicable policy and the one which has received most attention and discussion. It is also the policy which is most surrounded by confusion and disagreement. As Walker notes, there is agreement that it is a major goal, but virtually none on what it means.[11] The idea of community is itself one of the least understood but most widely used – and abused – in the lexicon of social welfare policy[12] [doc. 11]. One of the most recent manifestations of this confusion and uncertainty arises from the emphasis on care *by* the community, rather than *in* the community. Unlike Bayley's original formulation [doc. 12], care by the community presently seems to mean that problems should be absorbed as much as possible by relying on unpaid help in families and neighbourhoods rather than on the provision of public services. If, indeed, this is what it does mean, it raises very serious questions about the extent and adequacy of such unpaid help.[13] But this is merely to emphasise another perennial feature of community: political aspirations and policy intentions have consistently been complex and subject to confusing and often rapid change.

One way of handling the confusion surrounding the concept might be to define community care rigorously and then to examine it in detail. Definitions, however, reflect purposes and the meaning of community care has varied so much precisely because different groups at different times have used it as a term to cloak differing intentions.[14] Let us proceed to tackle the problem in another way, therefore. Let us begin by examining how caring does, and in future may, happen in the real world and subsequently superimpose a selection of policy intentions expressed over the past twenty years or so onto this background.

When talking of care we are referring to the personal, domestic and social tasks and activities necessary to the notions of a normal way of life prevailing in society in respect of those people for whom it is most likely to be a problem – children, the frail elderly, the chronically sick, the handicapped, etc. A vast amount of such care is likely to be *self care*, just as it is for people who do not suffer such disadvantages, but self care will not always be possible at a sufficient level and care has then to be provided by others. The others are most likely to be members of the person's immediate family. As Moroney demonstrated, and others have subsequently elaborated in detail, the family remains a bastion of care.[15] Beyond it, however, there is the possibility of help from neighbours, friends and other members of the local community. Self care backed up by this range of helpers constitutes what is now commonly referred to as the informal caring system.

Informal care, apart from self care, is predominantly – though not exclusively – care provided by women and, of course, it is care for which they do not normally receive payment. It is also characterised by a low level of formal organisation. It typically consists of the actions of individuals or small groups. However, a large amount of additional help is made available, with varying degrees of organisation, by volunteers who may work through voluntary bodies or state services. To it must be added that help which people buy on the private market in the form of domestic and personal assistance. Taken together, informal care, help provided by volunteers, and commercially purchased care, seem to constitute what is meant by care *by* the community. Its hallmark is that it does not involve the state in expenditure – or is believed to involve only very marginal expenditures. What is left is statutory and voluntary provision. Of course, much of the work of formal voluntary organisations is funded other than by the state, and state services may make charges and thereby pass part of the cost back to consumers. Nevertheless, where the state is a principal paymaster for the care delivered, the tendency now is to talk of care *in* the community: services are delivered to people who continue to remain in their own homes, but at a cost to public expenditure.

It is by no means certain that the above distinction between care in the community and care by the community is what everyone has in mind when using the terms, but it is does seem to reflect the principal contemporary purpose of stressing the distinction – which is to contain the cost to the state. By way of contrast, the different types, or 'systems', of caring (informal, volunteer, commercial, formal voluntary, and formal statutory) can be identified with much greater confidence. The boundaries are difficult to draw at the margin in most cases, but the basic differences arise from the variation in the motivation and rewards experienced by the person doing the caring and the level and form of organisation through which the care is activated.

The patterns of care described above are well established, but are surprisingly little understood. In particular, little attempt has been made in the past to study the nature of care within families. Only recently has there been a real concern to explore such crucial questions as: at what cost to the people involved is care provided within the family and what factors may influence the ability and willingness of kin to care for each other in the future? That the costs of caring can be high, especially for women, has rapidly become a more commonplace assumption; though the range, intensity and consequences of the costs – to health, social life, career and finances – has only begun to be explored.[16] Similarly, the costs borne by the cared-for themselves have remained unstudied and only emerge infrequently in reference to 'granny-bashing' and other expressions of strained relationships.[17]

One of the implications of these costs is that the willingness to bear them as the price of caring may be highly sensitive to changes in family structures and norms. The impact of increased levels of divorce and remarriage on the pattern of kinship obligations to care is one clear example of uncertainty about the future. Another is the future availability of employment opportunities for women and the extent to which the expectation of paid work will continue to rise among women. Set alongside this is the durability of gender roles in the face of high levels of unemployment: will more men undertake caring roles and, if so, will they only do so where these roles approximate to 'real work' – either paid or voluntary? These questions are crucial because, in the absence of influential public policies, they point to the factors which will shape the 'caring capacity of the community' in the future.[18] But public policies may be influential and questions arise about how far it may be possible to encourage, support, underpin or, indeed, undermine, the willingness of people to care for others. There are many possible forms of intervention which might encourage caring: tax concessions, well-targeted support for carers, well-orchestrated attempts to enhance people's sense of obligation to care for kin or strangers. What we need to do for the moment, however, is to consider the terms in which community-care policies have been couched in the recent past and to discover the intentions which have lain beneath these policies.

A major and recent shift in community-care policy has already been identified: that of emphasising care by the community rather than care in the community. That the new emphasis is problematic is clear from our comments on the costs and uncertainties of care by kin. It must be added that enthusiasm for neighbouring and volunteer work of various kinds has generated more activity and heated debate than real knowledge of the limits of these means of meeting caring needs. Research has begun to produce valuable results, but it has as yet taken little of the uncertainty out of the policy issues.[19] In particular, it has not suggested that care by the community is viable in the absence of the more traditional approach of developing strong, formal services in the community.[20] The new conventional wisdom is that such formal services should support and sustain informal care rather than operate as if informal care did not exist. What this suggests is that having concentrated for several decades on expanding formal services within the community, there is now a need to find the most productive balance and relationship between formal and informal care. Let us therefore consider what formal services have been at the heart of community-care policy in the past.

We earlier indicated that community care blossomed at different times and in different ways for the key client groups in the personal social services. The early commitment in child care was to boarding-out as an alternative to residential homes and to modifying residential care so as to make it a more effective approximation of family life. It later took the form of a drive to reduce recourse to penal institutions. In the case of the elderly, the early emphasis approximated the second of the three aspects of child-care policy – the search for a homely atmosphere in residential care. The first post-war commitment was to move away from the institutional inheritance of the Poor Law by building new, smaller homes. The second development was the expansion of domiciliary and day-care services: small dwellings for one or two person householders; and sheltered housing, as alternatives to residential homes. The third was the concern to reduce the need for long-stay care of the elderly in hospitals and to avoid the 'silting-up' of beds in both acute and geriatric wards. In the case of mental illness and handicap, this issue of hospital beds was at the heart of policy from the very beginning.

The various strands of community-care policy can therefore be summarised thus:
1. to avoid unnecessary hospitalisation;
2. to switch demand from the NHS to local (especially local-authority) services;
3. to avoid unnecessary care in institutions including local-authority residential care;

4.   to humanise residential care and make it more 'home-like';
5.   to avoid unnecessary public expenditure on formal services.

The last of these is comparatively recent in a well-developed form. The first four of these objectives dominated thinking in the post-war decades up to the mid-1970s, but they were not entirely compatible in practice. Collectively they pointed to the need to develop services in the community, especially on the part of local authorities, but they have confronted local authorities with three rather different kinds of demand:

1.   to meet unmet and growing demands for community services so as *to help prevent demand for institutional care*;
2.   to provide services – including institutional care – in order to limit dependence on penal institutionals and to *facilitate the transfer of existing long-stay NHS patients* into community settings;
3.   to *meet unavoidable demand for institutional care* in increasingly humane environments.

The easiest way for local authorities to conceive of community care was to see the reduction of residential provision as the clear policy goal. The way forward was then to develop social work, domiciliary and day care within SSDs and to encourage the provision of appropriate housing – including sheltered housing – by housing departments. Even this simple approach involved responding to two problems – meeting *new* needs (especially among the growing, and increasingly very elderly, populations of old people) and substituting community-based packages of care for *existing* clients of residential care. The complicating factor grafted onto this local authority viewpoint was that central-government policy involved a substantial increase in demand in order to keep juveniles out of penal institutions and in order to move many very dependent people into the ambit of the local authorities.

The role of institutional provision by SSDs has therefore been a source of potential stress and conflict. It has been epitomised in the child-care field by the problems surrounding secure accommodation and by the so-called 'silting-up' of many children's homes with children from ethnic minorities. The extent to which residential care is a necessary component of services for the frail elderly, the mentally handicapped and the mentally ill has been a similar source of dispute and doubt. To the extent that hostels, group homes and residential homes are necessary, however, the DHSS view of community care has imposed an enhanced demand for these types of facilities on local authorities who, from their own perspective, are engaged in trying to reduce their reliance upon them. The growth of private residential care has muddied the waters even where it has reduced the immediate demand on local authority provision. The result has been a degree of policy confusion as well as planning complexity. This has not been eased by the argument that growing numbers of very dependent people – especially very frail old people – require nursing care of a kind not originally envisaged as a part of the local authority approach to residential care. Consequently, much residential care has been steadily moving towards the model of nursing care associated with the NHS, at the same time as policy has emphasised the need to shift NHS patients to the local authority.

The simple fact is that the local authority and the NHS models of community care have been somewhat different and have implied different developments within local government; but both have been overlaid in the case of the elderly by the increasing level of physical – as well as domestic and social – dependence of the very old. Community care in the form of care *in* the community has been a dominant goal, but its meaning has indeed been unclear and subject to variation.

The motivations behind community care have been as problematic as the implications. One driving force has been the perception that people who spend long periods in institutions become dependent upon institutional routines and correspondingly less able to exercise personal initiative or choice: they become institutionalised. The avoidance of institutionalisation most clearly took the form of trying to avoid care in institutions. That this was so was partly the result of the strength of the condemnation of those institutions subject to close scrutiny through research or following public scandals,[21] and partly due to the belief that care in the community would be cheaper than care in institutions. It was the confluence of these arguments, in most cases, which drove community-care policy forward. But alternative arguments have been available, even though their impact on policy has often not been great.

One alternative strand of thinking has emphasised the need for institutional reform. It has taken practical shape as in the development, for example, of therapeutic communities in hospitals (and in a few cases in penal institutions).[22] It has also emerged in academic research.[24] In both cases, however, the basic proposition has been the same: that the 'boiler house' view of institutions reflected the unsatisfactory state of institutions in the immediate post-war years and took no account of the possibility of developing radically different and better forms of, and uses for, institutional provision. The impact on policy of this line of reasoning has been comparatively modest. It has surfaced at different times in enthusiasm for hostels, as opposed to residential homes, in the therapeutic community model, and in the notion that residential environments may often be best used as a short-stay resource rather than as a long-term expedient. A second strand of thinking has reinforced some of these arguments by questioning the cost advantages of care in the community. The argument has not been that residential care costs have been exaggerated, but that the cost of providing *comparable* levels of care in the community have been underestimated.[24]

This, of course, reveals the essential reason for the limited success of attempts to rehabilitate the image of residential institutions as positive options. Care in institutions has tended to be an inclusive package with little flexibility in the services made available or the costs incurred, whereas community based services are far more finely divisible. In the jargon of 'fast-food' restaurants, 'portion control' – and therefore cost control – is much easier in community services. It also reveals the attractions and dangers of care *by* the community: the opportunities for spreading public services thinly are further increased as is the possibility of shifting the costs of care to unpaid carers. One message is clear, the motivations behind and the outcomes of policy need to be as closely studied as the stated intentions of policy. The outcomes of community-care policies – or at least achievements to date – will be studied in some detail in Chapter 8.

REFERENCES

1. HALL, P., 1976 *Reforming the Welfare*. Heinemann
2. HERAUD, B., 1970 *Sociology and Social Work: Perspectives and Problems*. Pergamon Press; SMITH, G., 1970 *Social Work and the Sociology of Organisations*. Routledge and Kegan Paul; KOGAN, M. and TERRY, J., 1971 *The Organisation of a Social Services Department*. Bookstall Publications; FOREN, R. and BROWN, M. J., 1971 *Planning for Service*. Charles Knight; BILLIS, D., BROMLEY, G., HEY, A. and ROWBOTTOM, R., 1980 *Organising Social Services Departments*. Heinemann; SOCIAL SERVICES ORGANISATION RESEARCH UNIT AND BRUNEL INSTITUTE OF ORGANISATION AND SOCIAL STUDIES (BIOSS), 1974 *Social Services Departments: Developing Patterns of Work and Organisation*. Heinemann
3. PACKMAN, J., 1975 *The Child's Generation*. Basil Blackwell and Martin Robertson
4. TOWNSEND, P., 1970 *The Fifth Social Service*. Fabian Society

5. BALDOCK, P., 1980 'The origin of community work in the UK', in Henderson, P., Jones, D. and Thomas, D. N. (eds), *The Boundaries of Change in Community Work*, NISW no. 37. George Allen & Unwin, pp. 23–5

6. KAHAN, B., 1974 'The philosophy of the social services department', in Brown, M. J. (ed.), *Social Issues and the Social Services*. Charles Knight

7. TOWNSEND, P. op.cit. (ref. 4)

8. WEALE, A., 1978 *Equality and Social Policy*. Routledge and Kegan Paul

9. WEBB, A. L. and SIEVE, J. E. B., 1971 *Income Redistribution and the Welfare State*. Bell

10. WEBB, A. L. 1980 'The personal social services', in Townsend, P. and Bosanquet, N. (ed.), *Labour and Equality*. Heinemann

11. WALKER, A. (ed.), 1982 *Community Care*. Basil Blackwell and Martin Robertson; PARKER, R., 1981 'Tending and social policy', in Goldberg, T. and Hatch, S. (eds), *A New Look at the Personal Social Services*. Policy Studies Institute

12. PINKER, R., 1982 'An alternative view', in Report of the Committee (Chairman: P. Barclay) Appendix B *Social Workers: Their role and task*. Bedford Square Press

13. WALKER, A. (ed.) op.cit. (ref. 11)

14. Ibid.

15. MORONEY, R., 1976 *The Family and the State: Considerations for Social Policy*. Longman

16. EQUAL OPPORTUNITIES COMMISSION 1980 *The Experience of Caring for Elderly and Handicapped Dependents*. Survey Report, EOC; FINCH, J. and GROVES, D., 1980 'Community care and care in the family: a case for equal opportunities?', *Journal of Social Policy* 9(4) pp. 487–511; NISSEL, M. and BONNERJEA, L., 1982 *Family Care of the Handicapped Elderly*. Policy Studies Institute

17. GASTMAN, M. L., 1980 *The Battering of Mrs. Scarffe: A Case to Answer*. New Age: STEVENSON, O., 1980 *The Realities of a Caring Community*. Eleanor Rathbone Memorial Lecture

18. PINKER, R. A., 1978 *Research Priorities in the Personal Social Services*. SSRC; EVERSLEY, D., 1982 'The demography of retirement prospects to year 2030', in Fogerty M. (ed.) *Retirement Policy The Next Fifty Years*. Heinemann

19. ABRAMS, P., 1977 'Community care: some research problems and policies', *Policy and Politics* 6(2) Dec.

20. CHEESEMAN, D., LANSLEY, J. and WILSON, J., 1972 *Neighbourhood Care and Old People*. Bedford Square Press

21. TOWNSEND, P., 1962 *The Last Refuge*. Routledge and Kegan Paul; ROBB, B., 1967 *Sans Everything*. Nelson
22. HINSHELWOOD, R. D., 1979 *Therapeutic Communities: Reflections and Progress*. Routledge and Kegan Paul; JANSEN, E., 1980 *Therapeutic Community Outside the Hospital*. Croom Helm
23. KING, R. D., TIZZARD, J. and RAYNES, N. V., 1971 *Patterns of Residential Care*. Routledge and Kegan Paul
24. PLANK, D., 1977 *Caring for the Elderly*. Greater London Council

Part three
CONTEMPORARY ISSUES

Chapter five
BEYOND THE STATE

That the personal social services must be seen as a mixed economy of welfare is a statement of fact, not value. In Chapter 2 we indicated that all five forms of non-statutory responses to social needs are currently of importance: the private sector; voluntary organisations; voluntary workers; mutual aid groups; and informal care. What we must now do is examine the rash of prescriptions for change which has appeared in recent years. Each of the suggested lines of development envisages the maintenance of some form of mixed economy, but each also asserts the need for significant change. There has been a fairly widespread expression of concern that the future cannot and should not simply reproduce the mixture as before. Before considering the arguments, however, let us briefly note the present currents and trends within the present mixed economy – in so far as they can be discerned.

CURRENT TRENDS

The private sector is changing rapidly. Private residential care, in particular, has been growing and it is moving towards greater corporate organisation. However, if, for example, registered child-minding and paid foster care for 'hard to place' people (such as physically or mentally handicapped teenagers or adults) is included, there is also an increasing amount of very small scale 'private' provision to be taken into account. The future of private provision depends to a considerable extent on trends in the disposable income available to vulnerable groups needing help, but also on the quality and level of provision available outside the private market. An improvement in the first and/or a decline in the second would be likely to lead to further growth in private provision. At the moment, however, we possess remarkably little information at the national level from which to forecast the future significance and development of private provision.

Factual information is also quite difficult to locate on the current position with respect to other forms of non-statutory provision. The combined voluntary and paid work force in the traditional voluntary sector is certainly large enough to rival that deployed through SSDs.[1] Voluntary provision is therefore important. It is also showing every sign of growing; but differential changes are probably taking place. Many local authorities have had to reassess their practice of placing – and paying for – people in voluntary residential facilities. The same is true of local authority grant-aid support for voluntary organisations: it is an area of potential savings in hard times. Nevertheless, the voluntary sector as a whole has received additional benefits in the form of increased flows of central government cash – especially directed at the reduction or masking of unemployment. Moreover the number of voluntary workers giving their time to work in the social welfare field is large and is also more likely to be rising than falling.[2] One of the major problems is the uneven distribution of voluntary organisations and voluntary labour, rather than the scale of the effort.[3]

Mutual aid is by its very nature difficult to monitor. There are national organisations and bodies which operate on the mutual aid principle of emphasising the understanding, knowledge and helpfulness which sufferers of a problem or condition can themselves offer to other sufferers. Nevertheless, much mutual aid is a local and group phenomenon, rather than a national one. It seems to be growing rapidly as a style of organising and focusing help, though there is evidence that the edifice often rests on the shoulders of quite small numbers of particularly active members and is also unevenly distributed.[4] At the time of writing, the DHSS is about to make the first direct financial commitment to fostering support services for mutual aid. Although the sums will be minimal, the growth of mutual aid could be considerably strengthened.

Informal care is similarly to be seen as both rugged and yet fragile. Official policy and the optimistic approach to utilising 'community resources' detects a capacity for expanding or otherwise improving informal care.[5] The more sceptical view sees changes in 'the family' and in 'communities' as evidence of a possible reduction in caring capacity. Hard evidence on the changing dynamics of informal care is still difficult to come by. We know that a majority of families and many friends and neighbours do offer help, where required, to socially dependent people. The help made available shows no obvious or immediate sign of abating nationally and at the individual level there is a tendency for help to increase as need arises up to the point at which the limit of endurance for each individual carer and each caring network is reached. That informal care is a fragile resource can be inferred, however, from the central importance of (unsupported) women in informal caring and the costs which are often imposed on them by such caring;[6] the availability of female carers in the future and their willingness to bear the costs of caring are large unknowns.[7] It can also be inferred from the limits to neighbourliness, which many commentators see as considerable.[8]

Our understanding of the present position is clearly fragmentary and an unsatisfactory basis on which to build confident and detailed policies for the future. But this does not mean that there is an absence of policy proposals. Two have been in particular evidence. The first – welfare pluralism – emphasises the merits of multiple sources of help and service. The second – which we might call 'public sector disengagement' – places the emphasis on limiting the role of the state as the provider of services. What they share, apart from a superficially similar concern with informal care, is a strongly critical attitude to the role of the state and particularly towards centralised state control over service development and provision. But before we consider each in turn, it is necessary, at the outset, to emphasise that collective provision for social need does not necessarily imply identical roles for the state in financing, providing, and policing. State *financed* care could, in theory, be *provided* by voluntary and private bodies. The role of the state in *policing* standards and safe-guarding rights would then be at a premium and state provision could be minimal in the form of a 'safety-net'. Alternatively, state *finance* could fund competitive *provision* by statutory, voluntary and private services. In this case, state provision could remain important but it would not be a monopoly and it could possibly be highly decentralised. The theoretical options are therefore numerous and potentially complex.

In practice, however, the long history of British social policy has been one of an increasing identification of collective provision with bureaucratically organised state services which command a near-monopoly of formal provision. This has been less true of the personal social services than of other areas. But subtle variations tend to be lost sight of when arguments command passionate support; recent debates have therefore been characterised by a critique (of centralised state social service monopolies) which has easily spilled over into a more general scepticism or hostility towards the role of the state in general.[9]

WELFARE PLURALISM

The welfare pluralist approach contains two messages which need to be considered separately even if they are to be seen to be complementary. Both have implications for state services: the first implies a different role within a given pattern of care; the second implies a relative reduction in the extent and significance of state services which would turn imply changes in role. The two messages, it should be added, are often conflated by advocates of welfare pluralism; the distinction is our own rather than one recognised by all authors in this field. The first simply recognises the fact of an existing plurality of statutory and non-statutory ways of meeting social need and argues that this does not presently work well as an integrated system. In particular, the *role* of state provision is seen to be inappropriate and in need of change: state services often fail to relate to or reinforce non-statutory and informal care. This may be seen as a call for reformative change in state services – perhaps quite far-reaching – designed to make the existing system work more coherently. However, the second message is that the existing *pattern* of services is itself inappropriate for the future and that, in particular, the alternatives to state action have to be strengthened [doc. 13]. In the case of this second message, therefore, the centre of attention is clearly on the alternatives and on changing the inherited structure of provision.

The first of these approaches proceeds from a recognition of the already crucial contributions of family and informal care and voluntary provision. The diagnosed problem is that of a barrier between state services and other forms of help. This barrier is seen to arise from the tendency among policy-makers and practitioners in the statutory services to see the state, and therefore themselves, as at the centre of the caring network. This 'stato-centric' view of the world is reinforced by the professionalisation of state services which results in 'trained incapacity': an inability to see problems through ordinary people's eyes and to support them in their own problem-solving rather than to impose professionally approved solutions on them.[10] Even if professional dominance is not the order of the day, the professional worker in statutory services may provide clients with little that is directly and immediately of relevance.[11]

The obvious reformative conclusion is that this barrier can only be removed if the state services are recast. Bayley identified attitudinal and role changes essential to this process and summarised them in his call for an effective interweaving of statutory and other forms of care.[12] Others have emphasised the problems of achieving changes in attitudes and roles without first effecting changes in structures and in organisational principles.[13] Highly local forms of statutory services organisation – popularised in the idea of 'patch' based working – are seen to be essential, but so is a repudiation of centralisation, hierarchy and stiffly bureaucratic principles of organisation and management.[14] These ideas have been received by politicians with varying degrees of enthusiasm. The power to act rests with local authorities, however, and there have been only a few examples of thorough-going attempts to achieve a highly decentralised system of organisation throughout a whole SSD. More isolated developments provide the main opportunities for monitoring these innovations.[15]

The second approach to welfare pluralism is to be distinguished because it advocates a strengthening of the alternatives to the state as principle provider of formal services, not just changes in the role of the state services and their methods of working. This line of argument may spring directly from political ideology or from a more pragmatic awareness of scarcity in the public sector: need exceeds present and projected future levels of public expenditure. Given the acceptance of a shortfall in statutory services, the development of alternatives is seen as a simple matter of necessity.[16] This 'scarcity push' factor may in turn be reinforced by a 'client-preference pull' factor: people tend to prefer care which is seen to be as flexible and as un-bureaucratic as possible. This argument may then lead to the assumption that extending and augmenting informal care is the ideal way forward, if it can be achieved.

Whether or not these arguments are accepted as appropriate, they seemed to be at the heart of the strong preoccupation with Neighbourhood Care which was promoted by Mr Ennals during his term as Secretary of State for Social Services in the late 1970s.[17] Statutory support for and stimulation of 'good neighbours' was seen to be both a feasible and desirable response to the acknowledged limitations of state services.[18] Whether the strategy was in practice feasible was certainly questioned. Abrams' initial argument, that state services could as easily swamp and destroy informal care as stimulate it, was a particularly important corrective to the blithe assumption that the state could, at minimal cost, galvanise any part of the 'care system' into greater activity.[19] What Abrams most crucially noted was that state services and neighbouring may depend upon quite different values and forms of motivation. To conceive of them as complementary parts of a 'system' which can readily be orchestrated by the state may therefore be profoundly misleading. His work gradually led him to modify this initial scepticism,[20] but the issue which he raised remains as a salutory signal set at caution on the route to welfare pluralism. In particular, it suggests that we should look critically, for example, at attempts rapidly to expand 'voluntary service' as a response to the 'waste and social threat' inherent in mass unemployment.[21]

The Good Neighbourhood Scheme was one example of an attempt to strengthen the alternatives to state provision, but it did not proceed from an assumption that a move away from state services was to be valued in its own right. The inadequate supply of state services and the apparently low costs of neighbourly care were the primary reasons for advocating a somewhat changed pattern of responses to need. However, the case for a radical shift away from state services has been argued in recent years. One of the first, trenchant, presentations of such a view argued for a large-scale expansion of voluntary services.[22] The starting point was a wide-ranging critique of state welfare and a cataloguing of its failings and defects. To a considerable extent the voluntary sector was seen not to suffer from those defects – bureaucratic rigidity, insensitivity to clients' needs, the production of standardised services, an unwillingness to innovate and an inability to engage people in a participative style of running services – to which state services were seen to be prone. Alongside this critique there was a belief in the advantages and safeguards of a pluralist system which permits a wide cross-section of people to participate in public life and to influence policy-making. As in the report of the Wolfenden Committee,[23] welfare pluralism was therefore seen as one bulwark against the encroachments of a centralised and monolithic, or corporatist, political system. There is a real danger that this style of argument exaggerates the merits of voluntary organisations and overplays the failures of state services while underestimating or ignoring the possibility of change within these services.[24] There is also an assumption that the perceived merits of voluntary organisations could survive, unscathed, a substantial growth in the voluntary sector.[25]

There is another, and intrinsically very interesting, element in the argument, however. It is that many of the demerits of state service arise from the power of monopolies to go their own way and take little heed of what consumers want. Promoting welfare pluralism by expanding voluntary provision has therefore been seen as a means of breaking the state monopoly without creating a large private sector. The argument is that the voluntary sector can and does espouse the same values as the state services – including the service ethic, as opposed to the profit motive, and a belief in equality. The implicit suggestion is that healthy competition between basically compatible sectors will not lead to the 'second class' state residual services which could result from a large expansion in the private sector.[26] This strand of welfare pluralist thinking therefore offers 'competitive efficiency without tears'. It is a middle-way response to both the free market critique of state welfare and the condemnation of the free market which Titmuss developed so strongly.[27] The crucial gap in the thesis is the specification of the precise mechanisms for achieving 'competitive efficiency' by expanding voluntary provision. The classical notion of competition embodied in free market principles is that independent suppliers of a good engage in direct competition for consumers. The consumers, as a result, enjoy choice and the rational exercise of that choice is the bedrock of the competitive process. The problem posed for social policy is that direct competition depends on what one might call 'purposive duplication'. Services have to be established in the same localities for the same client groups if such choice is to exist. This may be possible in so far as voluntary provision can expand without support from public expenditure, but large-scale duplication paid for from public funds – for example, voluntary and statutory social-work services for families operating alongside each other – seems much less defensible. It also presumes a significant increase in total expenditure, at least in the first instance. Consumer choice resulting in the withering away of unattractive provision, but based on a degree of continuing duplication and competition, sounds interesting in theory, therefore, but unlikely in practice. The visceral reaction in the public sector is to avoid duplication and to seek coordination, not competition. To change that outlook would be expensive. To do so would also pose real questions about how to achieve 'fair' competition between statutory and voluntary services. But what the argument for competition underlines is the feeling that the innovative and cost-conscious qualities of the entrepreneur are needed in social welfare, even if the profit-maximising drive is to be avoided.

However, the recent past history of voluntary provision has been characterised by a completely different approach which can best be labelled as 'segregated markets' or 'product differentiation'. Voluntary and statutory services have tended to offer slightly – or substantially – different types of provision, or have catered for different client groups. In either case, they have rarely been designed purposively to compete for consumers in the same locality. Would extending the voluntary sector within these existing 'rules of the game' facilitate greater competititve efficiency? It might. In so far as statutory and voluntary policy-makers have a national or regional perspective, they may well respond to alternative services which are not direct local competitors but which have gained a clear reputation for excellence and which therefore present an indirect challenge or an innovative model.

At the heart of these ideas about welfare pluralism there is a single diagnosis: the need for stronger pressure, especially on statutory bodies, to provide services in a more responsive and cost-effective way and to challenge ineffective and inefficient ways of working. A large element of voluntary expansion is seen as the guarantor of change in the state services. But given that few local authorities would fund directly competitive – as opposed to complementary – services, much voluntary service funding would need to come from sources other than those local authorities. Charitable giving is under strain and unlikely to support such developments; the only real alternative would be direct central government support for local voluntary services. To an extent, central government support has in recent years grown through such schemes as Opportunities for Volunteering and Manpower Services Commission programmes. However, the extent to which these monies have merely offset reductions in the value of local authority financial support as times have become harder is not known.

Overall, local voluntary action does seem to have grown in vitality and in some cases the rate of change has been impressive. Whether this means that the voluntary sector now acts as an altogether more potent spur to statutory services is difficult to gauge. That competitiveness exists cannot be denied and a case certainly can be made for the beneficial impact of welfare pluralism on statutory services. However, we have no solid evidence on how far the reality is one of beneficial competitiveness, of competitiveness which is firmly curbed and held in check by a defensive statutory sector, or of a planned and productive partnership. The early indications of how *Care in the Community*[28] is working out in practice, suggests that the opportunity for partnership could easily decline into defensiveness and mutual suspicion.

CONTRACTING OUT

The danger of making easy generalisations about the present nature and future promise of non-statutory welfare provision is revealed by the idea, and the practice, of 'contracting out' – or purchase of service contracting (POSC).[29] Contracting out is not a new idea. It exists on a significant scale and is a primary way in which local government relates to the voluntary sector. Judge has shown that in 1978–9 at least 11 per cent of SSD current expenditure was devoted to purchasing services – especially those provided by voluntary organisations.[30] Residential care was very much to the fore, as it was in direct service provision by SSDs. Contracting out on this scale is at the very heart of the existing mixed economy. But what purpose does it serve? Can we throw any light on the merits or demerits of strengthening the alternatives to state provision by examining the reasons why local authorities presently pay for services produced and delivered by others?

Let us first consider the possibility that contracting out makes for greater cost effectiveness. From a purely theoretical point of view it could do so for any one of the following reasons. Contracting out could:

1. utilise service providers who are inherently more efficient than the state;
2. tap community resources – individuals, groups and organisations – characterised by a modicum of altruistic concern and a willingness to move beyond a restrictive, 'rate for the job' approach to providing help;
3. sponsor competition between the non-statutory providers.

The first of these possibilities would appeal to those with a strong faith in the natural superiority of voluntary organisations or of private enterprise. Contracting-out could use and could underpin expansion in either or both of these types of non-statutory provision. Mere belief in their superior efficiency is not enough, however, and the evidence brought together by Judge does not support the view that a considerable increase in contracting-out would necessarily result in more cost-effective services.[31] Though voluntary provision is often seen to be comparatively inexpensive, effectiveness is inherently difficult to measure. Similarly, there is evidence of some effective, good-quality private residential provision, and also of lower costs, but to argue that private provision is cheaper than state (or voluntary) provision at any given level of effectiveness is a different matter. The cost-effectiveness of private provision may also depend crucially on the state of competition and the enforcement of standards.[32]

The second possibility has an air of reasonableness about it – within unknown limits. Foster parents, for example, may often be an important source of contractual care augmented by a genuinely altruistic commitment to giving far more than is implied in the contract. Nevertheless, it is important to keep the point in perspective. State employees are not necessarily devoid of altruistic commitment merely because they are public servants. Whether contracting-out does, or could, produce a *net increase* in altruistic commitment and therefore better value for money is far from clear.

The third possibility exists, but is less than convincing. As we have noted, purposive duplication is rare and a network of multiple suppliers competing to provide services financed by the state is an abstract concept rather than a strong possibility or reality. Moreover, competition could as easily lead to a lowering of standards as to a promotion of cost-effectiveness. Only rigorous state monitoring of standards would be likely to guarantee that services were of an acceptable quality. As Judge notes, both the British and the USA literatures tend to show that state monitoring of the quality and appropriateness of services provided by present contractors is haphazard and lacking in rigour.[33]

The interesting feature of contracting-out is that it emphasises a division of labour between financing, providing and policing services which could in principle allow the overall shape of service provision to be planned and controlled by statutory agencies without them being monopoly suppliers. If developed rigorously, contracting-out would therefore seem to offer the possibility of furthering welfare pluralism without sacrificing the opportunity to plan and coordinate. Two objections remain, however. The first is that an expansion of contracting out which led to much closer monitoring would not necessarily be an unalloyed blessing – not least in the voluntary sector. The present scale of much voluntary provision, and the comparatively modest levels of public funding involved, provide for a large degree of flexibility and discretion. A rapid expansion of publicly funded voluntary provision could decisively change the relationships between these sectors.

The second objection is that if the cost-effectiveness gains to be made from contracting out are less than clear-cut and certain, the purpose of expanding it is unclear. Apart from cost effectiveness, the primary explanations of existing contracting-out arrangements identified by Judge are that they can foster the provision of specialised services for particular groups, provide consumer choice, stimulate innovation, and become institutionalised as a local tradition. The last is not a rational justification and none of the others necessarily suggests the need for a wholesale and rapid shift in the role of the state to that of service funder, but not provider. A possibility which Judge does not note is that non-statutory provision may be seen as a way of reducing the strength of public sector trades unions or of avoiding the constraints they place on service development. To advance such an argument, however, is to ignore the speed with which voluntary organisations have become unionised in recent years and the potential for unionisation in a private sector which employed full-time staff and moved beyond the cottage-industry stage. For the present, these trends and possibilities can only be guessed at. What is clear is that contracting-out has served a useful role over many years, but that there is every reason to explore its potential cautiously rather than invest high hopes in it or engage in a gratuitously ideological battle over it.

DISENGAGEMENT

The possibilities noted above could all be seen as a partial disengagement of the state, but they would seem to pale into insignificance compared with the philosophy of the first Thatcher Administration. In 1979 the state was seen to be an inherently suspect vehicle for providing social care and public expenditure was earmarked for tight control: 'rolling back the frontiers of the state' was to be a watchword. But what, in reality, was the policy and what has come to pass?

Whether the Thatcher Administrations have disclosed a clear philosophy of state disengagement in the personal social services is certainly open to doubt. At first an endorsement of the voluntary sector and informal care was centre stage. No minister could refer to the personal social services without 'beatifying' these forms of non-statutory provision. But whether there was a firm policy beyond the rhetoric was difficult to determine. Moreover, if there was a policy, could it be argued that it was a bi-partisan approach – an inheritance from the Callaghan years of Labour government. It was a Labour Home Secretary, Merlyn Rees, who had characterised voluntary organisations as 'The essential partners of the statutory authorities' and argued that 'Whatever the scale of statutory provision, we cannot do without the extra contribution from the voluntary sector.'[34] Indeed, Patrick Jenkin – the first Secretary of State for social services under Mrs Thatcher – had criticised Labour's Good Neighbourhood Campaign for its apparent preoccupation with the search for a 'cheap pair of hands'.

That there was a difference in philosophy is reflected in the way in which the Conservatives had gone beyond the idea of partnership with the voluntary sector and the need for an *extra* resource. They had firmly modified the ancient order by endorsing rather than merely tolerating the private sector and by displacing *both* statutory and voluntary services from the pivotal role: informal care was the focal point of their attention. The Prime Minister argued that 'the statutory services are the supportive ones, underpinning where necessary, filling the gaps and helping the helpers'.[35] Mr Jenkin made the point slightly differently: 'We cannot operate as if the statutory services are the central provider with a few volunteers here and there to back them up ... We should recognize that the informal sector lies at the centre with statutory services and the organized voluntary sector providing back-up, expertise and support.'[36] [doc. 14] Insofar as this was a recipe for 'rolling back the frontiers' it was based on a view of the statutory role *changing* rather than disappearing altogether. A supportive, 'back-up' role for SSDs was envisaged. State provision of service was to be of reduced significance: 'a long stop for the very special needs going beyond the range of voluntary services'. One senior official expressed the change of philosophy more sharply: 'I do not therefore have difficulty in accepting the role of the State as residual – the voluntary sector must to some extent return to providing and paying for services which we have come to expect from the State.'[37]

While a basic change in philosophy was apparent, therefore, the practical implications remained vague and uncertain. The same senior official argued that 'This cannot in practice mean a large shift in responsibility but it will represent a departure from the values of the past decade.'[38] The Secretary of State outlined a pragmatic strategy of 'stimulating the voluntary and informal and the private sector [to] clarify the role of the statutory sector'.[39] The indeterminate nature of these policies reflected deep-seated ambiguity and uncertainties in the broad philosophical approach itself. There were certainties about the need for change, but not about the route to be followed or the end result to be achieved.

None of this is very surprising. The Thatcher era crystallised a long-nurtured critique of both public provision and public expenditure. These attitudes immediately appear to reinforce each other, and in large measure they do, but in the personal social services there is also a choice to be made between them. To reduce state *provision* requires an initial and substantial *increase* in expenditure in order to build up voluntary and/or private provision and to underpin informal care. To cut public *expenditure* is to weaken state services and therefore to throw additional burdens on the existing informal and voluntary sector, but also to reduce the ability of local authorities to support them financially and in kind.

This dilemma is readily evaded in political rhetoric by relying on three comforting myths: that people have become neglectful of their social obligations to kin and neighbours and that a vast reservoir of informal care can be tapped simply by enforcing these obligations; that 'genuinely voluntary' provision, staffed by volunteers and paid for by charitable giving, can be rekindled with little difficulty; and that people served by the personal social services can afford to buy services privately. However, even the briefest examination of the real world reveals the fact that these are myths. Totally insensitive action which greatly increased the burdens on families and voluntary services could easily result in greater – not fewer – demands on statutory services, including hospital services and the social security system. Neither officials nor ministers could wholly ignore this possibility even if they wanted to do so. Ministers have been faced with two ways of resolving their dilemma: to proceed with cuts in state expenditure and services without worrying about the consequences, or to use such cuts rapidly to build-up the voluntary or private services by channelling money directly to them rather than relying on local authorities to support or patronise them. What has emerged is a mish-mash of approaches, but none of them has been pursued wholeheartedly. Public expenditure on statutory services has been curbed but not to such an extent that the role of the SSD has changed decisively away from the traditional service-giving approach. Some additional monies have been routed to the voluntary sector, but voluntary organisations are hardly more popular than statutory services if they require public monies – as virtually all do. The private sector has received a filip from changes in social-security policies, but no coherent strategy has emerged.

Ironically, but perhaps least surprisingly, it is informal care – the nub of the philosophically preferred model of care – which has received least attention in practice. The need to support informal care is now universally acknowledged, but to do so would be both expensive and comparatively difficult in professional and administrative terms. There can be no doubt that individual SSDs are trying to make progress on this front, but expenditure constraint tends to put greatest pressure on those activities which are already at the margin. Highest priority must continue to be accorded to socially dependent people who totally lack informal care and support.

The nearest approach to a concerted strategy, or model, for the future remains the idea of a 'mixed economy of welfare' in which the statutory role ceases to be wholly – or even primarily – that of service providing. In 1985 Mr Fowler sharpened and restated what has come to be known as the 'enabling role' – the new model of how SSDs ought, ideally, to work. While accepting that no single externally imposed model would be appropriate, he argued that 'three paramount responsibilities' rested with each social service department.

- *First*, to take a comprehensive strategic view of *all* the sources of care available in its area.
- *Second*, to recognise that the direct provision of services is only *part* of the local pattern and that in many cases other forms of provision are available.

● *Third*, to see a major part of its function as promoting and supporting the fullest possible participation of the other different sources of care that exist or which can be called into being.[40]

The 'enabling role' represents a strand of continuity and considerable consensus running through the debate about state social services. It links directly with the welfare pluralist debate discussed earlier rather than with the rhetoric of 'rolling back the frontiers'. The difficulty, of course, is that the latter survives and continues to visit uncertainty and demoralization on the state services. It countermands the necessity to increase expenditure on the personal social services in line with need. And it fosters a continuation of the haphazard development of the 'mixed economy'. There has been no sense of direction and SSDs can very reasonably ask what it is they are supposed to be enabling to happen in their enabling role. That the welfare system has become more mixed in recent years is undeniable, but to what purpose and with what consequences?

REFERENCES

1. REPORT OF THE COMMITTEE ON THE FUTURE OF VOLUNTARY ORGANISATIONS (Chairman: Lord Wolfenden), 1978 *The Future of Voluntary Organisations*. Croom Helm; WEBB, A., DAY, L. and WELLER, D., 1976 *Voluntary Social Services Manpower Resources*. Personal Social Services Council; WEBB, A. L. and WISTOW, G., 1986 *Planning, Need and Scarcity: Essays on the Personal Social Services*. Allen & Unwin

2. WOLFENDEN COMMITTEE, op.cit. (ref. 1); HADLEY, R. and HATCH, S., 1981 *Social Welfare and the Failure of the State*. George Allen & Unwin; HATCH, S., 1980 *Outside the State*. Croom Helm; HATCH, S. and MOCROFT, I., 1983 *Components of Welfare*. Bedford Square Press

3. HATCH, S. and MOCROFT, I., 1977 *Policy and Politics*, vol. 6 no. 2, Dec.; ABRAMS, P., 1977 'Community care: some research problems and politics', *Policy and Politics*, vol. 6, no. 2, Dec. ROBINSON, F. and ABRAMS, P., 1977 *What We Know about the Neighbours*. Rowntree Research Unit

4. See RICHARDSON, A. and GOODMAN, M., 1982 *Self Help and Social Care: Mutual Aid Organisations in Practice*. Policy Studies Institute

5. WOLFENDEN COMMITTEE, op.cit.; COLLINS, A. and PANCOAST, D. L., 1976 *Natural Helping Networks: A Strategy for Prevention*.

National Association of Social Workers, Washington; LEAT, D., 1978 'Homing in on a "hurrah area"', *Involve*, **4**, Spring, pp. 12–15; THE VOLUNTEER CENTRE 1976 *Creative Partnerships: A Study in Leicestershire of Voluntary Community Involvement*. The Volunteer Centre

6. NISSEL, M. and BONNERJEA, L., 1982 *Family Care of the Handicapped Elderly – Who Pays?* Policy Studies Institute; GLENDINNING, C., 1983 *Unshared Care: Parents and their Disabled Children*. Routledge and Kegan Paul

7. PARKER, R., 1981 'Tending and social policy', in Goldberg, T. and Hatch, S. (eds), *A New Look at the Personal Social Services*. Policy Studies Institute; ROSSITER, C. and WICKS, M., 1982 *Crisis or Challenge? Family Care, Social Policy and Elderly People*. Study Commission on the Family; PARKER, G., 1985 *With due care and attention*. Family Policy Studies Centre

8. DENNIS, N. 'The popularity of the neighbourhood community idea', in Pahl, R. (ed.), 1968 *Readings in Urban Sociology*. Pergamon, pp. 74–92; DENNIS, N., 1968 'Who needs neighbours?', *New Society*, 25 July, pp. 8–11; ROBINSON, F. and ABRAMS, P., op.cit. (ref. 3)

9. WEBB, A., 1980 *Collective action and welfare pluralism*. Association in Researchers in Voluntary Action and Community Involvement (ARVAC); WEBB, A. L. and WISTOW, G., 1982 *Whither State Welfare? Policy and Implementation in the Personal Social Services*. Royal Institute of Public Administration

10. ROBINSON, T., 1978 *In Worlds Apart*. Bedford Square Press; WILDING, P., 1982 *Professional Power and Social Welfare*. Routledge and Kegan Paul

11. BAYLEY, M., 1973 *Mental Handicap and Community Care*. Routledge and Kegan Paul

12. BAYLEY, M., 'Helping care to happen in the community', in Walker, A. (ed.), 1982 *Community Care*. Basil Blackwell and Martin Robertson; BAYLEY, M., 1977 *Community-Oriented Systems of Care*. Report to the Personal Social Services Council

13. HADLEY, R. and McGRATH, M. (eds), 1980 *Going Local: Neighbourhood Social Services*. Bedford Square Press; HADLEY, R. and HATCH, S., 1981 *Social Welfare and the Failure of the State*. George Allen & Unwin

14. HADLEY, R. and HATCH, S., op.cit. (ref. 2)

15. PARKER, P., SEYD, R., TENNANT, A. and BAYLEY, M., 1981 *Preliminary Findings From Baseline Data*. Neighbourhood Services Project Dinnington Working Paper; COOPER, M. and

STACYE, G., 1981 'Translating community based care into action', *Community Care*, 12 Feb.

16. DAVIES, B., 1980 *The Cost-Effectiveness Imperative: The Social Services and Volunteers*. The Volunteer Centre

17. DHSS, 1977 *Good Neighbour Campaign*. Local Authority Circular, 77,(22), Health Circular 77 (5)

18. MARPLAN LTD, 1979 *Good Neighbour Campaign: Summary of the Findings of Six Local Case Studies*. Prepared for the Good Neighbour Campaign by Marplan Ltd

19. ABRAMS, P., 1977 'Community Care: some research problems and policies', op.cit. (ref. 3)

20. ABRAMS, P., 1978 *Neighbourhood Care and Social Policy*. Volunteer Centre; ABRAMS, P., 1981 *Action for Care*. Volunteer Centre

21. WEBB, A. L., 1986 'Expectations, volunteering and the role of the state', reprinted in Webb, A. L. and Wistow, G., 1986, op.cit. (ref. 1)

22. GLADSTONE, G., 1980 *Voluntary Action in a Changing World*. Bedford Square Press

23. REPORT OF THE COMMITTEE ON THE FUTURE OF VOLUNTARY ORGANISATIONS (Chairman: Lord Wolfenden) 1978 *The Future of Voluntary Organisations*. Croom Helm

24. WEBB, A. and WISTOW, G., 1982 op.cit. (ref. 9)

25. Ibid.

26. TITMUSS, R. M., 1968 *Commitment to Welfare*. George Allen & Unwin

27. Ibid.

28. DHSS, 1981 *Care in the Community: A Consultative Document on Moving Resources for Care in England*. DHSS

29. JUDGE, K., 1982 'The public purchase of social care: British confirmation of American experience', *Policy and Politics*, **10** (4) pp. 397–417

30. Ibid.

31. Ibid.

32. WEBB, A. L., 1985 'Alternative futures for social policy and state welfare', in Berthoud, R. (ed.), *Challenges to Social Policy*. Gower; *see also*: CHALLIS, L., 1982 *Private and Voluntary Provision for the Elderly*. Centre for the Analysis of Social Policy, Bath University, mimeo; CHALLIS, L., DAY, P. and KLEIN, R., 1984 'Residential care on demand', *New Society*, 5 April; JOHNSON, M., 1983 'A sharp eye on private homes' and 'Controlling the cottage industry', *Community Care*, 4 and 25 August; LE GRAND, J. and ROBINSON, R. (eds), 1984 *Privatization and the Welfare State*. Allen and Unwin;

Social work, social care, and social planning

McLACHLAN, G. and MAYNARD, A. (eds), *The Public/Private Mix for Health*. Nuffield Provincial Hospitals Trust

33. JUDGE, K. op.cit. (ref. 29)
34. HMSO, 1976 *The Government and the Voluntary Sector: A Consultative Document*, p. ii
35. THATCHER, M., 1981 *Speech to WRVS Conference*
36. JENKINS, P., 1980 *Speech to the Conference of the Association of Directors of Social Services*, 19 September
37. UTTING, B., 1980 'Changing ways of caring', *Health and Social Services Journal*, 4 July, p. 882
38. Ibid.
39. JENKINS, P., op.cit. (ref. 36)
40. FOWLER, N., 1984 *Speech to the Social Services Conference*

Chapter six

ORGANISATION, MANAGEMENT AND PARTICIPATION

Should social workers be managed? By whom and how? To whom should they be accountable? Is it appropriate for them to be 'at the bottom' of hierarchical organisations? These are not new questions; they have reverberated through decades of discussion about the profession, its role and its relationship to government.[1] However, the questions were sharpened at the time of Seebohm and they were refocused once again by the Barclay Committee.[2] In both cases there were strong suggestions that the social worker's duty was to individual clients and to whole groups or communities and that professionals must therefore be accountable to the client and community. In practice, however, social workers almost always find themselves in a position of direct accountability to 'management'. The style of management in local government and voluntary organisations may differ, with the latter tending to be less 'bureaucratic', but the basic principle is the same. Social workers cannot simply do as they wish, or as their clients demand. Both Seebohm and, more explicitly, Barclay came to the conclusion that social workers had a dual responsibility – downwards to the client and upwards to 'management'. The trick is to strike the balance.

We would not disagree with this view, in principle, though it begs many questions and presents enormous difficulties in practice. What we would argue, however, is that the basic issues are rarely identified at all clearly or placed in the wider context of how the personal social services are organised and managed nationally as well as locally. Moreover, such discussion as there is tends to be confined to the position of social workers and does not extend to the position of social work assistants, home helps, care assistants or other staff. Our task in this chapter, therefore, is to express as clearly as possible those problems of organisation and management which affect all workers, and clients, of the personal social services. Our aim is not to provide blueprints or detailed solutions, but to establish a framework of basic ideas against which competing arguments and suggestions can be viewed.

What we also hope to demonstrate is that one cannot ask questions about immediate issues such as the organisation and management of social work without considering the much broader questions of the role of central government and the control and use of resources. The first of these broader issues is examined in Chapter 7, the second will be dealt with in Chapter 8.

PRINCIPLES OF ACCOUNTABILITY

Let us begin with a simple typology of organisation based on the question: who benefits?[3] The question is designed to identify the prime beneficiary and is normative; it is asking who *should* benefit from the operation of the organisation. The clear implication is that different types of beneficiary might imply different patterns of organisation and accountability. The typology can be presented as in Fig. 6.1.

It is important to emphasise that these are simplified 'ideal types' and that multiple roles are what give rise to problems in practice. Even profit-oriented organisations, for example, may need to be account-

Primary interest group	Type of organisation	Dominant form of accountability
1. **Owners**	Business (e.g. private, profit making organisations)	Hierarchical to owners
2. **Members**	Mutual benefit (e.g. mutual aid groups, trades unions)	Participative democracy
3. **Public in contact/ consumers**	Service (e.g. professional services – including social services)	Direct to client
4. **Public at large/ community**	Commonweal (e.g. central and local government)	Hierarchical to community representatives (e.g. a bureaucracy under political control)

Fig. 6.1

able to interests other than owners or shareholders. Accountability to the community at large is formal and mandatory in the minimal sense of having to submit proper accounts for public scrutiny, but the need to demonstrate 'informal accountability' to the community on environmental issues and to demonstrate a sense of social responsibility is real even if it tends to degenerate into public-relations exercises. However, what the typology does underline is that different types of beneficiary do indeed imply different types of accountability, and accountability fundamentally affects the form of organisation adopted.

Accountability in business is most typically achieved by placing a hierarchical bureaucracy of paid staff under the control of representatives of the prime beneficiary: a board representing shareholders. Authority and hierarchy are an essential ingredient in such accountability. An action decided upon by representatives of the primary interest is an authoritative decision and the person(s) enacting the decision will be accountable to those representatives for the conduct of the action. However, this does not necessarily mean that a complex bureaucracy is inevitable, the decision may easily be implemented by a single person or a small group of people working directly to the authoritative representatives (for example, in a very small company). Large bureaucratic structures are common because of the scale of operations which often results, but they are not an inevitable consequence of the hierarchical nature of accountability to authoritative decision-takers.

The example of mutual-benefit associations provides a useful contrast. The ideal case is one in which all the members of the association meet together and make unanimous decisions. The unanimous decision is then enacted by all members and, while it is authoritative, there is no real need for a formal system of accountability because all members have a direct interest in implementing decisions. The clear route for any dissenting member is resignation and the formation of a new group. Nevertheless, such an association may become quite large and wish to delegate some decision-making to an executive committee or some such authoritative group. It may also wish to establish a clear division of labour and authoritatively instruct some members, or even employees, to implement decisions with a speed and reliability which might be unattainable if implementation depended upon all members acting in appropriate ways. The distinction between a mutual-benefit association and a more traditionally bureaucratic organisation may therefore become blurred in practice. Both may have decision-making structures and a clear division of labour. The distinction in principle is clear, however. Mutual benefit associations are voluntary and consensual in nature, no-one is coerced into membership nor is membership based on payment for labour; the ideal of unanimously approved actions designed to benefit all members remains to the fore. Moreover, the distinction between provider and helper is nonexistent in mutual-aid groups, they are one and the same. Members share their problems, their experiences and their skills.

This brings us to what appears to be the typical case of a personal-social-services organisation – the service organisation. The case for it is that it is a means by which people with specialist knowledge and skills can make these available for the direct benefit of individuals or small groups. If sufficient people share an identity of needs and interests, they might best be advised to form a mutual-benefit association if, between them, they also possess – or can obtain – the skills needed to resolve problems. The growth of mutual aid and self help precisely reflects a process of redefining problems and re-identifying lay skills which make this process seem feasible. If community of interest, or the availability of skills and other resources is a stumbling block, however, a mechanism is needed to ensure that those with specialist skills act solely in the interests of clients – the members of the public with whom they are in contact. A form of service organisation is necessary in which the ideal is unambiguously that of direct accountability to the consumer or client. Much of the resistance to private (for profit) welfare provision arises from the assumption that statutory and voluntary provision approximates this ideal whereas the private sector subordinates consumer interests to the search for profit. By way of contrast, the liberal economic viewpoint stands this argument on its head and asserts that the private market confers power on the individual consumer whereas statutory provision gives pride of place to the decisions – including the self-interested decisions – of paternalistic politicians and experts rather than to the consumer interest. That the service ideal is far from simple to achieve in practice is certainly revealed in the history of the professions. The problems need to be considered carefully because they directly influence the nature of personal social services organisations.

SERVICE PROFESSIONS AND ORGANISATIONS

The simplest form of service is that in which an individual with a specialist skill makes the skill available to another in need of it in such a way as to ensure that the receiver retains control of the interaction. Paying for the service may seem to be the obvious and strong form of control. However, three quite separate, but often confused, problems arise. The first is that of the vulnerability of the client, the second that of 'contamination' of the service ideal by the profit motive, and the third that of the client's ability to pay. Each of these suggests the need for some modification of the simple position of buying and selling services, but they are different arguments for seeking alternatives to a market in services and they may point to different solutions.

In the first case, the consumers of a service may be vulnerable and unable to retain control of the service relationship for one of two reasons. They may be deprived of the capacity to exercise good and authoritative judgements about their own best interests by reason of age, infirmity, lack of intelligence, emotional turmoil, or simply by the overwhelming nature of their problem which seems to leave them with no choices, no dignity and no right to expect any help on their own terms.[4] The second form of vulnerability arises from the nature of the service provided and takes the form of ignorance. A mysterious and esoteric body of knowledge and skill may be necessary to respond to a problem, or even to understand and appreciate the problem. In such circumstances, control of the service relationship is inherently unlikely. These forms of vulnerability describe the position of many if not most of the consumers of the social services – including the personal social services.

The historical answer to this dilemma has been to invent the notion of professional service. The essence of this is simply that part or all of the responsibility for ensuring that the service is in the interests of the consumer is transferred from the consumer to the specialist helper. The essence of a professional, from this perspective, is that he or she accepts an overriding commitment to pursue the consumer's best interests.

The problem with this solution, of course, is that a professional who sells skills to clients for direct cash payments (e.g., a lawyer) represents a clash of two ideal types of accountability. Such a professional is motivated both to act in the best interests of the client in providing a service, and for himself as owner in running a business. The theoretical safeguard, that competition between professionals will ensure that control remains with the client, is attenuated by the client's vulnerability and the professional's power. The typical response to this problem is for the profession as a whole to vet and accredit professionals so as to safeguard the client. A degree of accountability by the individual professional to the community of professionals is established.

However, one likely result is the creation of a monopoly or cartel which actively restricts competition: professionals may collectively act in the business mode even in the very process of apparently developing new forms of safeguard for the client. This is one of the criticisms levelled at lawyers, and at doctors in countries with private health systems.[5]

One solution to this dilemma, it can be argued, is to relieve professionals of the need to make private profit by paying them from the public purse. A category of *public service professional* can be invented, therefore, especially in those cases where clients are most vulnerable. This solution 'de-contaminates' the professional–client relationship by removing the cash nexus. The obvious problem is that such professionals may continue to act in the business mode, but in relation to the public purse rather than the client's private purse. They may use their monopoly power to advance their position and interests within the framework of a public service. The medical professions, for example, and most especially dentists at the present time, have been criticised for distorting policy-making and demand within the NHS in pursuit of their own interests. The obvious alternative to a public service is a voluntary, or non-profit-making organisation. Clients may be self-financing or financed through the public purse, but the organisation has to pay its way. It has an interest in controlling the total demand for resources generated by professional decision-making.

The problem of financing client demand underlines the crucial significance of the third form of client vulnerability: the inability to pay. Specialist skills are comparatively scarce and expensive, but the needs to which they are a response are by no means distributed in proportion to the ability to pay for help. A public service or a subsidy from the public purse may be justified, therefore, as a means of meeting those needs for which society accepts a moral responsibility. However, the fact of subsidy inevitably raises the question of accountability. The powerful argument for providing a public service, rather than merely subsidising needy people, is that it may simultaneously solve the problems of need, of the moral contamination of service by the profit motive, and of public accountability for public money.

This lengthy digression is necessary because so much nonsense can emerge from discussions of the nature and role of the professions in the social services. What we have now revealed is a set of arguments for multiple accountability within publicly subsidised services. At least *three* forms of accountability are essential: that to individual needy people; that to the whole population of actual and potential clients/consumers; and that to the public purse for the cost-effective use of money.

It could be argued that the professional worker is wholly accountable to the individual consumer and that the service as a whole must bear the responsibility for the other two forms of accountability. If this argument is accepted, the implication must be that the professional worker is accountable downwards to the consumer but that professional discretion must be constrained by rules and top-down decisions in such a way as to safeguard the use of resources and to achieve a fair distribution of them between consumers. An alternative view is that there can be no such sharp division of accountability and that everyone in the service organisation – including the professional worker – must keep all three forms of accountability continually in mind and constantly renegotiate guidelines and decisions so as to keep their various responsibilities in balance. The first solution distinguishes sharply between professional discretion and 'top-down' controls; the second envisages a more 'organic' approach which is flexible but which places the burden of multiple forms of accountability on everyone, and at all times.

One of the gross distortions of reality which can arise in discussions of the professional role in the social services, is the notion that professionals have an overriding duty to respond *solely* to the consumer's interest and that hierarchy and managerial constraints get in the way. The truth is that 'top-down' forms of decision-making are one – undoubtedly imperfect – way of trying to cope with the three-fold pattern of accountability inherent in publicly funded social-service organisations. If service organisations can maintain a balance through other mechanisms, there need be no presumption in favour of top-down decisions and structures. Indeed, many smaller voluntary organisations do manage to operate in a more organic way. Nonetheless, three problems must be acknowledged: the history of the professions suggests that keeping multiple accountability in mind at all times is difficult for workers faced by the immediacy of individual or group need; the scale of organisation is obviously a crucial factor in designing forms of organisation and management; and public services involve a more complex form of accountability than that which affects most voluntary organisations. Public services are unambiguously responsible for promoting the common good, whereas even voluntary organisations in receipt of public subsidies can concentrate their attentions on comparatively small groups of consumers and give only limited thought to the wider public/good – if they so wish.

PUBLIC, OR COMMONWEAL, ORGANISATIONS

The task of government, at least in liberal democratic theory, is to act in the interests of the community as a whole or, through electoral politics, in the interests of a majority of the electorate. The pattern of accountability implied is, of course, the opposite of that located in the professional service ideal of 'downwards' accountability to individual clients; it is upward – probably through a substantial bureaucracy – to community representatives. This upward accountability can be seen to revolve around several key issues: the value base of action; the objectives underlying action; and the priorities adopted. Any commonweal organisation must involve control over these crucial matters of values, objectives and priorities if the interests of the public at large are to be safeguarded. The public as taxpayer is making resources available and has an inalienable right to express opinions about the total amount of resources to be made available and the broad pattern of priorities to be followed in their use, but the public equally has a right to decide in general terms what the service organisation should be doing, to what effect, and how it sets about its task. Accountability for values and objectives – not just for public money spent – sets the public service apart and has profound organisational implications.

The most obvious sense in which this is true of the personal social services is in the matter of social control. As we noted earlier, social control may serve a variety of interests but it is a dimension of personal social services work in which the commonweal interest, and accountability to politicians, is necessarily to the fore. Perhaps the most pervasive influence on the organisation of public social services, however, is the emphasis placed on equity. Unlike private and voluntary organisations, where selectivity is permissible, public services – and therefore their professionals – cannot concentrate on and be accountable to their *current* clients to the exclusion of potential clients. Every pound, or hour of professional time, spent on a client is at the expense of other potential or actual clients. Consequently, services have to be delivered in an equitable manner; to put the commonweal uppermost is by definition to give equal consideration to all in need and not to give preference to those clients who happen to have gained access. The corollary is bureaucracy. A bureaucratic form of organisation is the inevitable choice when large-scale service provision has to be combined with hierarchical accountability to the politicians who represent the public at large.

BUREAUCRACY, HIERARCHY AND MANAGEMENT

To use the term 'bureaucracy' is to cue in the related terms 'hierarchy' and 'management'. All three tend to be misunderstood and to need explanation. Let us first attempt to free these terms of pejorative overtones and to concentrate on their technical meanings.

A system of accountability upwards and delegation of authority downwards is a necessary corollary of representative democracy. Authority has to be delegated if large amounts of work are to be done, but accountability to legitimate decision-takers has to be retained. It must be emphasised that this is all that is meant by hierarchy in this context.[6] It is not used to mean, and it does not necessarily have to imply, differences in prestige, status, or income. Nor does it necessarily imply that subordinates are closely controlled, with very limited discretion. A hierarchy of accountability is compatible with very considerable discretion providing the pattern of accountability is clear. Moreover, hierarchy in this sense does not necessarily entail a long chain of command, as opposed to a short one, nor an authoritarian or dictatorial approach to management.

For example, the hierarchy in a voluntary organisation may be very short and minimal. It may only appear as a division of functions between a board taking decisions and a single worker enacting them. The fact of hierarchy does not necessarily imply a managerial leviathan. Providing one person is accountable to a legitimate decision-taking body, there is hierarchy and there is management. However, staff working to the decision-taking board or committee will typically be more numerous than this and will, therefore, involve more complex managerial relationships. A member of staff responsible for another person's work is in a managerial relationship to that person and the accountable person is managed. At its simplest, therefore, *management* is the term used to describe the relationships entailed in implementing hierarchical accountability within a body of workers. The most senior manager – the chief officer – is directly accountable to the board or committee in which decision-making power resides. However, defining management in a precise way indicates that 'the management' is not a hierarchically or geographically separate entity located at headquarters. *All* staff who have others accountable to them are managers [doc. 15].

Having distinguished the analytical meanings of hierarchy and management from the colloquial manner in which 'the hierarchy' and 'the management' are used to designate, and often to denigrate, those above us and under whom we labour, we must now similarly release the term bureaucracy from its pejorative connotations. Bureaucracy is the term applied to a particular way of organising. Its hallmarks are the establishment of clearly delineated offices, or posts, specified job descriptions, known conditions of service, and ordered systems of appointment, promotion or dismissal. The essence of bureaucracy is the *routinisation* of the delegation of authority and the enforcement of accountability. It is to be distinguished from the defects of rigidity, inefficiency and autocracy which is associated with its use as a pejorative term. It may be difficult in practice to avoid many of these defects, especially once a bureaucracy becomes large and unwieldy; in principle, however, bureaucracy is a form of organisation which might lead to many and varied patterns of working.

The key variables which are likely to determine the character of any particular bureaucracy are its size, the nature of the work undertaken, the pattern of centralisation and decentralisation, the amount of discretion given to workers, and the style of management. The last three may be significantly affected by the first two, but they are worth treating as independent factors.

Decentralisation is often linked with discussions of participation, but this can be misleading. The reason for the linkage is that centralisation implies that decision-making will be remote from people 'on the ground' and participation and decentralisation are easily lumped together as solutions to this problem. They are different things however. Centralisation and decentralisation merely refer to the concentration, or delegation, of areas of decision-making authority. They are 'measures' of the amount of authority delegated. Strong decentralisation involves delegating substantial areas of authority as near as possible to the periphery of the organisation. It may also mean 'going local': locating workers with delegated responsibility in small localities.[7] In its ultimate form it would involve dispersing most decision-making power to 'coal-face' workers located in small 'patches' and would involve a very high level of discretion for workers. Accountability would still operate, however. Moreover, participation could be very limited; the 'coal-face' workers could choose to make their decisions for themselves without involving other workers, clients or members of the public.

Discretion is a crucial factor in that it determines the amount of 'space' within which people operate, but it must be distinguished from participation because it entails accountability for the decision taken. Workers with considerable discretion are not 'participating', they are making decisions properly delegated to them. From the worker's point of view, therefore, more, or better defined, discretion – rather than participation – may indeed be the answer to some of the perceived defects of hierarchy. Nonetheless, significant and well-defined discretion may also be the key to participation and to reconciling accountability downwards to the client with accountability upwards. This is a point to which we will return. For the moment it is sufficient to note that given a fair degree of discretion, hierarchy need not mean rigidity – especially if the discretion is located at or near the coal face.

Important as structures are, managerial style is also crucial. An authoritarian and inflexible style of management may seem to typify large organisations, but this is by no means inevitable. Management styles can be arranged on a continuum from the exploitative-autocratic to the democratic.[8] A truly democratic approach implies the actual sharing of decision-making. The central question, therefore, is who should share in decision-making, and how? The answer in a representative democracy is that all the people share in decision-taking, but through the election of politicians. Consequently, it cannot be right simply to introduce a truly democratic style of *management* in which managers share decision-taking with, say, all staff, or some groups of staff, or some groups of clients. To go down this road is to reduce staff accountability to politicians and to impose a veto on what politicians can do in the name of the community. To introduce an element of participative democracy into representative democracy is not easy and it cannot be achieved by just changing the *style* adopted by managers. We will return to this point later.

A consultative style of management, on the other hand, implies that the legitimate decision-maker will make the actual decision, but only after seeking the advice and opinions of those affected. The merit of a consultative style of management is that while discretion is a source of responsiveness towards the client, it can only operate within the limits set by decisions made at higher levels. One crucial set of decisions is that which sets the broad parameters – including the allocation of resources – within which fieldworkers are to operate. These decisions are often made by committees and boards, but they are also concentrated at the chief officer level and may extend well beyond the organisation to include decision-making by superordinate bodies such as central government. A consultative or responsive style of management may therefore facilitate the incorporation of the field worker's knowledge of client's problems in higher levels of decision-taking and maximise the chances of discretion being a genuine and productive source of responsiveness to client need.

PROFESSIONAL AUTONOMY OR BUREAUCRATIC CONTROL?

The problem facing the public social services – and voluntary services to a lesser extent – is clear. They are service organisations operating within a commonweal framework. Accountability is rightly owed to *both* the client and to the public at large. The traditional, but imperfect, solution to the first need is that of professional autonomy bounded by an ethical code; the traditional solution to the second, also imperfect, is hierarchical accountability to a body of community representatives. How can the two be reconciled in practice?

If we look at the full range of social services, four main types of accommodation are seen to be possible. They are substantially influenced by the type and scale of the organisation's prime task and they involve different degrees of centralisation and different levels of discretion, or autonomy, for fieldworkers. They can be roughly ordered as a continuum running from the 'pure' commonweal bureaucracy (in which political control over decisions is maximised and implementation involves minimal discretion) to the 'pure' professional service (in which professional autonomy is as complete as could be imagined in a public organisation). Between these limiting cases lie two variants: the discretionary bureaucracy and the managed professional service. All four are presented diagrammatically in Fig. 6.2. The solid lines represent patterns of accountability. The broken line in the case of the professional services indicates a *policy* relationship, not a hierarchical, or accountability, relationship; the broken circles represent professional–client interaction. The position in public services accountable to politicians is used as an illustration, but voluntary organisations with lay boards – and even private services – involve essentially similar issues.

The case of the pure professional service is not, in fact, very relevant to the personal social services. As much as social workers may aspire to this ideal of professional practice, the only chance they may have of attaining it is by stepping outside the public sector. Some voluntary organisations come reasonably close to it, but even so they work through some form of hierarchical accountability to a board of lay representatives. A clear pattern of upward accountability is present in most cases, therefore. Consequently, social work does not enjoy the strong form of professional autonomy which medical doctors defend through the concept of clinical freedom. The essence of the doctors' position, which social workers have not achieved, is freedom from managerial control in interactions with clients. Doctors are still subject to some of the constraints of a commonweal organisation, of course.

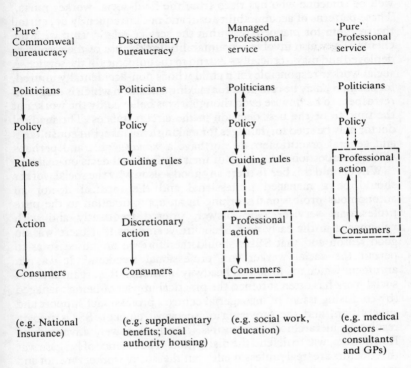

Fig. 6.2 A Social Service Typology

They are only able to work with the resources made available to them. A consultant can only use those beds at his disposal. Nevertheless, the freedoms are large, including large areas of control over vital resources such as the medicines prescribed and even over strategic policy via involvement or influence in decision-making forums.

By way of contrast, the position of the social worker in the statutory services, and many voluntary organisations, has best been described as that of group autonomy. Social workers are, by and large, an example of a managed profession in which hierarchical accountability is through other – superordinate – members of the same profession and thence to lay representatives. (However, residential, day and domiciliary workers may well be accountable to managers who have not risen from these practitioner ranks and their ultimate manager may well be someone who has risen from the field-social-worker ranks.) These patterns of accountability can, and not infrequently do, curtail the freedom for manoeuvre within the service relationship with the clients. They also involve accountability for the use of the resources deployed and may – crucially – extend to the outcomes of the service. A social worker responsible for a child who is non-accidentally injured, for example, may be censured for making a decision which is judged in retrospect to be unwise even though it was believed by the worker at the time to be the best decision in the circumstances. The medical doctor may be sued for damages for making a mistake, but consultants and general practitioners do not have a *manager* able and perhaps willing to question the quality of their professional decision-making.

Why should this be? Is there any good reason why the social worker should be a managed professional and the medical doctor an autonomous professional working in an approximation to the pure professional service? One answer, uttered frequently and with vehemence in the early post-Seebohm years, was that there was no good reason and that SSDs should therefore be organised so as to permit the social worker full professional freedom.[9] It was an argument which made no real headway. Although the organisation of social work has often softened the practical impact of being managed (by confusing issues of managerial control, professional support and supervision, and the provision of specialist advice), SSDs remain resolutely hierarchical *in principle*. Another answer, advanced by Rowbottam, was to defend the distinction. The essence of his case was that doctors are 'real professionals', but that social workers are not and are therefore appropriately subject to hierarchical forms of organisation.[10] Unfortunately, this argument is circular and rests upon an outmoded search for the essence of full professional status in the characteristics of the profession. At worst, the argument is that medical doctors are not managed because they are full professionals which can be seen by the fact that they are not managed. Although Rowbottom's argument was far more sophisticated, it does not resolve the dilemma. Social workers in the statutory social services are managed for a very simple reason, as we have indicated. They are workers within a commonweal organisation in which accountability ought to be, and appropriately is, upwards to community representatives. This may not be ideal from the point of view of all social workers, but that is not the point. Within our notions of democracy, the public at large, or representatives able to retain public support, can legitimately say that that is how social workers will work. It is perfectly reasonable and right to argue that the professional service ideal points to a different way of working and that some accommodation between the two would be appropriate. But if social workers wish to argue for *complete* professional independence the logical step must be to provide such a service without public money and without public control.

What this suggests, of course, is that doctors are a special case against the grain of the commonweal model. Indeed they are. Doctors are different from social workers not because they are more fully professional, but because they have won a political argument which social workers have not even broached. They have collectively convinced us that if left to do their job in peace they can themselves resolve any divergences of commonweal and service (client) interest. Indeed, they have succeeded in reducing awareness of such divergences to a minimum. They have additionally exerted the political power residing in the public acceptance of, and dependence on, their role so as to fend off many attempts to impose direct public accountability (e.g., the resistance to local-government control over the NHS). But this is to say that their 'full professional status' is merely the outward sign of a political battle which was won in the past and *not* a logical base for a particular form of organisation designed to guarantee this status. Whether one concludes that social work should be allowed to escape the commonweal model in the same way, or that doctors have inappropriately escaped it at some cost to the wider community interest, is a matter of personal perspective. Our view is that the latter is the case.

In practice, group autonomy is an accommodation which does enable real degrees of professional freedom for social work and which makes for a working reconciliation between the commonweal and service ideals. But it is an uneasy compromise at best and is bound from time to time to result in outbursts of conflict and dissatisfaction – from elected politicians, the public at large and social service staff. One of the most evident and damaging defects of the compromise is the fact that the public management of the social services operates far too much through crises. Public accountability is exercised over the general quality and direction of activity through Social Services Committees, but the value conflicts between the public and the professionals are so great, the level of trust so low, and the stakes so high – especially for the most vulnerable in society – that crises and scandals continue to be occasions for severe conflict. Of course, it could be argued that we have it about right in the personal social services and that the real problem is the lack of 'management by crisis' in medicine, the law and other services.

However, there is one good reason for arguing that scandals in the personal social services reveal a hypocritical tendency for public over-reaction. The simple fact is that our system of public accountability does not ensure that resources are sensibly compared with and traded off against the risk of failure and scandal. If we spent all our national resources on child care we could probably reduce non-accidental injury very sharply, if not eliminate it. Given that we choose not to do this, however, we must accept that a risk of 'failure' is inherent in our resource decisions. The real question is not whether better social services can prevent crises but whether at the given level of expenditure we can reasonably expect a better quality of child care, for example, while also maintaining existing levels of cover for the old and the handicapped. This view of the opportunity cost of reducing the risk of child abuse is conspicuous by its absence in the furore which surrounds scandals. We would argue that it is this failure in public accountability, not the managed status of social workers, which most threatens the conduct of social work and which undermines the compromise struck between the ideals of professional accountability to the client (service) and of accountability to community representatives (commonweal). It is also a failure in organisation and management which highlights the importance of central as well as local government to the immediate and day-to-day environment in which SSDs operate.

One of the sharpest challenges to the local-authority model of the managed professional has come from community work; it is important to the debate on community social work. Many community workers tend to see their role almost exclusively in terms of accountability to the local community. This may extend to an active role in articulating community criticism of local, and central, government. It should be emphasised that this does not necessarily mean that the community worker is more responsive to the client interest than the social caseworker, for example. While working with an organised group of people who are criticising the state is certainly a far more visible and overtly conflictual way of responding to such interests than is working with individual clients, it is the manner in which the client interest is represented, rather than the principle, which differs. Nevertheless, community workers have avoided taking on the most overt social-control functions and have typically been far more 'detached' from their employing agency than have their casework colleagues. Should this be taken further? Does it mean that they, at least, should be 'full', rather than 'managed', professionals? Once again, the answer must be that if they work for a public service they must be accountable 'upwards'. They must, for example, be accountable for the quality and effectiveness of their work. Conflicts of interests and values are inevitable and likely to be disruptive and painful at times, but this does not invalidate the principle of accountability to the public at large. Indeed, where the employing authority wholly accepts and supports community-work objectives and values, this could logically mean holding the community worker accountable for his or her effectiveness in *supporting* criticism of agency policies.

While the dominant form of organisation in SSDs is that based on the managed profession, the case of the community worker emphasises the fact that there is a mixture of organisational models. To take another example, home helps tend to be regarded as 'street level bureaucrats' who possess some discretion, rather than as (managed) professionals.[11] The precise nature of the difference is a moot point, but the traditional core of the issue is the extent to which discretionary decisions involve the flexible implementation of rules or the exercise of individual judgements based on specialist knowledge and skills (e.g., on matters of diagnosis and response). The more clearly professional position of the social worker is also emphasised by differences of status and by group autonomy: as we have noted, directors of social service were almost all practising social workers at one time, not home helps. This is not to say that these differences are immutable, fully justifiable, or universally accepted. Indeed, there may be very good reasons for having directors with home-help or day-care experience if the social maintenance function of the personal social services is as important as are the social control and social change functions. For the moment, however, there are differences in the organisation of social work and home help and these differences illustrate the fact that the personal social services operate on a variety of organisational models – not just one.

Indeed, one can go further and note that secretarial and clerical staff work within an approximation of the 'pure bureaucracy' with – in principle – only very limited discretion. That these organisational differences are important was well revealed by Hall's work on the role of receptionists.[12] The receptionists were clerical staff acting as 'street-level bureaucrats' and one might on the face of it expect them to have had very limited autonomy or discretion. In practice, their work required more than the implementation of rules and a considerable degree of discretion was a possibility. What Hall demonstrated was that receptionists tended to expand their role to such an extent that they began to act in ways similar to professional social workers. They overtly, or otherwise, began to make 'diagnostic and referral' decisions. Whether their lack of the professional's training and ideology made them over-responsive to the organisation's needs and less sympathetic to the clients' interests is arguable, but it is undeniable that their role revealed the complexity and the subtlety of social-service organisation and the extent to which the clash between the commonweal and the service models is the core problem which has to be resolved in theory and in practice.

PARTICIPATION: AN ALTERNATIVE TO HIERARCHY?

We have mounted a defence of hierarchy, in the sense of accountability upwards to community representatives, precisely because it has been fashionable to deride it. In the early 1970s when Social Services Departments were being established, the critique of hierarchy most commonly took the form of a call for participation. It was a movement of ideas which subsided and became relatively dormant as the new departments grappled with service development and resource constraints. It did not disappear, however, and it has resurfaced in a variety of forms. A key feature of the interest in participation is that it seems to offer an alternative, or corrective, to hierarchy. It challenges the admittedly imperfect compromise between service accountability and commonweal accountability which we have been identifying as the typical reality in the personal social services. Given that our present way of doing things is by no means the best or the only way, it is important to be clear about the essential nature of participation.

Most discussion of participation tends in the first instance to be a critique and a protest. It is essentially a statement of who has inappropriately or unjustly been excluded from decision-making; specific alternative ways of proceeding tend to take second place to this statement of dissatisfaction. To make progress, however, we must identify concrete possibilities. There are two basic versions of the idea of participation: one strong, the other much weaker. The stronger, and more immediately satisfying, is that of a participative democracy in which everyone decides about everything. It goes to the heart of one of our problems: the weaknesses and defects of our system of representative democracy in which decisions which rightly belong to all members of the community are concentrated in the hands of a small number of elected politicians who may be far from responsive to our own wishes or even to those of the majority. In a participative democracy the central question of how authoritative decisions are to be made is resolved by giving everyone an authoritative voice.

Two problems arise. The first – for those who dislike hierarchy – is that participative democracy need not do away with hierarchy. This form of democracy changes the decision-making process, but once everyone has decided on the objectives to be pursued they might still choose to appoint someone to see that they are implemented, and give that person the power to employ accountable – and therefore managed – workers. However, the workers may themselves have helped to set the goals rather than having simply chosen a set of political masters through the ballot box.

The second problem is that of feasibility. The essence of participative democracy is that everyone must have the *same* right to a say and this is very difficult to ensure once one moves beyond the confines of a small cooperative, a commune, or a mutual-aid group. The provision of pathways and park benches in a small community may easily be the subject of participative democratic decision-taking. But even the smallest SSD presents different problems.

It may be tempting to argue that decentralised SSD offices could be run as cooperatives, but who would be given the right to participate in decisions: the professional workers; all fieldworkers; all workers including the clerical and domestic staff? Even opening decision-making to all workers of whatever grade would still involve the cardinal error of treating a public service as if it were a mutual-benefit association for its workers. It is a dangerous temptation. To be legitimate, participative democracy in an SSD office would have to give an equal say on all decisions to all workers, all clients, all potential clients and all members of the local community. It would also have to give a say to all citizens of the local authority as a whole – and of the nation – if they helped to contribute resources or could offer other grounds for having an interest in what happened in the locality. The problem of representing all these interests simultaneously is precisely why we have our present system of central and local democracy and central–local relations.

Given that the units of government appropriate to many of our needs and problems must be large and multi-purpose, there is no alternative but to depend upon a system of representative democracy. The essential requirement is to try to ensure that all interests have an equal chance of being heard, and the election of representatives responsive to all their constituents (and not delegates primed to mouth a script written by some part of that constituency) is the solution which we have adopted. Participative democracy is not a generally available *substitute* for this system. But nor can it be used as an *ad hoc complement* to representative democracy, for it is axiomatic that elected representatives, and only elected representatives, are the legitimate decision-makers. Participation in political decision-making by anyone else – including chief officers – begins to undermine the democratic system by giving 'double representation'. There is therefore no good argument for social workers to participate in political decision-taking by having membership of social services committees, for example, as opposed to acting as advisers.

There is equally no good argument for giving particular client groups automatic membership of councils or committees. It may reasonably be argued that some minorities are almost always excluded from expressing their interests and that disabled people, for instance, ought always to be co-opted onto social services committees so as to supplement the imperfect processes of representative democracy. The problem is the sheer range of groups which can credibly claim to be under-represented. Which types of disability can any one disabled person understand and represent, for example? The search for participative additions to the basic system of representative democracy could, in principle, lead to a roccoco edifice without satisfying anyone. This argument does not in any way preclude consultation or the creation of direct channels through which staff and clients can forcibly lobby decision-makers; but it does suggest that simply adding layers of 'participation' to the existing political system is no solution to the problem of dual accountability to clients and community. Our conclusion does not mean that our present system of government is the only possibility, let alone the ideal. If our concern – and it is a concern which is at the heart of many discussions of participation – is to enable the maximum number of people to have the maximum possible control over their way of life, the need is to promote and safeguard autonomy. Individual autonomy, it is often argued, is best promoted by allocating a minimal role to the state and maximising individual decision making through the market. Such autonomy is not to be underestimated; even the smallest communal group may impose tyrannies which the individual with some resources may escape via the market. The price of a house was the price of independence from a suffocating extended family for Mr Biswas.[13] Nonetheless, individual freedoms are not sufficient. The message within the notion of participation is that communal autonomy can promote collective control over the local way of life.

In practice, the British governmental system tends to curtail, not promote, local or communal autonomy. We have inherited a unitary model of government in which sovereignty is undivided and located at the level of the nation-state. Parliament and Crown are the source of legislative power and there are no rival sources of legislative power at the subnational – or local – levels. Local government can act only because it has been given the power to do so by Parliament. This immediately means that hierarchy is unavoidable in local government. No matter how infrequently or lightly it may be exercise, accountability to central government and Parliament is a central feature of our constitution. Of course, local authorities are democratically elected and claim legitimacy for their actions from that fact, but their autonomy is bounded and there is no authority beyond Parliament capable of underpinning it. This position could be transformed or at least modified, but for the moment there exists an inescapable structure of subordinate and superordinate bodies and recent change has been towards more, not less, central control from Whitehall and Westminster.

A more decentralised, or devolved, system of government could make a contribution to greater communal autonomy. The call for welfare pluralism highlights another possibility. Creating the space for a multitude of non-statutory, especially non-profit, ventures and organisations would be a move in the direction of greater collective involvement in shaping our way of life – providing the organisations were open rather than self-perpetuating oligarchies.

The second message contained in our discussion is that a secondary, or weaker, notion of participation is equally important: those who are not – and who accept that they are not – legitimate decision-takers may still want to claim opportunities to *influence* the decisions. A participative or consultative style of management concedes this in an informal sense, but it may also be possible to allow for it more formally if appropriate structures and processes are created.

The obvious example is that of *advisory* committees of residents and users in homes, hostels and day centres; staff advisory committees are another. Such advisory mechanisms may be highly valuable in situations where areas of autonomous decision-taking cannot be specified and where influence and the exchange of ideas is the most that can be achieved. Two preconditions are paramount. The first is that the interests in question should be accurately and genuinely represented in mechanisms for participatory *influence* as they should be in participatory decision-taking. A comparatively small, homogeneous and known population is obviously easier to involve than a larger, amorphous and unknown one. In this sense, residents or users of day-care facilities present fewer problems of participation than would clients and potential clients of a local office or team. The greater the problems of formal participation, the more likely it is that any participation will be purely informal, underpinned by a supportive managerial style.

The second precondition of participative influence is the most crucial, however. It is the one which we have already began to emphasise. The decision framework established 'at the top' must both allow for *decentralisation* and be *as explicit as possible*. If the officer in charge of a day centre, for example, has considerable and explicit discretionary decision-making power, the participation of staff and clients is possible through informal consultation or more formal advisory processes. But involving others becomes impossible or unacceptable if the officer in charge has little discretion or uncertain discretion. Certainty is necessary on what is fixed, what is negotiable, and what may be altogether devolved.

It is in this context that our present system of public accountability is so unsatisfactory. It involves comparatively few explicit measures of success and some significant and unpredictable opportunities for disastrous failure. Our capacity to reconcile representative democracy with greater communal, or group, autonomy and participation is therefore curtailed from the top.

One example of the problem, and of a potentially valuable way forward, relates to the need to control resources. Fieldworkers in the personal social services are inevitably gatekeepers. They cannot avoid rationing a variety of resources – ranging from their own time, to access to specific services and facilities. The scope, nature and implications of such discretion are typically blurred, however, because few decisions about the commitment of resources are clear-cut or clearly understood. The real cost of home help, or residential care, is not known by the fieldworker and the supply of these resources is therefore controlled from the top. The result is that most decisions which fieldworkers need to make, except perhaps the allocation of time, are conditional and subject to approval or are 'centralised' to some degree. Experiments with 'shadow-pricing' attempt to overcome this by making fieldworkers aware of the cost of different services and by giving them 'budgets' within which they can make authoritative decisions on particular types of cases. Making costs and expenditure limits known creates room for greater discretion at the field level, but it also immediately opens up the possibility of client participation in the development of a planned response to problems. If the choices which exist can be precisely specified by the fieldworker – and the implications of decisions can be controlled – the decisions themselves can be more participative.

The Kent Community Care Project is the by now famous example of such an experiment.[14] It is limited in scope, but its value is that greater participation can be seen to depend on an explicit delineation of the limits and the degrees of freedom residing in decision-taking. It is a conclusion which applies at all levels. If the *boundaries* within which a decision must be taken can be specified in such a way as to safeguard other legitimate interests, a small group of people (clients, workers, or both) can participate so as to influence that decision and in appropriate cases they can make the decision itself in a participative, democratic manner. To take an obvious example: given rules and limits which safeguard the safety of all, the daily routine and way of life lived in a hostel can be determined democratically and participatively. Clear rules and boundaries can create, rather than limit, room for choice and for decentralised decision-making. This is a matter of developing an appropriate managerial approach and accountability system. But it also exphasises the importance of the service provided. Hostels offer more room for decentralised decision-making than do hospitals; group homes offer more again.

The call for 'participation' underlines the need to manage organisations so that they contain room for decentralised choice. Perhaps the most fundamental message, however, is that individual and group control over life-space and life-style should not be infringed unnecessarily in the first place and should be strengthened wherever possible. This should be a fundamental objective for the personal social services, as well as a principle of organisation within them.

REFERENCES

1. ETZIONI, A., 1969 *The Semi-Professions and their organisation*. New York: The Free Press; HERAUD, B. J., 1970 *Sociology and Social Work*. Pergamon; ALGIE, J., 1970 'Management and organisation in the social services', *British Hospital Journal*, vol. 80, pp. 1245–8; KOGAN, M. and TERRY, J., 1971 *The Organization of a Social Services Department – A blue print*. Bookstall publications; WEBB, A. L., 1971 'Social services administration: a typology for research', *Public Administration*, vol. 49, Autumn, pp. 321–39; WARHAM, J., 1977 *An Open Case*. Routledge and Kegan Paul; PAYNE, M., 1979 *Power, Authority and Responsibility in Social Services*. Macmillan; SMITH, G., 1979 *Social Work and the Sociology of Organization*. Routledge and Kegan Paul
2. REPORT OF THE COMMITTEE, 1982 (Chairman: P. Barclay) *Social Workers: their role and task*. Bedford Square Press

3. BLAU, P., SCOTT, W., 1963 *Formal Organizations*. Routledge and Kegan Paul; WEBB, A. L., 1971, op.cit. (ref. 1)

4. TITMUS, R. M., 1976 *Commitment to Welfare*. Allen & Unwin, 2nd edn, especially ch. 21; WEALE, A., 1978 'Paternalism and social policy', *Journal of Social Policy*, vol. 7, no. 2, pp. 157–72

5. WILDING, P., 1982 *Professional power and Social Welfare*. Routledge and Kegan Paul

6. ROWBOTTOM, R., HEY, A. and BILLIS, D., 1974 *Social Services Departments: developing patterns of work and organization*. Heinemann; BILLIS, D. *et al.* 1980 *Organising Social Services Departments*. Heinemann

7. HADLEY, R. and McGRATH, M., 1980 *Going Local*. Bedford Square Press

8. LIKERT, R., 1967 *The Human Organization*. New York; McGraw-Hill; BRYMAN, A., 1986 *Leadership and Organization*. Routledge and Kegan Paul

9. For a discussion of the confusion among practitioners on this issue, *see* DHSS, 1978 *Social Services Teams: The Practitioner's View*. HMSO, especially ch. 8

10. ROWBOTTOM, R. W., 1973 'Organising social services: hierarchy or . . . ?, *Public Administration*, vol. 15, Autumn, pp. 291–305

11. HILL, M., 1982 'Street level bureaucracy in social work and social services departments', in Lishman, J. (ed.) *Social Work Departments as Organisations*. University of Aberdeen Research Highlights 4

12. HALL, A. S., 1974 *The point of entry: a study of client reception in the social services*. Allen & Unwin

13. NAIPAUL, V. S., 1969 *A House for Mr. Biswas*. Penguin

14. CHALLIS, D. and DAVIES, B., 1980 'A new approach to community care for the elderly', *British Journal of Social Work*, vol. 10, no. 1, pp. 1–18

CENTRAL GOVERNMENT AND LOCAL SERVICES

The personal social services are largely a local phenomenon. Statutory provision is concentrated in local-authority Social Services Departments (SSDs) and only a very small amount of provision is undertaken on a regional or national basis. Voluntary provision is more diverse. Many voluntary organisations appear to be national in character (e.g., Age Concern, Dr Barnardo's). However, this can be profoundly misleading in some cases because a clear national voice on policy issues may obscure the fact that local groups have considerable, even total, autonomy. There are nationally provided services of varying sizes (e.g., The British Association of Adoption and Fostering is a 'resource centre' which also runs a small national service for children who are difficult to place), but most service delivery by voluntary organisations is locally administered. The centre of gravity of voluntary, like statutory, provision tends to be in localities. At present, the centre of gravity of the private sector is also local, but there are some networks leading up to the national level.

CENTRAL-LOCAL RELATIONS: STRUCTURES AND PROCESSES

Despite the concentration of service delivery at the local level, central government has a profoundly important impact on the personal social services. To explore this impact is to venture into the field of study which political scientists refer to as central–local relations.[1] However, there is a tendency to use this term to mean the interaction between central and local government; an interpretation of the term which, from our point of view, would be too narrow. We need in fact to lay the foundation for some understanding of how central government affects the whole mixed economy of the personal social services, nationally and locally. We cannot hope to discuss all the elements of central–local relations in detail, but it is important to emphasise that neither local authorities (or their SSDs), nor voluntary and private services, operate in a local vacuum. Their policy-making worlds, and space for manoeuvre, are moulded in complex ways.

The picture is an exceedingly intricate one and we have tried elsewhere to express these intricacies in terms of four sets of ideas[2]:

1. policies and policy implementation;
2. channels of communication;
3. arenas of debate and action;
4. policy streams.

Policies and policy implementation

The idea of policy is a source of considerable debate and confusion because the term is widely used but with considerable variations in meaning. We will use it simply to mean authoritative statements of intended courses of action which provide a framework for detailed decision-making. It is important to note that such a view of policy sees it as the expression of consciously articulated choices, but it does not necessarily imply that policy is imposed 'from the top'. Statements of intended courses of action may be authoritative for a variety of reasons: their authors may be the legitimate holders of leadership roles or offices, or their authors may be a democratic assembly or decision-making group of some kind.

Policy may therefore be determined bottom–up as well as top–down and by democratic processes as well as by bureaucrats. However imperfect local democracy may be, for example, local government policies are nevertheless the product of a democratic process if they are determined by members in committee or council. As we suggested in Chapter 6, an altogether smaller and simpler 'organisation' – such as a self-help group – may achieve a far more direct form of democracy based on participative decision-making by all members of the group. Moreover, bottom–up influences may also have an impact even in hierarchically structured bureaucracies in which some, or all, policies are made by officials in the most senior posts or by their political masters; bureaucracies do not have to be impervious to the upward flow of ideas and it is wise of decision-makers to gather knowledge from wherever it is available. But the essential point is that the *manner* in which policies are formed is not implied in the concept of policy.

It is presently fashionable to see policy-making and policy implementation as a 'seamless web': no clear distinction between the two can be discerned in practice.[3] From this point of view, policies are being made and remade even as they are implemented, and the very process of implementing one policy may gradually generate a new way of working which eventually emerges as an established policy in its own right. This obviously makes good sense and is well illustrated by the way in which a heavy pressure of demand is accommodated. Fieldworkers and their immediate managers – even clerical staff and receptionists – ration scarce services in the face of excess demand; an official policy about priorities at the field level may be one result, unofficial but enduring agreements about rationing strategies may be another. Whatever the outcome, the relationship between 'policy' and 'policy implementation' is clearly close and complex; it would be a gross over specification to suggest that policy is 'made' somewhere by one set of people and then 'implemented' somewhere else by another set of people.

Nevertheless, it equally makes good sense to distinguish between these ideas. Fieldworkers in SSDs, and in voluntary organisations, do primarily see themselves as working within a broad framework of policies established by 'policy-makers' who operate at higher levels in the organisation. Some of these policies may be made just above the levels of the fieldworkers, in their own agency, but others may be set by central government or by national headquarters in the case of a national voluntary organisation. The fact that professional workers have at least some, possibly considerable, discretion and that they may themselves 'make' some policies or 'implement' given policies in such a way as to change them significantly, does not imply that these distinctions should be abandoned completely.

The position which we will adopt is, therefore, as follows. All organisations, especially those employing professional staff, tend to evolve and adopt ways of working in such a manner that it is difficult to know how or where many changes in practice were agreed – or even if they were agreed. Many changes, and ways of working, simply 'emerge'. In addition, however, there are other influences on the way work is done and one of them certainly is policy which comes down from 'on high' and which commands action. Such policy may be the result of autocratic decision-making, of democratic debate and participation, of consultation, or of bottom–up influences, suggestions and pressures. But, however it was made, once a distinctive policy has been sanctioned from 'the top', implementing it is certainly a top–down process: particular staff are given the responsibility of getting on with it – usually through a hierarchy of accountability.[4] Even so, implementation is not straightforward and the policy may be substantially modified in practice, it may be sabotaged, or it may simply run into the sands. It may, perhaps rarely, work out exactly as planned.[5]

Rather than *assert* that there are personal social services policies which determine practice, or that there are practices which in effect become policies, or that there is conflict and mismatch between policies and practices, it is therefore useful to pose several simple questions and to keep them to the fore.

1. To what extent are the personal social services characterised by clear, coherent policies?
2. How are such policies made, by whom, and at what level?
3. What efforts are made systematically to implement such policies, through what process and to what effect?
4. To what extent are fieldwork practices shaped by such clear, coherent policies and to what extent are practices shaped by tradition, custom, individual discretion and the pressure of local and short-term pressures?
5. Do these patterns, systems of policy-making and policy-implementation processes vary greatly by field, by organisation, and from time to time?

Against this background it can be argued that personal social services policy-making occurs in central government in general terms, and in local authorities and voluntary organisations in more specific terms. The autonomy of local government and voluntary organisations is such that government can only conceive and implement broad policies about child care, or community care, or privatisation, or prevention. An essential feature of the implementation of nearly all central-government policy in this field is that, for anything to get done, the local field organisations have themselves to formulate and then implement their own detailed policies. The central government is at several removes from the action, but so too are the senior decision-makers in local government or the voluntary sector. The personal social services are characterised by significant degrees of professional autonomy and fieldworker discretion. It is therefore important to identify and understand the channels of communication and influence through which 'the top' can influence field action – and vice versa.

Channels and arenas

Government has a variety of ways of articulating and communicating policies: legislation, white papers, policy documents and ministers' speeches. It also has 'levers to pull' in the form of decisions about resources, planning processes and guidelines and the mobilisation of advisers and inspectors. Local government and voluntary organisations, in turn, have their own equivalents of these ways of expressing and attempting to implement policies. Because the fieldworker has some – perhaps considerable – autonomy, training and the reinforcement of particular values or views of the world are also significant. In principle each of these channels of communication and influence which link 'bottom' and 'top' can be two-way: the traffic can run up as well as down. The horizontal traffic from one organisation or individual to another at the same 'level' is also important. But to say that traffic can run in different directions – not only from top to bottom – does not imply that power or influence are evenly dispersed. Once again the balance of power is a matter for observation and research, not a matter of definition and assertion.

A useful way of imposing some order and form on the many channels of communication and influence is to note that they can be broadly allocated to three 'arenas' of debate and action: the governmental; the professional; and the political. The first of these is the most closely organised; we will return to it below and identify some of the important channels of communication within it. Let us first outline the other two more briefly.

In the case of the personal social services, the professional arena is rather loosely defined and organised. Social work is not one of the most tightly and powerfully structured professions and other groups of personal social services staff are organised to varying degrees. Nevertheless, it is not at all difficult to see that social work, for example, does exist as a profession independently of the SSDs, the DHSS, and other agencies which interact in the 'governmental' arena. Some of the nodes of this professional arena are readily identified. They include The British Association of Social Work, The Central Council for Education and Training in Social Work, The National Institute for Social Work, and the professional journals and magazines. Quite how the professional and governmental arenas interact is not well documented. There has been virtually no research on the topic.[6] Nevertheless, government certainly is attentive to the messages conveyed – not least through journals and magazines. It also attempts to influence these messages; as, for example, in the setting up of the Barclay Committee which was clearly intended to have an impact on professional thinking about the future role of social work.

The workings of the political arena are, in detail, even more difficult to identify and specify than those of the professional arena. The political parties are a major means by which a broad ideological consensus is achieved between centre and locality, but direct communication only operates *within* each political party. Inter-party communications on policy issues are focused through intermediate bodies such as the local-government associations, as well as through exchanges in Parliament and local councils. Operating alongside these networks are the media – which embrace one of the important groups of actors who move in and out of each of the arenas we have identified.

It is impossible to generalise about the extent to which the influence of the centre over the localities – and vice versa – is effected through the political or professional, as opposed to the governmental, arena. What is clear is that policy formation and implementation are not wholly or even primarily contained within the latter. The governmental arena may be most important in the sense that it encompasses the major official channels and conveys official statements of policy, but the other two are often crucial precisely because they provide a forum within which ideas, attitudes, values and priorities can crystallise. These more amorphous determinants of behaviour can be every bit as important as policy statements and official channels of communication and command.

Policy streams

That it is unhelpful simply to conceive of central government as making detailed policies which localities implement is apparent. Local government, other agencies, and field staff, all have differing degrees and types of autonomy which cumulatively falsify such a picture. We have argued that the reality encompasses upward processes of influence as well as authority operating downwards, and it also involves considerable lack of clarity about and contradictions between policies. If we are fully to reflect these contradictions, however, we have to add a further idea to our conceptual framework: that of 'policy streams'.

In speaking of 'policy' we have used the term in what has become the conventional manner in relation to the social services. The word tends to be used to refer to the specification of service objectives and ways of attaining them. Policy is 'obviously' about those needs (e.g., of old people or families with children) which we intend to do something about, and the service outputs required to meet those needs. However, it is helpful to speak of these as *service or output policies*. Alongside them must be set *resource policies*: policies about how much to spend, on what, and how. They are every bit as significant as policies about services, or outputs.[7] Moreover, service and resource policies may be developed in isolation from, and be in conflict with, one another.

There can be no assumption that service policies will be matched with the resource policies necessary to give them life; there is no law of political and administrative behaviour which guarantees that these 'streams' of policy will be well coordinated and compatible.

At least two other 'policy streams' need to be added to the two above: *governance policies* and *policies in related areas of provision*. The first concerns general principles about how to organise and manage government and government business. In the 1960s and 1970s governance policies included a strong commitment to a substantial if not dominant role for state services, a belief in the value of comprehensive forward planning, and – less consistently explicit – a strong tendency towards central guidance or control. In particular, planning provided one approach to coordinating resource and service policies. In the early 1980s these elements of governance policy have been sharply reversed and the ruling ethos is apparently one of state disengagement, avoidance of '*dirigiste*' planning, and decentralisation – except in the field of resource control.

While specialised structures and processes are typically developed to handle both service and resource policy-making and implementation, governance policies tend to arise in less predictable ways and through *ad hoc* decisions and policy processes. For example, the principles of organisation on which local government and the NHS were restructured in 1974 were broadly in line with government thinking about public-sector management across a wider front, but they were also a one-off response to the need for structural change in those particular organisations. The dominant principles of the present day which we mentioned above emanate from the government as a whole and from its basic philosophy, but they too affect different areas of government to differing degrees. They are widely diffused from a central ideology and from the Prime Minister's office, but they take a variety of forms in different fields of application.

Policies in related services do not constitute a distinctive type of policy. They too may be divided into the component elements of service, resource and governance. Nevertheless, it is important to draw attention to them because they are a major source of potential confusion and complication. We have indicated that consistent attempts have been made to link developments in the NHS and the personal social services, and the direction of influence in this case has been clear: the personal social services have been seen as important to the realisation of aims within the NHS.[8] But social security policy, for example, is not necessarily devised with a keen eye on its implications for the personal social services, despite the fact that the implications can be substantial. Policy in the field of housing, law and order and policing may be equally important – but even more independent and difficult to influence. There are barriers to coordinating policies across different fields of activities even within one government department; inter-departmental barriers are even greater. Some real coordination is achieved on occasions, but the interaction of related services tends to be unpredictable rather than well understood or well managed. Indeed, there is every reason to assume that coordinated decisions may be the exception rather than the rule.

The idea of 'policy streams' is not merely an analytical device, therefore; it highlights potential lines of conflict and contradiction. For example, resource and service decisions tend to be made through different mechanisms involving different actors and branches of government. Moreover, these institutional differences tend to be underpinned by the specific values and views of the world upheld by the various types of actors involved: the Treasury and the economists and financial specialists whom it nurtures and to whom it listens inhabit a different milieu to the doctors, nurses and social workers who interact in and with the DHSS. Rather than assume that there is something called 'policy', therefore, it is important to ask how many such streams of policy there may be, how distinctive and autonomous they may be and whether multiple policies and decisions result in a coherent – or confusing and incoherent – environment for local social services managers and professionals. In principle there are at least three broad possibilities: that different streams of policy operate in isolation from one another and produce compatible policies and decisions fortuitously, if at all; that they are coordinated through administrative routine (e.g., by committees which span different streams) or by more systematic administrative devices such as planning systems; or that politicians enforce cohesion by sub-ordinating all decisions to a single set of objectives, values and theoretical perspectives.

The purpose of developing these ideas is to emphasise the fact that far from there being a single coherent policy or set of policies for the personal social services, reality is more likely to take the shape of 'streams' of policies which are often quite strongly insulated one from another, which may contain highly contradictory elements, and which will certainly interact in ways which cannot readily be predicted in advance but which must be understood if we are to have a clear notion of how the personal social services 'work'. One key question is how, and how often, central government manages to 'get its act together' such that policies within the different streams complement each other and present local agencies and actors with a coordinated and coherent set of limits, commands, guidelines and suggestions within which to act. Ten minutes discussion with staff at almost any level in SSDs, or voluntary organisations, will tend to produce the conclusion that it never happens. That is to minimise the success of the DHSS over the last decade or two, but it does emphasise the fact that policy coordination is a difficult and hard won, rather than an automatic, product of central–local relations. Coordination is the 'holy grail' of administration; its very elusiveness is the spur to an essentially heroic, optimistic and eternally frustrated quest.

Substance can be added to this skeleton of ideas and concepts by considering the governmental arena in more detail. The general role of central government will be examined first, followed by a more specific look at the role of DHSS and of other central departments.

THE ROLE OF CENTRAL GOVERNMENT

The primary significance of central government is that it shapes and elaborates the legal framework, created by Act of Parliament, in which local authorities, voluntary organisations and private services operate. The relationship varies in each of these cases. Local authorities cannot move without legislation: their power to act is only a power to do that which is specifically permitted or enjoined by Act of Parliament. Local government is the creature of legislation and therefore of central government. Legislation provides a broad framework within which there is a fair amount of room for manoeuvre, but the framework does nonetheless set the boundaries. The same is not true of voluntary or private services. No legislative sanction is needed for a group of people jointly to create a self-help group or launch a private residential home for old people. Non-statutory bodies are free to act as they will, providing they obey the law and work within any regulatory constraints. One example of such legally enforced constraints is the provision for registering private residential homes. Another arises from the fact that many voluntary organisations are charities; the status and tax privileges accorded to charities are defined by law and enforced by the Charity Commissioners.[9]

Tax privileges are one, important, source of 'public' financial support; they are public monies which government foregoes. More generally, central control of resources – which is the second means by which government has a major impact – takes several forms: direct grants (to local authorities and to a number of national voluntary organisations); social security benefits (paid to individuals but often used to 'buy' statutory, voluntary or private services); authorisation to raise loans (in the case of local authority capital expenditure); and tax concessions. It also, increasingly, takes the form of sanctions exercised against local authorities which exceed the total level of expenditure which central government considers as appropriate. The control of the flow of resources takes a variety of forms, therefore, and is pervasive. Resource distribution has a fundamental impact on local statutory and non-statutory services alike.

The responsibility for developing national (service or output) policies for the personal social services – and safeguarding standards – is the third component of the central-government role. The oversight of policy might in some circumstances amount to little more than keeping the legislative framework in good repair, although it tends inevitably to involve a good deal of 'secondary legislation': the elaboration of the legal skeleton through the formulation of detailed regulations. However, it can mean far more than that. Active ministers have the opportunity to shape and develop ideas, promulgate new policies, modify priorities and initiate legislative changes if the legal framework is considered to be appropriate. Policy is closely allied to the legislative framework, therefore, but it is a field of potentially more detailed interventions.

Similarly, policing standards can be an essentially reactive or low-key, or a more positive and dynamic, responsibility of central government. It can take one of two forms. The first and more traditional is that of maintaining standards of professional practice. This may involve the setting of minimum standards of performance such as those embodied in the statutory duty to visit foster parents or conduct six monthly reviews of cases where children are in the care of the local authority. It may also involve the use of a professional inspectorate. The Home Office's childcare inspectorate was a highly regarded safeguard of professional standards in the pre-Seebohm years. It was absorbed into the newly formed DHSS Social Work Service at the beginning of the 1970s and the emphasis shifted from inspection to one of advising and supporting local services.[10] The pendulum is now on the return swing and the Social Work Service has been renamed the Social Services Inspectorate.[11]

Concern with standards of performance can also encompass the level and balance of services provided, though the appropriateness of central government intervention in this respect is less unanimously agreed. One objection raised by cost-conscious ministers is that it can easily increase pressure to spend more money on services. Another objection is that it directly confronts and limits the autonomy which local authorities enjoy in shaping policy within the national framework.

Setting minimum standards and enforcing them would apparently not infringe local freedom to improve upon such levels of service, but it could in fact have real disadvantages, nonetheless. In particular, services such as home helps, meals on wheels, day care, residential care and field social work need to be 'packaged' and they are partly substitutes for and partly complements to one another. Minimum standards, expressed as required levels of *each* service, would therefore tend to imply rather rigid packages of, and relationships between, these services. The approach adopted in practice by the DHSS from 1972 until comparatively recently was to issue planning guidelines for each of the major services, but without specifying that the guidelines were minimal or that they were universally appropriate to local practice.

While the concern with performance standards has certainly been expressed at the level of service provision in the past as well as at the level of professional practice, therefore, the approach has been tentative. The emphasis seems now to have shifted decisively to a concern with professional standards, but even more clearly to a concern with cost-effectiveness; planning guidelines have become something of a footnote in the history of the 1970s. What this will mean for the role of the Social Work Inspectorate is presently unclear. The inspection of standards of professional practice has a long pedigree, but the promotion of cost-effective policies and practices is inevitably more complex and the meaning to be attached to cost-effectiveness is inevitably controversial.

We have identified four primary areas of central government involvement in the personal social services which we can now more conveniently summarise as three by combining the first two:
1. shaping the legislative framework and promulgating 'service' policies;
2. exercising control over resources;
3. monitoring standards of performance.

We have also identified one clear channel by which government relates to local authorities and non-statutory services: namely, the Social Services Inspectorate. But there is much more to the DHSS than the SSI. It is important to restore the perspective by sketching in a fuller picture of the interaction between the DHSS and the local personal social services.

The political, governmental and professional arenas are brought together within the DHSS. This is simply reflected in Figure 7.1,

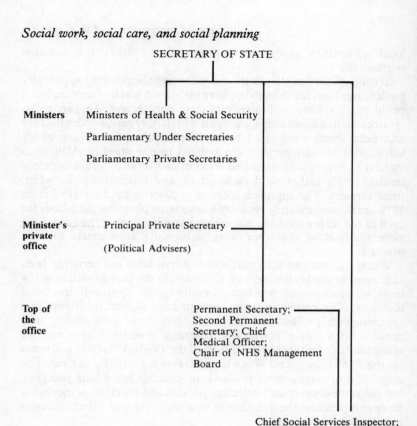

SECRETARY OF STATE

Ministers   Ministers of Health & Social Security

Parliamentary Under Secretaries

Parliamentary Private Secretaries

Minister's private office   Principal Private Secretary

(Political Advisers)

Top of the office   Permanent Secretary; Second Permanent Secretary; Chief Medical Officer; Chair of NHS Management Board

Chief Social Services Inspector; Chief Nursing Officer; and other chief professional officers

Fig. 7.1

which identifies the relationship between ministers (who have overall responsibility for the political direction of policy), the permanent secretary (who has overall administrative responsibility for the Department) and the professionals (who have a responsibility directly to advise ministers as well as a responsibility to work with administrative civil servants in the development and implementation of policies).

The basic structural features of the DHSS are further revealed by the allocation of responsibilities between the senior administrative civil servants. This is shown in Figure 7.2. As can be seen, the

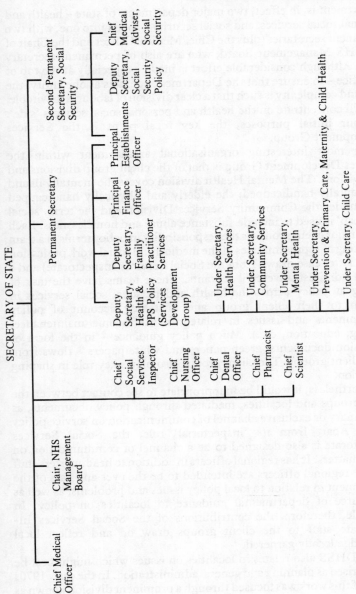

Fig. 7.2

Department is, in effect, two major departments of state – health and personal social services, and social security – rolled into one, with two permanent secretaries (plus the Chief Medical Officer and the Chair of the NHS Management Board, who are also of permanent secretary rank). Although considerable effort is made – especially at the top of the office – to ensure that the Department operates as one entity, the scale and complexity is such that a clear division of labour is inevitable. We will concentrate on the health and personal social services 'side'. For our initial purposes, the key focal point is the Services Development Group.

The most interesting organisational arrangement within the Services Development Group is that of the client group divisions and subdivisions. The Mental Health division covers the mentally ill and the mentally handicapped; the elderly and physically handicapped come under the Community Services Division and the term 'social handicap' is used to include substance abuse and homelessness. Each of the major client groups is the responsibility in policy terms of a team consisting of representatives of the medical and social work profession (in the latter case drawn from the Social Services Inspectorate) and a core of administrative civil servants. These teams have the task of looking at policy across the health and personal social services in relation to their client group and of taking account of policy developments and issues in related fields (income maintenance, housing, education, etc.). Much policy guidance – in the form of discussion documents, green papers and white papers – flows from these client groups. The client groups also play a key role in shaping legislation.

Nevertheless, it would be inappropriate to see contact between the client groups and localities, mediated through policy documents, as the primary or exclusive channel of communication on service policy issues. Apart from its 'inspectorial' role, the Social Services Inspectorate is also designed to be a channel of communication on policy matters. It has regional officers in addition to headquarters staff and the regional officers are intended to be the eyes and ears of the Department in relation to local policy issues and problems, as well as the source of departmental guidance to localities on policy. In principle, therefore, the contributions of the Social Services Inspectorate staff to the client groups draw on and reflect local knowledge locally garnered.

The DHSS also relates to localities on issues which might best be summarised as planning and general administration. In the early 1970s much of this work was focused through a prominent division known as

LASS: the Local Authority Social Services Division. It was the 'mirror image' for the personal social services of the structure of regional management operating in the NHS. A directly managed service such as the NHS requires a complex managerial structure, but in the case of the personal social services what was seen to be necessary was a focal point and channel of communication which was sensitive to the different kind of relationship appropriate to interaction between DHSS and local authorities or voluntary organisations. A large part of the work of LASS in the early years concerned the DHSS's attempt to develop a systematic form of forward planning in SSDs which would parallel that in existence in the NHS. LASS was also closely involved in other areas such as the launch of joint finance in 1967. Cuts in civil service manpower and changes in the distribution of work have led to the absorption of LASS within the Community Services Division. However, the fact remains that planning and general administration constitutes a relatively distinctive and clearly important area of central–local relations.

The process of developing a framework of legislation and 'service policies' is structurally much less complex than that of controlling resources – to which we must now turn. In the case of 'resource policies', the DHSS is relegated to a less central position. The resources available to a Social Services Department are primarily determined by the local authority of which it is part. The local authority's resource come primarily from local rates, from the block grant made available by central government, from charges levied on consumers of services and from several other sources of lesser important (such as urban aid or joint finance). The central-government grant is made to the local authority as a whole and is administered through the Department of the Environment (DOE), not the DHSS. Because the grant is unhypothecated (i.e, not 'earmarked' for particular departments or uses), the DHSS does not have direct control or influence over SSDs' budgets. Its involvement in the 'resource stream' is primarily at the central level and consists of trying to influence Treasury thinking about the level of funding which SSDs need if they are to fulfil their duties and carry out the main areas of policy appropriately. Much of this influence is focused and exerted through the Department's Finance Division.

The decision processes on local government funding are dominated by the Treasury and, ultimately, the Cabinet. The DHSS voice is but one source of influence on the eventual outcome. Another is the local authority associations and, for our purposes especially, their personal social services specialists. These associations (The Association of

County Councils and The Association of Metropolitan Councils) relate directly to the DOE and the DHSS and there is, in principle, a continuous process of communication about the needs and problems of local government. More formally, the Joint Consultative Council on Local Government Finance brings all central government and local government interests together. However, the sharp shift in emphasis from considerations of need to the squeezing of public expenditure – which began in the mid-1970s but accelerated rapidly after 1979 – has been accompanied and affected by a shift in power. The upward flow of information on need and its resource implications is much less effective than the downward flow of decisions about the expenditures to be sanctioned. This imbalance continues to be manifest even after the general decisions about the level of central support for local government have been made. The DOE, as the key channel of the resource stream, has its impact on Policy and Resource Committees and on local authority Treasurers; the DHSS can only advise SSDs on priorities, it cannot greatly influence the resources that are available to them.

Nevertheless, DHSS has not always had such a limited ability to control the use made locally of resource, nor is it totally without influence even now. Because the Rate Support Grant – which covers revenue expenditures – is outside DHSS administrative control, approval of capital expenditure was traditionally the key means by which SSDs could be directly influenced.[12] Capital expenditure was only the tail, but it was one way of wagging a substantially autonomous dog. Priority between different client groups, policies about the desirable structure and balance of service provision, and ideas about good practice within establishments such as day centres or homes could all be reflected, at least in part, through decisions to grant or refuse capital projects, and these decisions were channelled through the Social Work Service. However, capital expenditure controls became somewhat more responsive to local-authority priorities from the mid-1970s onwards and their importance diminished rapidly as the overall level of capital expenditure fell sharply.

The more interesting feature of recent years, therefore, has been the growth of DHSS influence over some areas of revenue funding. The most direct and obvious example is the expansion of DHSS funding of local voluntary activity through such schemes as Opportunities for Volunteering and Helping the Community to Care. The sums involved are trivial in relation to SSD expenditure, but they are potentially a very powerful means of shaping voluntary provision. The importance of income-maintenance benefits to many personal social services clients also ensures that the rules under which they operate have a crucial, though indirect, impact on statutory, voluntary and private services. These rules are largely controlled by DHSS.

CENTRAL–LOCAL RELATIONS: A SUMMARY

The position outlined can be summarised as follows. We have identified three broad arenas of interaction: professional; political; and governmental. We have also identified various areas of activity which involve interaction between central government and local agencies. They include: legislation and service policy formation; resource control; the safeguarding of standards; planning and general administration. In addition, we have noted that DHSS is the key central government department in relation to the personal social services and that it encompasses at least four identifiable channels of communication in the Service Development Group, the Social Service Inspectorate, the Finance Division and the Community Services Division. However, the control of resources is effected primarily by the Treasury through the DOE, not by the DHSS. The service and resource streams of policy do, therefore, flow through structurally different channels and there is ample room for them to carry divergent and incompatible messages.

A simplified version of part of this pen picture – the governmental arena – is presented in Figure 7.3. It includes a symbolic representation of the professional arena in the form of professional associations. The overlap is, of course, extensive and crucial. Professional workers are to be found in local authorities, voluntary organisations, in DHSS, and acting as advisers in the local-authority associations. The political arena has been lightly identified by noting the key locations in which ministers and local-authority members are to be found. Once again the political arena is woven through the governmental arena, but is not synonymous with it.

The governmental arena has been greatly simplified, but the main features of the DHSS and of the system of public-expenditure control have been identified. Authoritative and 'managerial' relationships are shown by solid lines, though in the case of local-authority associations, for example, the relationship is one of representation rather than managerial control. Relationships which are primarily advisory, consultative, coordinative or supervisory, but not clearly managerial, are shown as broken lines.

What the diagram cannot indicate is that the nature of the messages, and of power, is different in the two 'streams'. Service messages tend

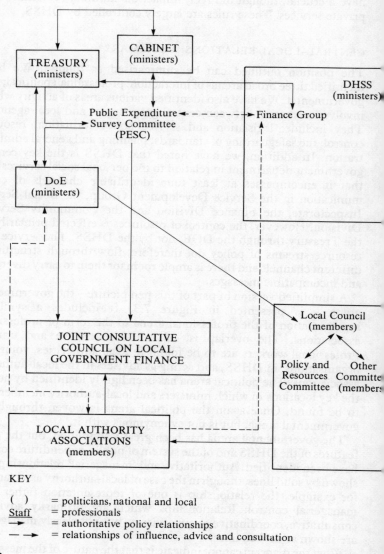

CABINET
(ministers)

TREASURY
(ministers)

DHSS
(ministers)

Public Expenditure ← - - - - → Finance Group
Survey Committee
(PESC)

DoE
(ministers)

Local Council
(members)

**JOINT CONSULTATIVE
COUNCIL ON LOCAL
GOVERNMENT FINANCE**

Policy and
Resources
Committee

Other
Committee
(members)

**LOCAL AUTHORITY
ASSOCIATIONS**
(members)

KEY

( ) = politicians, national and local

<u>Staff</u> = professionals

⟶ = authoritative policy relationships

- - → = relationships of influence, advice and consultation

Fig. 7.3

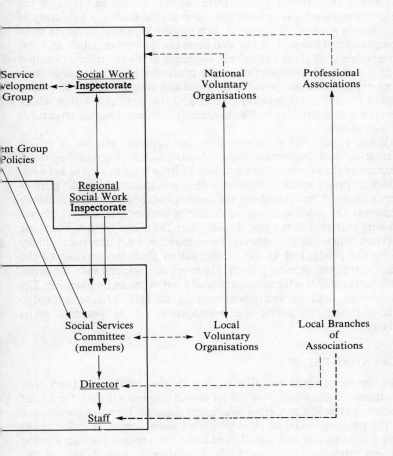

to be about broad goals, which are influenced by and filtered through the values of many groups – especially the key professions involved. However, resource messages can be determined far more completely by the ideologies, priorities and objectives of central government and presented in relatively precise terms as cash limits. In principle the resource stream is easier to command from the centre. The history of the decade since 1974 is one of increasingly vigorous attempts so to command it. However, it has also been one of a more subtle and less observable shift from the values, language and objectives associated with social need and with the service professionals to those associated with expenditure and with the financial and accountancy professions. Power resides in commanding ideas and the language within which issues are discussed, as well as in directly commanding the structures of government.

What Figure 7.3 does reveal is the complex nature of policy formation and implementation. Moreover, the diagram begins to emphasise the opportunities for 'lack of fit' within as well as between different policy streams. Resource decisions made within the public-expenditure system need not necessarily make sense of the multiple demands for resources arising from the service policies which are flowing and have in the past flowed, from the client groups. But these services policies may themselves be uncoordinated. Coherence is likely to be the product of an act of will rather than the product of the administrative machinery itself. However one understands the term, such an act of will is the very essence of what we mean by planning. Let us therefore ask how, and how effectively, the DHSS has attempted to plan for and coordinate the development of the personal social services.

PLANNING: THE 1970S

The surge towards social planning in the 1970s has been well documented elsewhere.[13] What we would emphasis is that, for a brief period, it offered a particular solution to those problems of governance in the personal social services which we noted above. A real attempt was made to guide individual local authorities to work within a broad national strategy which emphasised community care. However, the solution had a fair wind for only a very short period of time and from the mid-1970s onwards the story of planning in this field was one of trying to retain a degree of control over troublesome events. DHSS emerged with a fair degree of credibility, as did most local authority SSDs. Nevertheless, the credibility of the *idea* of synoptic forward planning suffered a more ignominious fate and it was a simple matter for the incoming Conservative government of 1979 to brush the vestiges of the system aside. To express distaste for the centralising and bureaucratic connotations of synoptic planning is not to create an alternative strategy for resolving underlaying problems, however. The Conservative response to the continuing need for some, albeit different, method of social planning will be outlined as a conclusion to our survey of this topic.

The enthusiasm for synoptic forward planning precisely identified policy coordination, central–local relations and local relations – between the NHS, local government and the voluntary sector – as crucial to progress. The 'priority' client groups – the elderly, mentally ill and mentally handicapped – had long been seen as a problem for and a drain upon the resources of the NHS.[14] Historically, large numbers of these people had been 'warehoused' in hospitals, not because effective medical treatment was available but because the functions of social care and control had been heavily concentrated in institutions over a long period of time. Medical developments and escalating costs in hospitals combined to push forward one part of the community care ideal: the reduction of the numbers of long stay patients in NHS hospitals. To effect this, the personal social services had to be planned in close conjunction with the NHS. Indeed, the abiding temptation in DHSS has been to treat the personal social services and community care as an adjunct to NHS planning: as merely a crucial footnote to the main story.

The centrality of coordination is clearly revealed. The need was to coordinate, in our terminology, service policy streams in the related areas of both the personal social services and NHS. Community care had to be matched to reductions in the numbers of long-stay hospital patients. In order to do that, however, there was an equally crucial need to coordinate resource and service policies. The money spent had to be sufficient to achieve the desired service developments and it had to be appropriately used. So much is obvious enough. The point of highlighting the issue of coordination across policy streams, however, is to insist that it is not easily achieved, let alone the automatic outcome of governmental machinery. Local authorities and local health authorities had to be induced to plan together, or at least to plan in compatible ways. Their own resource stocks and resource allocations had to be moved in the right directions and, within the NHS, greater prominence had to be given to the 'priority' groups. All this had to be achieved through the complex set of central–local relations outlined, taking full account of the fact that the NHS was centrally managed but effectively impervious to much DHSS direction because of the power of doctors while SSDs were within the politically independent local authority sector but were new and relatively open to influence and guidance.

The early and mid-1970s saw a real, though uphill, struggle to re-allocate NHS resources towards the less well financed regions and areas and towards the neglected client groups.[15] This sense of direction was imposed on and expressed through an elaborate forward-planning system which had been in the process of being developed for some years. Systematic forward planning backed up by a good measure of ministerial drive from the centre offered a means of changing thinking and of implementing broad goals and objectives. In the case of the personal social services, the need was to link SSDs with the NHS planning processes without contravening the semi-autonomous status of local government. The DHSS's call for ten-year forward plans from SSDs in 1972 provided the mechanism. Guidelines on the 'desirable' levels of provision in different types of service were issued, but they were clearly not imposed on SSDs. Although many local *health* authorities tended to see them as binding on SSDs and as a measure of the minimum levels of service to be attained by SSDs, they were intended as a basis for local thinking and planning. In principle, SSDs were being guided in directions which would correspond to the changes taking place in the NHS and were being encouraged to give due weight to the neglected client groups. The planning base for community care – seen as the transfer of social care tasks from the NHS to the SSDs – had been laid. That it was dominated by the need to coordinate across organisational boundaries between the NHS and the SSDs was reflected in the justifiable complaint that at the local level ten-year planning discouraged, rather than encouraged, corporate thinking across the whole range of *local authority* departments.

Ten-year planning was certainly about coordinating health and local authority social services, but it was also about coordinating resources and service policies. The DHSS encouraged SSDs to think in terms of a steady rate of growth of 10 per cent per annum in real terms. The object, therefore, was to guide foreseeable growth so that it could be used to achieve desired ends. But once the world economy had begun to tremble in 1973, the die was cast for the remainder of the decade. The struggle was on to retain a degree of coordination between resource and service decisions such that some vestige of the strategy for coordinating NHS and personal social services developments could be retained. The basic resource decisions – an imposition of an overall standstill in public-expenditure levels – were made in the

Cabinet, the Treasury and within the cabal of senior 'economic' ministers. All the DHSS could do was to argue a case for continued growth, allocate its own NHS budget appropriately, and advise local authorities on the need for protection for the personal social services.

Four key mechanisms were used in the struggle to keep planning and policy coordination alive. The first was to identify the minimum rate of continued growth in expenditure deemed necessary in the NHS and the personal social services if the inevitable growth in need and demand was to be met. The largest single pressure of this kind was that of demographic change (especially in the elderly population). This, combined with the stresses inherent in a newly reorganised and lately expanded service, resulted in the minimum rate of real growth for the personal social services being set at 2 per cent per annum – a slightly higher figure than for the NHS. Second, and within these overall targets for very limited growth, the DHSS further specified priorities within and between client groups in 1976 and 1977 through the medium of two priorities documents.[16] Although setting priorities across the health and personal social services as a whole perpetuated the sense of NHS domination in DHSS thinking, the exercise was widely seen as a positive and much needed response to the sudden collapse of planning for rapid growth.

The third mechanism, added in 1976, was joint finance. It was introduced to facilitate joint planning at the local level between local authorities and health authorities. Joint planning was an essential component of the strategy for coordination and the reorganisation of local government and the NHS in 1974 had provided a structural and legal base. Collaboration between the NHS and local government was required by law and DHSS provided guidance on the appropriate committee structure which might facilitate it. Nevertheless, joint planning remained an ideal in 1976; little had been achieved since 1974. Joint finance was therefore to be the catalyst for real progress in joint planning. In effect it was, and remains, an earmarked element of NHS budgets to be spent on jointly agreed projects developed and managed by local authorities, or voluntary bodies, but designed to bring benefit to the NHS.[17]

The fourth mechanism was a redesigned system of forward planning. The 1972 attempt to look forward for ten years had been determined by the needs of the NHS. It reflected the position of the NHS as a service which was directly managed by the DHSS and which involved very considerable and long-term capital, manpower and training decisions. The case for such a long-time horizon in the personal social services was less obvious; once the economic situation became unpredictable it was nonexistent. Each SSD had to face the uncertainty of changes in resource policies, and in political control, in its own authority, as well as changes in national policy towards local government. A revised planning system was therefore introduced in 1977 based on a three-year cycle; a shortened time-scale seemed more in keeping with the climate of uncertainty. The LAPS (Local Authority Planning Statements) system, as it came to be known, also involved the submission by SSDs of statements of general policy to DHSS as well as the more traditional submission of data on likely trends in service provision. But the time and mood for such forward planning had passed and the chore of putting submissions together was not welcomed by many SSDs. It seemed to many to be an unreal and unproductive activity; LAPS too was rapidly abandoned.

Taken together, these four responses to public expenditure cuts represented a fundamental change in the nature of planning and in the coordination of resource and service policies. The approach in the early 1970s had been need led: growth was to be used systematically to fulfil service objectives. By the mid-1970s an approach had been developed which could best be described as 'scarcity-need planning'. It was dominated by the scarcity of public money but, within the constraints imposed, a systematic attempt was made to respond to the most pressing needs.[18] The DHSS had given notice to the health authorities of what, managerially, it wanted to see happen and it had given clear guidance to local authorities of the priority it felt should be given to SSDs and to competing demands within their field of action.

The practice was not as coherent as were the principles. Local authorities generally gave greater priority to SSDs than the DHSS outlined as the minimum. Real growth exceeded 2 per cent per annum in the mid-1970s and most of the priority groups benefited from this preservation of growth. However, the pressure on public expenditure was exacerbated by high rates of inflation, and the production of services was steadily squeezed. These problems are discussed more fully in Chapter 8. In the case of Joint Finance the money was spent, but whether it benefited the strategy is a different matter. Given the resource pressures, the most realistic conclusion is that community services would have deteriorated even faster if joint finance had not been available.[19] There have been local innovations and cases of effective joint planning, but the overriding experience has been one of minimising the damage done rather than making major strides towards the promised land which systematically planned growth seemed to bring within sight at the beginning of the decade.

To review these planning experiences is not merely an exercise in writing history, however. Rather it is a case of exposing two of the central problems of the personal social services: *coordination* across professional and organisational boundaries is essential and the community-care strategy also requires at least some degree of coordination between resource and service objectives across the health and personal social services; *additional resources* are also essential if the personal social services are to pick up a large part of the burden of social care presently borne by the NHS while also responding to demand for social care arising in the community. But in practice, from the mid-1970s, forward planning provided only a limited base for coordination and resources were severely curtailed in real terms – joint finance transferred comparatively small sums from the NHS to SSDs. This was the situation which faced the new Conservative government in 1979, just as it had faced the departing Labour government.

The difference in 1979 was that the new administration was committed to more and tougher cuts in public expenditure and it repudiated the paraphernalia of systematic forward planning. This did not, of course, mean that ministers could dismiss the need for some form of social planning if they were to retain the community-care strategy. Indeed, the increased pressure which Conservative expenditure policies placed on local government simply exacerbated the problem. What, then, has transpired?

One answer is: 'not a lot'. Community care has primarily been retained in the particular sense that rhetorical support for it has not diminished. On the other hand, no convincing attempt has been made to offset the impact of expenditure cuts on SSDs and thereby square the circle. In this sense the need for social planning has not been recognised or, if recognised, has not been acted upon.

However, this picture has to be modified to take into account one important development: the development of the approach to *resource transfers* which was first expressed publicly in the consultative document *Care in the Community*, published in 1981.[20] The argument was a simple one and is a good example of an initiative which began in a few localities and was pushed onto the national agenda via articles by SSD staff in journals and by the lobbying of ministers. By the early 1980s there was very little evidence of joint finance having enabled unnecessarily hospitalised people to move into the community, despite the number who might reasonably do so. The obvious need was to move significant sums of money from the NHS to SSDs to enable such patient transfers to take place. If sufficient patients could be transferred to enable wards or whole institutions to be closed, the resource transfers could be self-financing. The possibilities were explored in the consultative document; the end product was changes in the legislative and policy framework enabling health authorities to transfer resources, official encouragement for them to do so, and more 'generous' support from joint finance for the development of the necessary facilities in the community. Resource and patient transfer are now real possibilities, but they are nothing like a complete answer to the more general need for a coordinated approach to service development and a resource policy which positively encourages a thorough-going commitment to community care.[21]

A different view of the Conservative government's impact hinges on the redefinition of community care. As we saw in Chapter 5, growing emphasis has been placed on care *by* the community and therefore on family and informal care, rather than on local authority provided services. The difficulty which this poses is that social planning for more informal care is quite different from that involved in building up local-authority services. Families are not direct agents of government policy: there are few 'levers' for government to pull.

If care by the community is viewed as a purely negative policy (i.e., as the rolling back of the frontiers of state provision on the assumption that families will cope) negative mechanisms may be all that are needed. Public expenditure cuts, if sufficient, could force the pace and direction of change. The question then is factual: has the government cut, or firmly controlled, SSD budgets? This is a question for Chapter 8.

A more positive view of care by the community would see it as one element in the welfare-pluralism debate: voluntary organisations, mutual-aid groups and volunteering would be expected to expand alongside and in support of informal care. However, as we have already implied, such a policy would also raise problems of implementation – even if it were coherently and consistently articulated. Central government has traditionally provided little *direct* financial support for voluntary organisations and virtually none for purely local voluntary provision. To increase local-authority support for the voluntary sector while reducing the local-authority expenditure base would require great central pressure and a degree of intervention in local affairs which the government has philosophically rejected. Exhortation there has been, but there has been no real pressure on local authorities. However, such a policy would presume that the government wished voluntary organisations to grow with additional help from the public purse. There has been only limited evidence to suggest that this is in fact desired. Government spokesmen have certainly argued that the real value of grant support to the voluntary sector has at least been maintained, but this claim does not suggest a strong commitment and it sits alongside a consistent refusal, for example, to relieve voluntary organisations of the burden of Value Added Tax.

One of the strongest developments on the voluntary front, which has also benefited agencies deploying volunteers, has been the growth of bespoke funding programmes designed to reduce or mask unemployment. Sums of new money which are substantial in voluntary-sector terms flowed through this route to local as well as national organisations. However, there has been little or no attempt to coordinate social service and employment policies. The monies have taken many voluntary organisations in new directions but there can be no guarantee that this will benefit community care or other personal social services objectives. The main programmes which have been focused directly on the personal social services by DHSS (Opportunities for Volunteering and Helping the Community to Care) have been on a small scale compared with Urban Aid and the work of the MSC and the Home Office Voluntary Services Unit.

The final interpretation to be placed on care by the community is that it implies a new partnership between SSDs and informal care – the former must increasingly support the latter – and that it makes room for further movements of patients from the NHS to SSDs. The first of these possibilities – a new partnership – highlights the problems of implementing policies which depend on changes in professional values and priorities. The need is to persuade SSDs and individual fieldworkers to give greater priority to supporting non-statutory services and informal help, and correspondingly less to direct work with clients. The Barclay Report was one exercise in trying to restructure professional agendas, the attention given to 'patch' has been another. Neither has been directly under the control of the DHSS and the impact of each remains unclear. As we noted in Chapter 5, the Department has favoured change in the role of the SSD and this has been made explicit by ministers. The impact of exhortation, combined with the general ideological and resource climates and the rethinking of traditional state services, may have a considerable impact in the long run. For the moment the outcome is uncertain.

What is clear is that a new conventional wisdom that the personal social services should not be 'stato-centric' and that SSDs should be 'enablers' is one thing, but to specify what this might mean in practice and how it might be achieved is another. There are four inherent difficulties in the proposition which will have to be faced if it is to be of any real significance. The first is whether an enabling role is at all possible given the pressure of demand and crisis work in SSDs. Does it imply a long-term decrease – or increase – in the level of demand on SSDs? The second concerns the skills required by practitioners. Is an enabling role to be prosecuted by the same mixture of casework, advocacy and gatekeeping skills necessary to contemporary social work – and to other groups of personal social services workers – or is it to be furthered by inculcating new skills? The third is a structural problem. Is 'enabling' something which can only hope to succeed in very small localities and does it therefore rest upon a resolute pursuit of decentralisation – or upon the development of new types of teamwork? The final difficulty is that of planning capacity and influence. Given a greater heterogeneity of voluntary and private provision, do SSDs need and can they have much strategic influence? The questions are not too difficult to pose, but the answers are presently far from clear and central guidance is minimal.

REFERENCES

1. Among the most helpful publications in this field are: JONES, G. (ed.), 1980 *New Approaches to the Study of Central Local Government Relationships*. Gower (for the Social Sciences Research Council); GOLDSMITH, M. J. and RHODES, R. A. W. (Issue eds), 1981 'Intergovernment relations in Britain', *Public Administration Bulletin*, no. 36, August; RHODES, R. A. W., 1981 *Control and Power in Central-Local Government Relations*. Gower; YOUNG, K. (ed.) 1983 *National Interests & Local Government*. Heinemann

2. WEBB, A. L. and WISTOW, G., 1980 'Implementations and central-local relations in the personal social services', in Jones, G. (ed.), 1980 op.cit. (ref. 1); WEBB, A. L. and WISTOW, G., 1982 *Whither State Welfare? Policy and Implementation in the Personal Social Services. Royal Institute of Public Administration;* WEBB, A. L. and WISTOW, G., 1985 'Structuring local policy environments: central-local relations in the personal social services', in Ranson, S., *The Changing Relationship Between Central and Local Government*. Allen & Unwin

3. BARRETT, S. and FUDGE, C. (eds), 1981 *Policy and Action: Essays on the Implementation of Public Policy*. Methuen

4. Much has been written on rationing; for an overview *see* FOSTER, P., 1983 *Access to Welfare: An Introduction to Welfare Rationing*. Macmillan

5. For an introduction to the problems of policy implementation *see* DUNSIRE, A., 1978 *Implementation in a Bureaucracy.* Martin Robertson; JENKINS, W., 1978 *Policy Analysis: A Political and Organisational Perspective.* Martin Robertson; WEBB, A. L. and WISTOW, G., 1982, op.cit. (ref. 2)

6. The influence of professionals on the Seebohm debate is the best charted part of this largely unexplored territory: HALL, P., 1976 *Reforming the Welfare: the Politics of Change in the Personal Social Services.* Heinemann; THOMAS, N. in Chapman, R. A. (ed.), 1973 *The Role of Commissions in Policy Making.* George Allen & Unwin; COOPER, J., 1983 *The Creation of the British Personal Social Services 1962–1974.* Heinemann

7. WEBB, A. L. and WISTOW, G., 1982, op.cit. (ref. 2)

8. PINKER, R. A., 1978 *Research Priorities in the Personal Social Services.* Social Science Research Council

9. For a discussion of charity law and its implications for voluntary organisations *see* THE REPORT OF THE GOODMAN COMMITTEE (Chairman: Lord Goodman) 1976 *Charity Law and Voluntary Organisations.* Bedford Square Press

10. UTTING, W., 1979 'The social work service of DHSS', *Social Work Service* no. 1, January; HALLETT, C., 1982 *The Personal Social Services in Local Government.* Allen & Unwin

11. DHSS, 1983 *The Social Work Service of DHSS: A Consultative Document.* HMSO

12. JUDGE, K., 1978 *Rationing Social Services.* Heinemann

13. GLENNERSTER, H., 1975 *Social Service Budgets and Social Policy.* Allen & Unwin; BOOTH, T. A. (ed.), 1979 *Planning for Welfare: Social Policy and the Expenditure Process.* Basil Blackwell and Martin Robertson; WALKER, A. (ed.), 1982 *Public Expenditure and Social Policy.* Heinemann; GLENNERSTER, H., 1983 *Planning for Priority Groups.* Martin Robertson; WEBB, A. L. and WISTOW, G., 1986, *Planning Need and Scarcity: Essays on the Personal Social Services.* Allen & Unwin

14. GLENNERSTER, H., 1983, op.cit. (ref. 13); WEBB, A. L. and WISTOW, G., 1985 op.cit. (ref. 13)

15. Ibid.

16. DHSS, 1976 *Priorities in the Health and Personal Social Services.* HMSO; DHSS, 1977 *The Way Forward.* HMSO

17. For a much fuller discussion of joint finance and joint planning *see* WEBB, A. L. and WISTOW, G., 1986, op.cit. (ref. 13)

18. WEBB, A. L. and WISTOW, G., 1982 'The personal social services: incrementalism, expediency or systematic social planning?', in

Social work, social care, and social planning

Walker, A. (ed.) *Public Expenditure and Social Policy*. Heinemann

19. WEBB, A. L. and WISTOW, G., 1983 'Public expenditure and policy implementation: the case of community care', *Public Administration*, vol. 16, Spring, pp. 21–44

20. DHSS, 1981 *Care in the Community*. HMSO

21. WEBB, A. L. and WISTOW, G., 1983 'Can you spare a policy?', *Social Work Today*, vol. 14, no. 28, pp. 10–12; WEBB, A. L. and WISTOW, G., 1986, op.cit. (ref. 13)

Chapter eight

NEEDS AND RESOURCES

What level and range of needs did the personal social services inherit in the early 1970s as they emerged from a history of fragmented provision? Have they been adequately resourced to meet these needs? Are needs being met more adequately or appropriately now than in the pre-Seebohm years? To answer these questions we need to say something about need and the way in which thinking has changed over the past decade or so. An obvious benchmark would seem to be the evidence on need brought together by the Seebohm Committee.

NEED: A VITAL BUT IMPRECISE CONCEPT

The Seebohm Report devoted separate chapters to the review of each of the main client groups and a discussion of needs figured in each of these chapters. Nevertheless, the Report was firmly criticised by some commentators for its failure to produce a clear picture of the need to be met.[1] This was partly because the individual assessments in the client-group chapters varied in quality, partly because a clear conceptual approach to need was lacking, and also because the Committee did not collate these separate discussions of need and translate them into a clear statement of the resources required if such needs were to be met. The simple explanation of the Committee's approach is that they bowed to the inevitable constraints imposed by the difficult economic circumstances of the time. The more revealing explanation, perhaps, is that their deliberations marked a watershed: the period was one of transition from the need-led policy-making and planning of the early decades of the Welfare State to a much more austere period characterised by a preoccupation with scarcity.

To place Seebohm at an historical watershed is not strictly accurate because planning based on ideas of need and a boom in much public expenditure briefly characterised the early 1970s. Nevertheless, there was a real sense in which the Report began by setting out evidence of new and unmet needs in the by-then traditional style of post-war social policy and ended by trimming its demands very modestly indeed to the prevailing context of economic change and short-term economic management. What it illustrated, above all, was that need is socially constructed. Need is not an attribute: a fixed characteristic. Need is a variable. We cannot, except arbitrarily, distinguish simply between the disabled and the non-disabled, for example. Nor can we assume that the label 'disabled' implies a fixed quantity of need and therefore a given right to resources. The boundaries which we trace when we specify what is to count as social need are politically negotiated boundaries. Moreover, when we move from the specification of a social problem to the specification of needs with resource price tags attached we are making a very complex set of related decisions.

To specify a need for a particular type of action or response we must have some body of theory – however implicit and ill-defined. Indeed, we must have a theory of the problem – what kind of problem it is – and also a theory of the solution – how it could be tackled effectively and in a socially acceptable way. In addition, to translate these ideas about problem and solution into a fairly precise statement of the kind and level of resources needed to produce the solution, we have to make judgements about priorities. The implication of using resources to resolve a particular problem in the specified way is that the resources cannot be used for any other purpose: to specify a level of need in terms of resources which we are prepared to commit to the task is to make judgements about opportunity cost.

The *social construction* of need can therefore be seen to involve two primary factors or dimensions. The first is the moral and political climate of the society. The second is the economic context and the interpretation of that context embedded in ideas about how the economy should best be managed. Both are crucial because social policy hinges to such a degree on decisions about whether or not to spend public money. It may be relevant to define need in ways which ignores the prevailing political and economic climate, but that is because arguments about need can be used as a form or moral and political persuasion. But once one reaches the point of making[2] decisions about what resources are to be spent on what, need has changed its function and has become the criterion of resource allocation. Need therefore fulfils two functions for us: a demonstrative function in which the role is to exercise moral and political persuasion; and an analytical one in which the role is to act as a substitute for the price mechanism in allocating resources between different uses. The first of these roles has been the most attractive to students of social policy, but the second is the more demanding – especially when resources are tight and the political climate is unsympathetic to social spending.

The Seebohm Committee chose to leap from the first approach to need – the specification of need in some manner which was independent of political and economic constraints – to the second. They chose to be cautious and not to collate their understanding of need as a prelude to political and moral persuasion. Consequently, the Report does not in fact provide us with a very clear benchmark from which to review shifts in need and in the success with which it has been met. Is it possible, in such circumstances, to say anything useful about need in the personal social services? We may be able to do so if we can first agree on the meaning to be attached to the concept of need.

Townsend suggested that there were three ways of identifying need: by examining the subjective views and feelings of consumers and suppliers of services; by noting the conventional or social views of need embedded in our culture; and by establishing an objective standard against which to measure needs and the quality of existing provision.[2] Subsequently, Bradshaw proposed a typology of need which has come to be regarded as an almost definitive statement.[3] He identified four interlocking perspectives: (a) felt need; (b) expressed need; (c) normative need and comparative need. Each of these approaches to definition has its own implications for measuring need.

(a) *Felt need,* which corresponds to Townsend's subjective need as identified by potential consumers, has been least studied. Consumer research was not directly undertaken or fostered by Seebohm and it remains the least favoured approach to understanding need in social policy. A limited amount of consumer research has been undertaken in the past decade, but the major contribution to this field has been made by pressure groups and mutual-aid groups articulating felt need quite directly. One area in which the importance of felt needs has at least been increasingly recognised is summarised in the call for formal services to interweave their provisions more systematically with the patterns of coping developed through informal care.[4] This particular strand in thinking about the role of formal services, which we noted in Chapter 5, implies that fieldworkers should constantly and consciously seek to discover the felt needs of people and their informal helpers, rather than impose a 'need profile' on them which largely reflects what the services have to offer in standardised form. Perhaps one of the best examples of felt need slowly percolating official thinking, however, is the area of physical disability. The achievements have been fairly modest but it cannot be doubted that the existence of some accessible, acceptable and adequate services can and does reveal more felt need – just as constraints on services depress and conceal it.

(b) *Expressed need* – or demand placed upon services – is a very imperfect reflection of felt need in many instances. This is particularly so if access to a service is restricted, and the freeing of access was precisely one of the underlying objectives of reorganising and developing the personal social services. A single local authority department embracing a range of services was seen to be easier to identify and approach. Whether the growth in demand which occured during the 1970s would have been the same without reorganisation is impossible to tell because so many factors have affected the need and demand for the personal social services. Nevertheless, it remains likely that the much closer accessibility provided by small, decentralised local offices would further increase demand, as Bayley's current research in Dinnington suggests.[5] It is also likely that much of the demand which such arrangements would call forth would be for basic advice and simple support. In other words, relatively inaccessible services probably encounter need when it has already built up to a fairly serious level. Hence the claim that a closer engagement with neighbourhoods and informal caring networks would prove to be more preventative- and – in the longer term – less crisis- oriented. This hypothesis remains to be fully tested, however.

(c) *Normative and comparative need* decisions about service delivery are certainly strongly influenced by demand, but the broad pattern of policy-making has been much less influenced by felt and expressed need than by normative and comparative need. The former refers to assessments of need made by people – researchers, politicians, professionals or bureaucrats – who stand at a remove from the need group. It corresponds in part to Townsend's notion of conventional views of need. The latter refers to comparisons made between different groups of people which reveal one group to be less well provided for or to be leading a less desirable way of life than the other. It has the advantage of demonstrating quite directly the unmet needs of one group of people – say the isolated elderly – by reference to the actual experience and ways of life of an essentially similar group of people – say old people living in sheltered housing with warden services. The 1960's were the fundamentally formative years for the personal social services in relation to the normative and comparative concepts of need. Estimates of unmet need for home helps, meals on

wheels, social work, etc. were made. Long-neglected areas of need –
most noticeably the problems of the physically disabled and the
mentally handicapped – were brought into the public arena. Last, but
by no means least, social problems and their traditional solutions were
re-assessed such that the need for new types of services was recognised
in respect of long-standing obligations. This process of redefinition
has already been referred to in Chapter 3; it particularly affected the
elaboration of community-based care as an alternative to institutional
provision for children, the elderly, the mentally ill and the mentally
handicapped.

It would be quite inappropriate to suggest that the understanding
and interpretation of needs has stood still since the early 1970s.
Analyses of existing needs are available for most of the client groups
and they chart changes in thinking. It must also be noted that some
problems have been newly recognised in the 1970s: the physical and
psychological abuse of women and, more recently, of some elderly
people, for example. In addition, the needs of people who are
themselves caring for elderly, handicapped or sick dependents have
begun to come to the fore. Nevertheless, the legislative framework of
the personal social services and the structure of need recognition
which it represents was substantially revised in the 1960s and has
largely remained steady since then. In terms of the official policy
framework our understanding of needs has changed comparatively
little over the past decade.

In need terms, the early 1970s was a period of quantification –
especially of normative and comparative need. This happened locally
and nationally, and in both cases, albeit imperfectly, the quantification
of need was related to the attempt to plan for the future. Locally, a
direct inheritance from Seebohm was the creation of a small but lively
body of researchers in the SSDs and in the voluntary sector. Much of
their work involved the measurement of local needs. The surveys
designed to assess need under the terms of the Chronically Sick and
Disabled Persons Act 1970 were the most obvious catalyst for this
concern, but the interest was much more widely based. Whilst this
interest has not disappeared, the role of SSD researchers has accurately
mirrored the transition from the emphasis on need to that on scarcity.
Research effort seems to have shifted firmly towards the provision
of management information and assessments of cost-effectiveness.
But this was, in part, an almost inevitable feature of the development
of forward planning in the SSDs: need assessment was routinised.

For many SSDs this routinisation was most clearly established by
the planning guidelines introduced nationally by the DHSS in 1972

when a new, systematic planning approach based on a ten-year cycle was introduced. What the DHSS did in effect was to mix the normative and comparative approaches to need as a basis for establishing guidelines for most of the basic items of personal social services provision. Thus, for the elderly, the guideline levels of provision per 1,000 population over 65 were: 25 residential places; 12 home helps; 3–4 Day Centre places; and 200 meals per week. Similar guidelines were laid down for each of the main services provided by SSDs.

That a concern with measures of unmet and newly emerging needs has gradually been swamped by concern with expenditure restraint during the years since 1972 was symbolically confirmed in 1981 when the planning guidelines were formally abandoned. However, the process has also been charted in another way. Pious hopes and expressions of 'blunt realism' about resources have replaced specific ambitions about the needs to be met in some recent policy documents. Cost-effectiveness and efficiency have displaced need as the core elements of official thinking. An emphasis on cost-effectiveness and efficiency is not to be decried. Indeed, it is an essential prerequisite of justice and equity. There is no merit whatever in wasting scarce resources and thereby depriving people who can benefit from them. Nevertheless, the eclipse of need as a focal point for policy-making and planning *is* to be decried. The value and analytical base of policy and administration ought, in our view, to give prominence to both need and the scarcity of resources.

By the early 1980s, therefore, the state of the personal social services revealed only too clearly the absence of what Townsend had called for at the beginning of the 1970s: a bench-mark of objectively defined and measured need against which to assess success and failure. But can need be measured objectively? Is it not the case, as we suggested earlier, that need is socially constructed and subject to change and redefinition? Townsend's answer was to assert that the interaction of inequality and deprivation provided the key to an objective identification of need. Inequalities consist broadly of differences in the resources and environments to which people have access – incomes, working conditions, homes – and differences in social integration. The latter category of inequalities includes the degree of social isolation imposed on the deaf, blind, or physically handicapped. In the 1960s it was also clearly seen to include the stigmatization of people dependent on substandard and unattractive services; in the 1980s it must be seen to include unemployed people who feel themselves cut off from meaningful work. This latter example emphasises the fact that such inequalities are likely to deprive many people of opportunities and life-styles which a major part of the society takes for granted: opportunities to be physically mobile; to be independent and not beholden; to feel a sense of social worth.

What Townsend was doing, of course, was to assert that the comparative approach could be used to establish an objective standard of the needs to be met. Both inequalites and deprivation are referred comparatively to the way of life enjoyed by the majority. Unfortunately, this does not in practice provide us with an 'objective' measure, unless we argue that absolute equality among all citizens is our benchmark and all deviations from it are to be taken to indicate the presence of need. Even if we could agree that absolute equality is a sensible and acceptable benchmark – and this is obviously a view which can be contested – we would still have difficulties. Like it or not, and some people are incensed by the very use of the term, we can at best ameliorate many needs and problems. This is especially true in the personal social services. We can never hope to achieve equality between a bereaved person and a person surrounded by rewarding social relationships – or between a blind or multi-handicapped person and a physically and mentally whole person. We can only attempt to reduce the deprivations which such conditions impose and perhaps offer some compensation for the fact that not all the deprivations can be made good. To guarantee that we will achieve equality of life-styles, satisfaction and happiness is beyond our scope no matter how unlimited the flow of resources.

Nevertheless, this comparative approach to need does provide us with a powerful corrective to a philosophy dominated by resource scarcity and cuts in public expenditure. There is every good reason for continuing to consider what inequalities and deprivations we ought to be seeking to reduce, despite – or precisely because of – the limited resources at our disposal. At the very least, we ought to make the most basic comparisons between those people who receive social service help because they are frail and elderly, or handicapped or homeless, and those people who face essentially similar problems but who do not receive help. In a time of austerity it is certainly worth asking the question: is our service cover deteriorating such that people who would have received help several years ago are now likely to be left to fend for themselves or to receive an inferior service? Such a limited approach to comparative need, though unambitious, would provide an objective assessment of how things are changing.

As we will indicate in our discussion of resource trends, the world has so changed within the short space of a decade that a taxonomy of 'cuts' is as essential now as a taxonomy of need was before. In such a climate, a preoccupation with achieving growth is supplanted by a defence of existing levels of provision. The success with which provision has been maintained must be central to the discussion of resource trends in recent years. The question to which we will return at the end of the next section is, therefore, the one with which we end this section: having begun – however inadequately – to respond to a wider and larger body of need in the early 1970s, have the personal social services been enabled to maintain a constant level of service as the pressure on resources has grown?

RESOURCES: THE NEED FOR GROWTH

Seebohm's analysis of shortcomings in the then pattern of social services highlighted inadequacies in the *amount, range* and *quality* of provision.[6] One of the major underlying explanations for these deficiences was the services' lack of resources in money and manpower. As a result, the Committee took up the need to attract additional resources into the personal social services as a central plank in its case for unified departments. Such a structure, it was envisaged, would not only offer better career opportunities for the staff; a department with responsibility for all the personal social services would rank as a major department in local government and its committee ought, in principle, to possess sufficient 'clout' to secure more resources. Seebohm's case for a unified department rested in part, therefore, on the grounds that it could act as a more powerful focus for resource growth.

In this section we will consider whether the Committee's approach has been successfully pursued. Was its case for additional resource accepted and, if so, to what extent have the personal social services benefited? What, in particular, has been the impact of the progressive tightening of public expenditure controls on the amount of finance available to the personal social services? To answer these questions we need to examine how the services have been treated over the post-Seebohm decade by both central and local government, since the former sets national spending guidelines while the latter determines actual levels of expenditure for each department.

CENTRAL GOVERNMENT PLANS

Although Seebohm did not precisely quantify the scale of resources required to remedy the deficiencies it identified, the response of central government was, by any standards, both speedy and substantial. Expenditure White Papers began to plan for large-scale growth in the personal social services immediately following the implementation of Seebohm. Thus the 1971 White Paper anticipated 'real' growth of 9.2 per cent for 1972/3 and an average compound growth rate of 6.8 per cent per annum in subsequent years.[7] The latter figure was increased to 8.5 per cent the following year,[8] while the ten-year planning circular confirmed that growth on this scale was to be a long-term feature of the personal social services: authorities were asked to submit plans on an assumption of 10 per cent annual compound growth rates for current expenditure throughout the ten years to 1982/3.[9] We must remember, moreover, that such growth rates were not merely a reflection of a less harsh climate for public expenditure than that to which we are now accustomed: the personal social services were being singled out for growth well in excess of that anticipated for other central and local government services.

Part of the explanation for this favoured treatment lay in a recognition of the shortcomings which Seebohm had underlined. However, central government was not merely responding to decades of neglect: differentially high growth rates for the personal social services were also seen as a positive means of promoting community care. Indeed the 1971 White Paper explicitly contrasted growth rates of some 9 per cent and 7 per cent for the personal social services with those of around 3 per cent for the NHS. The explanation advanced for building up the personal social services was that 'one of their major objectives ... is to shift the balance of care from hospital to the community'[10]. Resource growth in the personal social services was seen by central government, therefore, as an essential precondition for realising the major goal which spanned both the service and resource policy streams in the health and personal social services.

Such were the intentions of central government in the years immediately following the establishment of the personal social services. However, the history of social planning in the 1970s often seems to have been one of expectations being dashed, ambitious plans collecting dust, and good intentions remaining unfulfilled. Was the experience of the personal social services different from the norm? The fate of the planning initiative was noted in the previous chapter. Here we concentrate upon the resource experience of the personal social services over their first decade, an experience which we may summarise as one of both disappointment and yet exceptional achievement. The disappointment arises from comparisons with the high hopes of the early 1970s, while the achievement is evident from comparisons with the fate of other areas of public expenditure in the late 1970s. We may assess the extent of resource growth in the personal social services by measuring both the expansion of spending on the services themselves and comparing that with the wider pattern.

Ferlie and Judge's expenditure series (reproduced here as Table 8.1) provides a valuable starting point. It shows that total spending on the personal social services (at constant volume prices) almost doubled in both the 1960s and 1970s. Thus a rapid growth in expenditure was beginning even as Seebohm met (1965–8) and continued to take place while its report awaited implementation. Such growth took place, however, from a ludicrously small base. Until the late 1960s the equivalent of what are now the personal social services were the smallest of the social policy programmes. In 1955, for example, spending on school meals, milk and welfare foods was double that on the personal social services as a proportion of all public spending.[11] This gap was not closed completely until the late 1960s. Moreover, Ferlie and Judge's data series also reveals an uneven pattern of experience over the 1970s with over three-quarters of the growth in current spending being concentrated in the years up to 1976 and with capital expenditure peaking in 1973 and falling to a third of that level by 1977. As Ferlie and Judge conclude, 'the golden age for spending on the personal social services was quite clearly the first half of the 1970s'.[12]

Nevertheless, current expenditure did continue to grow during the late 1970s, though at rates well below the 10 per cent figure on which the ten-year plans were based. Indeed, that resource assumption was dead almost by the time the first plans reached the DHSS. Overtaken by the economic and fiscal consequences of the 1973 increase in oil prices, they remain (we must presume) interred in the Department's vaults as a final monument to the brief burst of optimism in which the personal social services were conceived and born. By 1976, a cooler, harsher realism had taken root in which the watchword was 'priorities' and the target 2 per cent growth per annum. This approach was annunciated in the 'Priorities' document of that year and its more limited growth target has since become the official benchmark for spending on the personal social services. More particularly, it represents the amount DHSS calculates to be necessary to maintain service levels in the face of rising need. It is in itself, therefore, a substantive expression of the changed fortunes of the personal social services in the second half of the post-Seebohm decade. In effect, by 1976 central government no longer sought to improve the overall range, quantity and quality of services – the Seebohm objectives. Rather, its horizon was limited to ensuring that services did not

Table 8.1   Indices of expenditure on the personal social services in the UK, 1953–79, at constant volume prices (1971 = 100)

Year	Current expenditure on goods and services	Gross domestic fixed capital formation	Total expenditure
1953	44.7	18.1	41.2
1954	42.4	23.6	40.4
1955	43.4	22.2	41.1
1956	44.1	20.8	41.6
1957	44.7	25.0	42.6
1958	45.3	23.6	42.8
1959	45.9	31.9	44.3
1960	48.4	36.1	47.0
1961	51.6	45.8	50.8
1962	55.3	56.9	55.9
1963	57.2	65.3	58.4
1964	59.2	70.8	61.3
1965	63.3	83.3	66.2
1966	67.8	79.2	69.9
1967	76.0	88.9	78.1
1968	79.7	100.0	82.8
1969	79.5	86.1	80.6
1970	91.8	87.5	91.2
1971	100.0	100.0	100.0
1972	112.1	91.7	108.8
1973	134.8	169.4	136.7
1974	154.7	144.4	151.5
1975	178.5	113.9	168.5
1976	185.0	115.3	174.1
1977	185.4	56.7	167.3
1978	196.9	72.2	179.1
1979	204.1	72.2	185.4

Sources: (1953–71) Unpublished data supplied by the Central Statistical Office on current administrative definitions;   (1972–79) Central Statistical Office, *National Income and Expenditure 1980* (HMSO, London 1980), table 9.4;   Deflators obtained from Central Statistical Office, National Income and Expenditure 1980 (HMSO, London 1980) table 2.6.

Reproduced from E. Ferlie and K. Judge, 'Retrenchment and rationality in the personal social services', *Policy and Politics*, **9** (3), 1981.

deteriorate. It should be emphasised, of course, that this restricted goal represented a clear acceptance that need for the personal social services was continuing to grow: the 2 per cent was intended, in roughly equal proportions, to meet pressures of demand from growing numbers of elderly in the population and of children coming into care.[13] At the same time, improvements in services could, in principle, be 'bought' through improvements in efficiency and effectiveness, including the substitution of low-cost service packages or the expansion of some areas of service at the expense of others.

Yet the priorities which had become the centrepiece of resource planning by DHSS by the mid-1970s provided little guidance to local decision-makers. Personal social services responsibilities encompassed virtually all the DHSS priority client groups. Indeed, in a very real sense the DHSS approach meant giving priority to the personal social services as a whole as a low-cost alternative to health services. From this perspective 2 per cent growth represented a continuing, though minimal, investment in community care. If no growth were made available, the personal social services could not meet increasing need while also making a contribution to the shift in the balance of care from hospitals to the community. This latter objective was also supplemented by growing amounts of joint finance – health service resources earmarked for expenditure on personal social services projects which benefited the NHS. It was certainly acknowledged that without minimal real growth in personal social services' expenditure to meet increased need it would be impossible to defend community care as a viable policy and certainly as a substitute for health-service provision. However, the election of a new government in 1979 was followed by the improbable combination of an apparent attempt to secure real cuts in personal social services spending with a reassertion of the importance of social-care alternatives to long-stay hospital provision. The 1979 Expenditure White Paper indicated cuts of 6.7 per cent for 1980/1 compared with expected spending levels for 1979/80.[14] Although spending plans for the years up to 1983/4 included growth allowances which restored personal social services spending to the 1979/80 level, this still constituted a real cut in services against the 2 per cent benchmark.

We may summarise the second half of the post-Seebohm decade, therefore, as a period when central government abandoned large-scale expansion in personal-social-services resources to meet multiple-service goals. Initially this was succeeded by a minimal growth target intended to maintain *service* levels against growing need and, later, by sufficient growth to reattain previous *spending* levels in the early 1980s following a sharp cut in 1980/81. What happened, in practice? How did local government respond to the plans and intentions of the centre? In particular, was 2 per cent growth attained and was the later cut in spending enforced?

LOCAL-GOVERNMENT PRACTICE

The very rapid growth attained in the early 1970s was itself considerably in excess of the figure contained in the Expenditure White Papers. Local government chose to spend far more on the personal social services than central government had anticipated. Real growth rates up to 1975 proved to be roughly double the White Paper forecasts and in 1973/4 peaked at the dizzy height of almost 20 per cent.[15] For local government, however, the year 1975 proved to be the fateful one in which the then Secretary of State for the Environment, Anthony Crosland, crisply announced 'the party is over'. From then on, control of local government spending was to be the target of successive central administrations and there was no prospect of double-digit growth being sustained. Indeed, the real question was whether even the 2 per cent figure could be attained, especially in the early 1980s.

Table 8.2 shows that the goal of the 'Priorities' document – 2 per cent real growth per annum in current expenditure up to 1979/80 –

Table 8.2 Net current expenditure on the personal social services (England)

	Excluding joint finance (%)	Including joint finance (%)
		Input volume 1983/84 prices
1977/78 on 1976/77	+1.5	+2.3
1978/79 on 1977/78	+3.8	+4.4
1979/80 on 1978/79	+4.6	+4.9
1980/81 on 1979/80	+2.7	+3.3
1981/82 on 1980/81	−1.3	−0.8
1982/83 on 1981/82	+2.2	+2.3
*1983/84 on 1982/83	+3.6	+3.7
1983/84 on 1976/77	+18.2	+21.6

* Provisional figures for 1983/84.

Source: *Parliamentary Debates (Commons)*, vol. 77, cols 221–222. HMSO, 1985.

was more than met. In other words more than sufficient growth was attracted into the personal social services to maintain service levels if the DHSS estimate was correct. The local authority record for 1980/81 was even more impressive: growth of some 3 per cent being achieved against the proposed 'cut' of nearly 7 per cent. It was not until 1981/2, therefore, that the sustained squeeze on local government spending undermined its ability to give favourable treatment to the personal social services and the first ever fall in current spending on these services took place. Yet it is by no means clear that this experience represented the end of growth: estimates of expenditure in the most recent years for which figures are available show a return to low rates of growth.

Our conclusion must be, therefore, that Seebohm's hopes for unified departments have been fulfilled in at least one respect. They have undoubtedly provided a powerful focus for the attraction of resources into the personal social services on a scale in excess of central-government plans and expenditures. The old departments had a similarly successful record, as Ferlie and Judge's data series shows, but we may reasonably question whether they would have been as powerful and cohesive a force in resisting the pressures of expenditure contraction in the late 1970s and early 1980s. A comparative measure of SSDs' success in securing resources for their services is provided in Table 8.3. There was a significant increase in the *proportion* of all public expenditure taken by the personal social services between 1970/71 and 1980/81 (from 2.6% to 4%). It also reveals the scale of their growth in relation to other areas of local government spending: the personal social services share almost doubled over that period. This is all the more impressive an achievement since it took place

Table 8.3   The personal social services and public expenditure as a whole

Share of net public expenditure	1970/71 (%)	1976/77 (%)	1980/81 (%)
Personal social services	2.6	3.9	4.0
National health service	19.9	19.4	20.9
Central government spending	64.5	66.9	72.1
Local government spending	35.5	33.1	27.9
Personal social services as % of:			
(i) Local government spending	7.4	11.8	14.4
(ii) NHS spending	13.2	20.1	19.2

Source: *Annual Abstract of Statistics*. HMSO 1982, Table 3.1.

against the trend of local-government spending, which fell markedly as a share of all public expenditure. In other words the personal social services more than held their own in a bleak local environment.

However, while it would be wrong to take too apocalyptic a view of the resource position in recent years, we should certainly not be too sanguine in our assessment of the situation. This is for three reasons. First, to secure a growth of spending of 1 or 2 per cent more than the DHSS benchmark is small consolation for those Departments who laid plans on the assumption of 10 per cent growth and who initially experienced even higher levels of increase in spending. We should not underestimate the frustrations and very real difficulties involved in making the rapid and forced transition from substantial to minimal growth which has been the lot of SSD managers and local councillors. It is too easy (if essentially accurate) to discuss this experience as 'only' cuts in growth. Expenditure constraint has not only been perceived and experienced locally as 'real' cuts, it has dislocated (and, indeed, undermined the credibility of) forward planning. It has also depressed morale and, on occasion, all but overwhelmed the management process.

Second, the data in Table 8.2 relate to the overall national situation and they conceal considerable variations in local experience. For example, they conceal the failure of a significant proportion of individual authorities (as many as 67% in 1981/2) to reach the 2 per cent in any given year. Even more fundamentally, they conceal the fact that 41 authorities failed to receive an average of 2 per cent growth per year over the whole period 1978/9–1983/4. In other words, almost two-fifths of all English SSDs received less growth over those years than was considered necessary to maintain service levels.[16] This shortfall is not only significant in itself but is also illustrative of a further feature of personal social services resources: their uneven geographical distribution. Territorial inequality is an inevitable concomitant of a system of local government finance which has in the past embodied a considerable degree of autonomy and permitted the majority of authorities to exceed DHSS targets. However, the present scale of territorial inequality is an issue which has exercised the Association of Directors of Social Services.[17] It has raised important but difficult issues about the role of the centre in maintaining minimum standards and ensuring some measure of geographical equity in access to personal social services.

The third reason for advising caution in interpreting data on the growth of resources in the personal social services is of perhaps even greater significance. Consumers of social services are directly interested in, and affected by, changes in the quantity and quality of services delivered, not of resources spent. Thus resource growth is important only in relation to what it buys and how it is allocated – the types of services produced and the client groups on whose behalf they are utilised. For example, our assessment of the recent resource achievements of the personal social services has rested, so far, on the assumption that 2 per cent growth was indeed sufficient to maintain service levels, not only in those client groups whose increasing needs it was nominally allocated to meet (children and the elderly) but also across the entire range of personal social services. In the final section of this chapter we consider whether resource growth of at least 2 per cent has been sufficient to maintain services overall and examine two further questions: which client groups have benefited from resource growth and whether it has promoted the expansion of community care, the major motive on the part of central government for allocating substantial increased resources to the personal social services. In other words, our focus shifts from the level of resource inputs to the level and pattern of service outputs [doc. 16].

HAVE SERVICE OUTPUT LEVELS BEEN MAINTAINED?

There are two senses in which services may be said to have been maintained: first in terms of their absolute level (the actual *number* of meals-on-wheels delivered, etc.) and second in relation to need, for which the best available – if still unsatisfactory – proxy is the size of the client-group populations. The latter is the more demanding measure when need is increasing. That the higher growth rates of the late 1960s and early 1970s were accompanied by increases in both absolute and per capita levels of service is not in a question, as Bebbington has clearly demonstrated in relation to the elderly.[18] We have also shown elsewhere that a significant growth of service provision took place across the full range of personal social services activities between 1971 and 1978.[19] The question remaining, therefore, is whether service levels were maintained in absolute and per capita terms during the most recent period. Let us first of all take the more demanding of the two standards against which service output levels may be measured and review the evidence for the maintenance of *per capita* levels of provision. As half of the 2 per cent growth was supposed to enable local authorities to maintain such levels of service for the elderly, we shall focus particularly upon this area of SSD responsibilities.

Table 8.4 provides data on trends in the provision of the main services for the elderly from 1975/6 to 1982/3 in relation to the growth of the elderly population. It reveals a steady decline in per capita levels of service for all areas of provision, except day care, since approximately 1977/8. Moreover, the scale of this decline is substantial: measured against the numbers of elderly over 75, on whom such services are largely concentrated, the fall in service cover is around 17 per cent for residential care and 15 per cent for meals and home helps (numbers and hours). Thus provision for the elderly has not been maintained at constant per capita levels despite the growth in personal social services' spending levels more than matching the DHSS estimate of the amounts required for this purpose. Only the provision of day care more than kept pace with the growth of the very elderly population (up by a quarter); though the decrease in the per capita provision of residential care has been accompanied by a very substantial increase in private care. As the production of service outputs failed to meet our most demanding yardstick, albeit that for which resource growth was intended to be sufficient, let us turn to our more limited standard and simply ask: has the *absolute* level of service outputs been maintained across personal social services provision as a whole?

Table 8.5 enables us to approach this issue by providing evidence on trends in absolute levels of service outputs over the period 1978/9 to 1983/4. The clear message of these data is of the failure to maintain service levels across the board, despite the maintenance of resource growth above the 2 per cent level in all but one of the years under review and despite a total real increase in expenditure of nearly 22 per cent. Broadly speaking, the pattern is one of decreases in residential services alongside increases in day services and domiciliary services (see also Table 8.4). Even so, not all of the growth areas show consistent increases. In addition, many of them seem to have experienced only modest growth in service levels, especially bearing in mind the scale of resource growth and the amount of resources which, in principle, might be expected to be released by reductions in residential services – the most expensive form of personal social services provision. In part the explanation for this state of affairs lies, as we have shown elsewhere [doc. 17] in the growth of unit costs caused by the tendency for public sector costs to grow more rapidly than inflation. This has meant that the personal social services require growth simply to stand still, even before the growth of need is taken into account.

It is clear from these data that even in the years when the 2 per cent resource growth target was more than met the personal social services failed to maintain absolute, let alone per capita, service levels across

Table 8.4 Provision of selected services to the elderly (England and Wales)

	Thousands	Indices of change							
	1975/6	1975/6	1976/7	1977/8	1978/9	1979/80	1980/81	1981/82	1982/83
Elderly persons									
Total age 65+ (000s)	6,811.2	100	102.8	102.8	104.8	105.3	107.6	106.3	110.9
Total aged 75+ (000s)	2,446.3	100	103.3	103.3	107.2	109.0	113.0	115.0	121.7
Residential care									
Total in care (000s)	120.3	100	104.0	105.5	104.8	104.1	101.6	103.2	100.9
Per 1,000 population 65+	17.7	100	101.1	102.9	100.0	98.9	94.4	97.1	91.5
Per 1,000 population 75+	49.2	100	101.0	102.0	97.8	95.5	89.8	91.1	82.9
Home helps									
Total number WTE (000s)	50.1	100	93.0	97.2	99.2	96.9	100.2	101.2	102.6
Per 1,000 population 65+	7.4	100	90.5	94.6	94.6	91.2	93.2	94.6	93.2
Per 1,000 population 75+	20.5	100	89.8	94.2	92.7	88.8	88.8	89.3	84.4
Total cases (000s)	670.5	100	102.9	107.8	109.2	114.0	107.1	132.3	109.8
Per 1,000 population 65+	98.4	100	100.2	105.0	104.3	108.3	99.6	124.5	99.9
Per 1,000 population 75+	274.1	100	99.6	104.3	101.9	104.6	94.7	116.8	90.2
Total hours service (000s)	80,622.3	100	99.9	101.7	102.8	103.2	103.9	100.0	103.5
Per 1,000 population 65+	11,836.7	100	97.2	100.0	97.1	98.1	96.6	94.1	94.1
Per 1,000 population 75+	32,956.8	100	96.7	99.5	94.9	94.8	92.0	88.3	85.1
Hours per case	120.2	100	97.1	95.3	93.1	90.6	97.1	75.6	94.3

Table 8.4 (continued)

	Thousands		Indices of change							
	1975/6	1975/6	1976/7	1977/8	1978/9	1979/80	1980/81	1981/82	1982/83
Meals									
Total number (000s)	41,276.0	100	100.2	99.4	97.5	103.9	99.9	99.5	103.8
Per 1,000 population 65+	6,060.0	100	99.9	96.8	93.1	98.1	92.9	93.6	94.4
Per 1,000 population 75+	16,872.8	100	99.4	96.2	91.0	94.8	88.4	87.9	85.3
Day care (England)									
Total available places (000s)	19.9	100	104.5	119.6	128.6	136.7	136.7	151.3	151.3
Per 1,000 population 65+	2.9	100	103.5	117.2	124.1	131.0	127.6	141.4	137.9
Per 1,000 population 75+	8.1	100	101.2	116.1	121.0	125.9	121.0	134.6	124.7

Note: The data for day care are drawn from DHSS sources and relate to all authorities in England. All other data are drawn from the CIPFA, 'Personal Social Services Actuals' for the relevant year and cover both England and Wales. The number of authorities making returns under each heading varies from year to year. Hence extreme caution should be exercised in making precise comparisons between years. The data may, however, be used to suggest the direction of broad trends.

Source: Update of A. Webb and G. Wistow, 'Public expenditure and policy implementation,' *Public Administration*, Spring 1983, Table 4.

Table 8.5 Trends in selected service activities 1976/77 to 1982/83 (England)

		Thousands	Rate of change per annum				
		1978/79	1979/80	1980/81	1981/82	1982/83	1983/84*
Res. – elderly	Occupied places	117.1	+1.5	-1.1	-0.5	-1.2	-2.8
Res. – YPH	Occupied places	10.0	-7.0	+4.3	-6.2	-0.8	-4.5
Res. – MI	Occupied places	4.9	+2.0	-12.0	+2.3	-4.6	-6.9
Res. – MH adult	Occupied places	12.0	+6.7	+5.5	+4.4	+5.7	+4.2
Res. – MH child	Occupied places	1.7	+5.9	0.0	0.0	0.0	-11.1
Res. – children	Occupied places	32.9	-1.2	-8.4	+11.1	-16.3	-9.9†
Day care – elderly	Available places	25.6	+6.3	0.0	+11.0	+0.3	+1.6
Day care – YPH	Available places	14.2	-6.3	+2.3	-2.9	-1.5	+3.1
Day care – MI	Available places	7.2	+6.9	+2.6	+3.8	+11.0	+3.3
Day care – MH	Available places	42.4	+0.2	+2.1	+4.1	+3.1	+1.7
Day nurseries	Available places	30.0	+1.0	-0.3	+1.7	-1.9	+0.7
Boarding out	Occupied places	34.3	+2.6	+1.7	+3.1	-1.1	+2.2†

* Provisional
† Highly Provisional

Source: *Parliamentary Debates (Commons)*, vol. 77, cols 223-4, HMSO, 1985.

the board. In other words, 2 per cent *appears* to have been an insufficiently accurate estimate, by even the most modest of standards, of the growth in resources required annually to prevent a decline in the level of service provision. We should be cautious before rushing too swiftly to such a judgement, however. In principle, the failure to maintain per capita provision for the elderly could simply reflect a decision to switch resources between client groups. In that case the levels of growth would not necessarily have been inadequate but simply used in ways different from that which DHSS apparently intended. At the same time, reductions in both absolute and per capita service levels might arise from decisions to substitute, for example, day and/or community services for residential care. In that case differential patterns of growth and reductions in service levels would reflect conscious changes of policy and not necessarily the inadequacy of resources. We shall explore these possibilities by reviewing the evidence for changes in priority between client groups and between types of provision.

CLIENT GROUP PRIORITIES: GAINERS AND LOSERS

We may make a broad assessment of changes in the share of personal social services resources allocated to each of the main client groups from the data in Table 8.6. It has not been possible to allocate all expenditures to individual client groups and, in addition, certain other categories of expenditure have been allocated on assumptions about service utilisation by client groups (as the notes make clear). Nonetheless, we may use the data with some confidence to indicate the scale and direction of change in patterns of expenditure. In fact, they reveal a largely stable pattern in the distribution of expenditure during the period 1975/6–1981/2.

The 16 per cent real growth in spending which took place between those years was allocated in ways which produced only limited shifts in the proportions of total expenditure devoted to the client group and other headings shown here. Within this overall pattern of limited change, however, the mentally handicapped emerge as the biggest 'gainers' among the client groups while social work secured a similar increase. The overall pattern of limited change is emphasised by the fact that, in both cases, the increase in budget share was under 2 per cent. The biggest single 'loser' was Administration which saw its share of total expenditure decline by almost 2 per cent. Close behind were the elderly with a decrease in budget share of more than 1 per cent. Although services for children also showed a small decrease, this

Table 8.6 Allocation of personal social services gross current expenditure by client group 1975/76 and 1981/82 (at 1981–2 prices)

	1975/76 (£m)	1975/76 (%)	1981/82 (£m)	1981/82 (%)	Growth 1981/82 on 1975/76 (£m)	Share of growth (%)
Elderly	704.2	38.0	788.3	36.7	84.1	28.5
Physically handicapped	86.4	4.7	96.1	4.5	9.7	3.3
Mentally ill	18.4	1.0	27.6	1.3	9.2	3.1
Mentally handicapped	107.5	5.8	165.8	7.7	58.3	19.8
Children	410.1	22.1	465.1	21.7	55.0	18.7
Social work	187.0	10.1	253.0	11.8	66.0	22.4
Administration	261.9	14.1	264.0	12.3	2.1	0.7
Training	13.0	0.7	13.1	0.6	0.1	0.0
Other	64.3	3.5	74.6	3.4	10.3	3.5
Total	1852.8	100.0	2147.6	100.0	294.8	100.0

Notes: 1. Expenditure on Home Helps has been allocated to individual client groups in proportion to their use of the service as shown in 'Health and Personal Social Services Statistics'.

2. Expenditure on aids and adaptations has been wholly allocated to the physically handicapped in the absence of data on utilisation across client groups.

Source: House of Commons Social Services Committee.

should be set alongside the increase in spending on social work. DHSS does not possess national data on social work activity. However, its own review of community care reported local studies which 'suggest that most (social work) time, perhaps 60%, is spent with children in care and with families'.[20] By contrast, the corresponding figure for the elderly was put at 15–20 per cent. The decrease in spending on children may, therefore, be more apparent than real – with the figure under the client-group heading reflecting changes in patterns of care rather than changes in priority.

What does this evidence suggest about personal social services priorities and the adequacy of resources? First, although none of the main categories of spending has been cut, there are marked variations in their rates of growth. For example, spending on mental handicap increased from a low base by almost a third, while spending on social work increase by more than a third and from a higher base. By contrast, expenditure on the elderly increased by little over a tenth, though from a much more substantial base than either of the other two. Differential priorities are most clearly demonstrated, however, by comparing the shares of total personal social services growth allocated to each budget heading with their respective shares of total expenditure in 1975/6. Thus the elderly received only 28.5 per cent of total growth over the period 1975/6 to 1981/2 compared with its 38.0 per cent share of all expenditure in 1975/6. In other words, the elderly clearly received a smaller share of personal social services growth than was necessary for them to maintain their previous position in the personal social services budgets. In this sense, therefore, the relative priority accorded to the elderly fell over the period 1975/6–1981/2.

As we have seen, the consequence of this fall in priority was that service levels were not maintained at either per capita or absolute rates of provision. At the same time, social work, together with services for the mentally handicapped (and mentally ill), secured significantly greater amounts of growth in relation to their bases and thus may be said to have been accorded higher degrees of priority compared with the elderly. In principle, differential rates of growth between client groups might not be inconsistent with the twin goals of maintaining services to growing numbers of the elderly and also improving their range and quality for the most under-provided client groups. The determining factor is, of course, the *total amount of growth available* for differential allocation between client groups. The position in the years reviewed here was one in which growth in expenditure, though in excess of the DHSS 2 per cent yardstick, was insufficient to achieve both ends. In practice the gains made on behalf of the mentally handicapped and social work, in particular, were at the expense of losses for the elderly – despite the apparent attempts to protect services at the expense of administration.

PRIORITIES BETWEEN TYPES OF PROVISION: SERVICE CUTS OR SUBSTITUTION?

We would not wish to imply that any cuts in expenditure or types of provision are of themselves necessarily damaging to the interests and quality of life of service recipients. To adopt this stance would suggest that existing service stocks and patterns of provision represent an optimal match between needs and resources. Apart from anything else, this would mean that there was no need for change or innovation. There are good grounds for regarding such a proposition with more than a little scepticism. For example, we have already noted that need is a socially constructed phenomenon. It follows, therefore, that ideas about how we should best meet need will change over time. The most appropriate responses to need in one decade may be considered professionally retrograde, ineffective or even damaging in the next. Understandings, objectives and fashions all change over time and new patterns of service provision achieve the status of conventional wisdoms. One of the clearest examples of the swing of the professional pendulum is to be found in the field of child care where, since the Curtis Report of 1944, the emphasis has successively swung between institutional and alternative forms of care.

To the extent that such changes in thinking are reflected in practice, we should expect to find, therefore, variations in the balance between the numbers of children in residential care and those boarded out (fostered). In current circumstances, a cut in residential provision, providing that it was matched by an appropriate increase in alternative placements for children coming into care, should be regarded as evidence for the successful operationalisation of the favoured professional paradigm. (Whether this constitutes a switch to a more effective means of meeting need is another matter, outside the purview of the present discussions.) Given this background, how should we regard the data on services for children contained in Table 8.5? They certainly place the fall in residential places (of some 40%) in a new light. This fall has not been compensated for by the increase in boarding out, though the proportion of children supervised has also increased. In other words, there is clear evidence of *substitution* rather than *crude service cuts* being put into effect. A final assessment of these trends would need to take into account, however, how far the latter increase is also part of the intended pattern of provision rather than a reflection of the absence of alternative placements. It should also consider whether social workers are adequate in number and capacity to supervise such placements at home as well as the increased number of fostering places. The importance of this issue is dramatically underlined by the sad and apparently unending catalogue of abuse cases which have taken place even while children have been under care of local authorities.

Despite these complexities, it is clear that substitution may be an explicit goal of policy and that trends in service provision should be interpreted in the light of changes in ideas about how need might best be met. Indeed, policy-making was underpinned throughout the 1960s and 1970s by the belief that the substitution of new service packages for old was the route both to improvements in the quality of life of dependent people and also to the more cost-effective use of resources. The case of child care is but one example of that multi-faceted policy which we know as community care. We may, therefore, bring together our discussion of trends in resources and provision by reviewing them against the goals of community care. This will also permit us to move towards a firmer assessment of whether the resources devoted to the personal social services over the last decade have been adequate in relation to need.

COMMUNITY CARE: AN UNDER-RESOURCED POLICY?

One of the central difficulties with community care is that it means all things (or certainly different things) to all men.[21] We have particularly sought to distinguish the usage of the term in an exclusively personal social services context from that where it is used in a sense which spans the health and personal social services as a whole. In the former case, it implies a switch in the emphasis between residential and other forms of provision. Its enactment involves according lower priority to the former than to those day and domiciliary services which may be used to substitute for it. A standstill or reduction in numbers of residential places alongside an increase in other forms of provision would suggest that such an approach was being put into practice. In principle, community care defined in this way could be achieved by switching resources between budget heads and, thus, without increasing overall personal social services expenditures. In practice, things are rarely so simple and we might expect to find that additional costs were necessary in the short term to finance the transistion to a new pattern of caring. In addition, we should remember that resource and service substitution is unlikely to be a self-financing route to the meeting of *growing* need. (In other words, a switch in the balance between residential and domiciliary care does not necessarily offer a cheap and painless means of meeting the demand for support generated by the growing numbers of dependent elderly.)

As we have already noted, there is evidence of a process of substitution taking place in the case of child care. This is not so in respect of the elderly, however: cuts in the level (absolute, in some cases, as well as per capita) of residential, home-help and meals services have all been taking place simultaneously. Only day care increased substantially, but this could be thought to counterbalance the decline in residential places only if considered a complete substitute for residential care, home helps and meals. Not only have the elderly been accorded a lower proportion of all personal social services expenditure, therefore, but this has been associated with an overall deterioration in service levels rather than a switch to apparently less costly packages of community care within the personal social services. Thus both spending and service levels have declined proportionately in the case of the elderly as other objectives have, in practice, been accorded higher priority in personal social services budgets.

Part of the explanation for this situation becomes clear when we examine service trends in relation to the second meaning we have identified for community care. This is associated with shifting the balance between hospital and other forms of provision. We noted that this goal was a major reason for the allocation of very high growth rates to the personal social services in the early 1970s and for preserving their growth rates in the mid-1970s. It has been particularly closely associated with the policy in the mental health field, but also has substantial implications for the elderly in terms of developing community-based services to reduce lengths of stay in both geriatric and acute hospital beds. Thus community care, in these terms, has traditionally been seen to imply, for the personal social services, a build-up of provision across all catagories of service for such client groups. Unlike our other definition of community care, therefore, this could not – even in principle – be implemented within existing personal social services resources, particularly given the growth of other kinds of need. Thus the substitution of personal social services for health service provision necessarily implies the need to inject additional resources into social care.

Our data showing the decline in per capita provision for the elderly suggest that the personal social services have not been able to effect any substantial shift in the balance of provision for this client group. Or, rather, that any such shift between health and personal social services provision as has taken place can only have been secured, at best, through some combination of spreading services more thinly and pushing demand onto other agencies such as housing authorities and onto informal care networks. At worst, the coincidence of the increase in client group numbers with a shift in the balance between health and social services responsibilities would mean a growth of need unmet and of families unsupported.

If, on the other hand, we turn our attention to the mental health field, a somewhat different pattern appears to emerge. The expansion of residential and day care for the mentally ill and mentally handicapped appears to be consistent with the personal social services' taking on an increased share of the overall responsibility for these client groups. The data on services for the mentally handicapped, in particular, are broadly in line with those for expenditure – which showed them to have secured the largest increase in client group shares of personal social services spending. Does this represent, therefore, a success for community care? On a superficial reading of the evidence, this certainly seems to be the case: the growth of personal social services provision has been accompanied by a reduction in hospital populations for both the mentally ill and mentally handicapped. Indeed these reductions have been even greater than the expansion of personal social services residential care. However, they have been achieved largely through the death or discharge of long-stay patients to lodgings and NHS hostels rather than by their transfer to local authority care.[22] The role of the personal social services has been to make provision for the growing numbers of persons already in the community who might otherwise have required hospital places.

Once again the growth of demand – caused especially by the increased longevity of the mentally handicapped – has defeated attempts to meet community-care objectives across the board. At a conservative estimate there are 5,000 mentally ill and 15,000 mentally handicapped patients (a third of the total) who remain in hospitals because alternative forms of provision are not available in the community.[23] As a result, DHSS has placed renewed emphasis on the need to transfer such patients to local authority care and has modified the joint finance arrangements in an attempt to secure this end.[24] Yet our data suggest that there are real costs attached to such a policy. Unless future growth levels are much higher than in recent years, the continuing expansion of provision for such groups is likely to be achieved at the expense of an erosion in the provision of services elsewhere including, for example, those mentally ill and mentally handicapped people – and their carers – already living in the community. If extra resources are not found, the only way out of this cul de sac – in principle if not in practice – is to use existing resources differently: to create growth out of the more flexible and cost-effective use of the finances and services we already have. How far is this possible?

RESOURCES: ARE THEY INADEQUATE OR INAPPROPRIATELY USED?

We may summarise the position we have now reached in our discussion of need and resources in the following terms: Seebohm sought to establish a structural base for the personal social services capable of attracting a substantial increase in their resources so that expanding and unmet need might be provided for within a framework of higher quality care. Up to the mid-1970s resource growth was considerable and it was possible for progress to be made across a number of fronts. Service levels more than kept pace with the growth in need and both expenditure and provision grew in relation to the NHS. However, it should be remembered that such growth was from a very low base. Thus, when growth rates were rapidly scaled down, personal social services stocks were still far short of DHSS guidelines and the lower growth rates of recent years have permitted only limited progress subsequently. Judged by this standard, personal social services resources remain substantially inadequate (Table 8.7). Moreover, our data have shown that some areas of provision have begun to fall back in absolute as well as per capita terms. The exception – where growth has been maintained – appears to show that community care across health and personal social services boundaries can be achieved only at the expense of declining service levels elsewhere, at least at present resource levels. Growth in excess of the official 2 per cent target has thus been inadequate both to maintain service levels and shift the balance between health and social care.

Our conclusion must be, therefore, that the personal social services have been unable to meet increases in need and provide care in the community for those who might most appropriately be provided for there. Even the modest advances which have been made towards reducing dependence on long-stay hospitals have been secured at the cost of a deterioration in service levels for the elderly. And in the meantime, significant numbers of the mentally ill and mentally handicapped remain unnecessarily in hospital in what are all to often

Table 8.7 Shortfall of personal social services provision against DHSS guidelines

Service	Appropriate population	Guidelines	Provision per 1000 appropriate population	
			Provision	Shortfall
Residential care places				
Elderly	65yrs plus	25.0	18.6	46,590
Mental handicap – adults	16yrs plus	0.78	0.32	17,970
Mental handicap – children	0–15yrs	0.44	0.18	2,920
Mental illness	Total population	0.30	0.11	9,350
Day-care places				
Elderly	65yrs plus	4.0	3.1	6,550
Mental handicap	Total population	1.5	0.81	33,950
Mental illness	Total population	0.6	0.11	24,110
Domiciliary services				
Home helps (wte)	65yrs plus	12.0	6.3	8,730
Meals/week	65yrs plus	200	118	596,880

Source: *Cuts in Public Expenditure: The Effect on the Personal Social Services*, Association of Directors of Social Services, 1980, p. 11.

unacceptable conditions. By any standard, therefore, the personal social services appear to have been and to remain seriously under-resourced, despite their privileged and protected position in local-government spending. Since we have reached this position after a period of continuing – albeit limited – growth, a scenario of zero or negative growth would be disturbing indeed.

One response to this situation is to argue that resources are not so much inadequate as badly used. The attack on waste and bureaucracy is one, often undiscriminating, expression of this view. Its influence may be reflected in the reduced share of expenditure devoted to administration (Table 8.6). At the least, this suggests an attempt to concentrate resources on services and an implicit belief that administration is a lower-order priority. There is, however, a rather more sophisticated version of the argument that resources are less than optimally used. This questions whether a closer match might be secured between provision and individual need. The issue revolves around the further question of whether the targeting of service delivery is sufficiently accurate. Do the most dependent elderly, for example, receive the highest inputs of home helps and meals services? Are less dependent groups receiving more services than they strictly 'need' or are 'entitled' to in comparison with more needy clients? More prosaically, can we be satisfied that the allocation of scarce resources is based upon a systematic assessment and re-assessment of need?

This is, of course, to open up a range of difficult technical – and moral – issues. While we cannot discuss, and still less resolve, all of them here, we may at least begin to identify some of the evidence on the match between need and provision. In the case of the home help service, for example, Bebbington[25] has shown that there is some evidence of significant mismatch. Based on a re-analysis of national survey data, he classified 30 per cent of home help and 20 per cent of meals services recipients as being in less than 'moderate' need. At the same time, 12 per cent and 15 per cent respectively of non-recipients of these services were classified as being in 'moderate', 'considerable' or 'severe' need. As we have noted elsewhere,[26] this evidence of mismatch between need and provision suggests there is some scope for securing greater effectiveness in the allocation of services to clients. If this were to be achieved it would have some mitigating effect on the falls in per capita levels of provision for the elderly shown in Table 8.4. The potential scope for improvements in the targeting of service delivery is by no means confined to the home help service, however. In the case of the elderly alone, studies of the meals and residential services have highlighted similar issues.[27] Thus, for instance, evidence from a census of residents in homes for the elderly conducted in four SSDs by Booth and his colleagues led them to suggest that "there may be a substantial proportion of people currently living in homes for the elderly who are not so impaired in their ability to cope with 'the practicalities of living' as to require the sort of total care and support generally provided by residential homes".[28]

Plank[29] suggested that half of the residents of old people's homes in his study were capable of looking after themselves. More recently Wade et al[30] have reported that a quarter of such residents were misplaced in the opinion of staff, though only 7 per cent were thought better suited to a less dependent environment; other residents, with high levels of dependency, were seen to require more rather than less supportive environments. This latter finding illustrates an important point: misplacement takes place across the whole spectrum of provision and does not merely apply to persons in receipt of residential care who might more appropriately be provided for "in the community". Indeed Wade and her colleagues concluded that there were so many anomalies in the matching of need to provision that "for the efficient and therefore most cost-effective use of the services and provision already provided, urgent re-thinking is necessary".[31]

Given the pressures which services are said to be under, how are such patterns of apparent misallocation to be explained or justified? It is possible to account for this state of affairs in two ways. First, there is the well known tendency for provision to attract need. Hospital waiting lists disappear with the opening of new beds or other facilities only to re-emerge as GPs realise that previously marginal cases now have a better chance of receiving services. Something similar was found in the case of old people's homes by Booth *et al*. Comparisons between levels of dependency among residents and availability of places between SSDs suggested that 'as the level of residential provision rises so homes tend to admit a greater number of independent residents'.[32] Part of our explanation for the mismatch between provision and need is therefore that there appears to be a tendency for demand to match supply rather than for supply to be provided in relation to identified need. Indeed, one of the most striking features of the expansion of provision in the personal social services is that it has tended to be made on the basis of *assumptions* about both need and demand rather than the identification of needs. What we are dealing with here is the long-term working out of the Seebohm failure to base its case for resources on even the beginnings of a systematic attempt to assess need. As a result, quantity has tended to be equated with effectiveness on the assumption that higher levels of provision are necessarily a good thing. It is not difficult to understand how this should have become the dominant criterion for service expansion in a context characterised by a visible growth in client group populations and the death of sophisticated need studies.

Our second, and not unrelated, explanation for the mismatch between need and provision lies in the weaknesses of service allocation procedures. Two weaknesses, in particular, may be identified. First, there is mounting evidence that once services have been allocated they are rarely withdrawn, despite changes in need levels. For example, although there has been an increase in the use of residential services to supply short-term care for all client groups, it remains largely true that residential places are allocated for 'life'. Often the response to short-term crises, residential provision becomes a permanent solution to a problem which may no longer exist. Yet discharge from residential care is comparatively rare. In a similar vein, Hedley and Norman[33] found the review of long-term home-help cases to be rare and Davies[34] has strongly criticised the absence of systematic review procedures for recipients of meals on wheels. Again, it is not difficult to understand why this should be the case. In a caring service, providers are reluctant to deprive clients of services once their entitlements have been established, as Hill reported in respect of the meals service.[35] Such a reluctance is almost inevitably reinforced by the lack of agreed operational procedures for reassessing service recipients once provision has been made.

We must be cautious of concluding, however, that a perfect match between need and provision can be secured and maintained. As Hedley and Norman note, some degree of mismatch is the inevitable concomitant of a flexible response to need. The real question, therefore, is whether a *better* match can be attained. Of this there can be little doubt. The evidence we have discussed clearly suggests that there is scope for at least some increase in the effectiveness of service allocation through building in more systematic reassessments of need among service recipients. At the same time, the studies we have been reviewing identify a second and more fundamental weakness in service-allocation procedures. They show that the mismatch between need and provision arises not only from the absence or inadequacy of *review and reassessment* procedures but also from similar deficiencies in the *initial* allocation of services to clients. Thus, for example, Hedley and Norman reported that few authorities in their study had laid down explicit criteria for allocating home-help hours. As a result priorities were not set and need was not assessed, the allocation of hours being left to the 'professional judgement' of staff. Even where assessment forms did exist, they tended to be used more to record allocation decisions than as aids to the assessment of need or priority.[36] The position with regard to meals and residential services is not dissimilar. Connolly and Goldberg suggest that research on the meals service has revealed a pattern in which detailed consideration of alternatives at the point of initial referral is rare, where systematic assessment and balancing of one person's need against another's is virtually absent and where reassessment rarely occurs.[37]

At the same time, the allocation of places in residential homes varies widely between authorities. In some it follows a detailed and multi-disciplinary process of observation and assessment. In others it may be largely determined by a single social-work visit. Admissions may also be dependent less on the severity of individual need than the desire of staff to maintain some arbitrary notion of the desirable balance between male and female, or more and less dependent, residents. Indeed, the overall impression gained of the allocation of services is of a process which is overwhelmingly more random than systematic. As a result, and as the studies of misplacement reveal, people with similar characteristics ('needs') are to be found in widely different circum-stances: in hospital, residential homes, sheltered and ordinary housing, with more or less formal and informal support.[38]

There can be little doubt, therefore, that the present procedures for matching individual need to resources leave much to be desired. More systematic and rational assessment, review and allocation practices would clearly produce a more effective targeting of resources and services. This would lead, in turn, to an enhanced level of client welfare, particularly since 'too much' care can be as damaging to individuals as 'too little' if it undermines autonomy and establishes or reinforces dependency on others. On the other hand, we should not assume that evidence of services being inappropriately deployed necessarily means that there are substantial financial savings to be derived from more effective targeting. The net effect of reducing misplacement in a care system may be entirely marginal in terms of resources released. The pack may simply have been reshuffled. For this reason, among others, attention has increasingly focused upon the creation of new options and patterns of care as the route to meeting the growth of need from increasingly limited resources.

NEED AND RESOURCES: THE SEARCH FOR NEW OPTIONS

The search for new options is in some respect a more challenging and more fundamental exercise than the reallocation of existing services to achieve a closer match with need. One of the most important starting points for this approach is the belief, as expressed by Challis and Davies, that in the future we will not be able to cope with increasing and changing needs 'using the same mix of services as we have during the early seventies'.[39] Although Challis and Davies were particularly discussing the position of the elderly, the case for innovatory service packages as a response to the growth of need out-stripping that of resources has also been advanced in other fields.

In essence, the argument is that the present range of services is not only poorly targeted but also too narrow and inflexible. For example, elderly people are, in effect, offered either three or four hours of domestic assistance per week or total care in a home. Similarly, the parents of mentally handicapped children all too often face the 'choice' of placing their child in residential (or hospital) care or carrying on unsupported at home. This, in turn, leads to individual cases being assessed in relation to the narrow range of options available rather than on the basis of individual needs. At the same time, the absence of adequate alternatives outside residential care may lead to a deterioration in functioning until residential care appears to become the only viable option. In other words, the present pattern of service can be seen to create its own demand: to oversimplify slightly, if only residential care is provided clients will come to require it.

These considerations, often stimulated by a wider concern for cost-effectiveness, have led to growing experiments with a diversity of alternative services including short-stay residential care, adult fostering, group homes, very sheltered housing, 'super' home helps, the payment of neighbours, sitting services, street day care and good-neighbour schemes. There is, it would seem, no shortage of potential means for enriching and broadening the range of options which SSDs might offer their clients in a climate of resource scarcity. Indeed, that climate has provided a valuable stimulus to such experimentation. To the extent that such innovations provide improvements in the range and quality of care provided, the end of very rapid growth may be seen to have had a positive impact on both the personal social services and those they serve. The mass production of standardised services based on assumptions about levels of needs and individuals' preferences is a luxury which can no longer be indulged. On the other hand, when resource pressures become so great that the search for cost-effectiveness is replaced by narrow cost-cutting, the capacity and will to innovate is undermined. As the personal social services began their second decade, it was the tension between these two forces which seemed most likely to determine how far and in what manner individual need would be met in the 1980s.

REFERENCES

1. TOWNSEND, P., 1970 *The Fifth Social Service*. Fabian Society
2. Ibid.
3. BRADSHAW, J., 1972 'The concept of social need', *New Society*, 30 March
4. BAYLEY, M., 1973 *Mental Handicap and Community Care*, Routledge and Kegan Paul; BAYLEY, M. 'Helping care to happen in the community', in Walker, A. (ed.), 1982 *Community Care*. Basil Blackwell and Martin Robertson
5. PARKER, P., SEYD, R., TENNANT, A. and BAYLEY, M., 1981 *Preliminary Findings from Baseline Data*, Neighbourhood Services Project Dinnington Working Paper
6. SEEBOHM, F., 1968 *Report of the Committee on Local Authority and Allied Personal Social Services*, Cmnd 3703. HMSO, pp. 74–8
7. TREASURY, 1971 *Public Expenditure to 1975/6*, Cmnd 4829. HMSO, p. 53
8. TREASURY, 1972 *Public Expenditure to 1976/7* Cmnd 5178. HMSO, p. 73
9. DHSS, 1971 *Local Authority Social Services Ten Year Plans 1973–1983*, Circular 35/72. Department of Health and Social Security
10. TREASURY, 1971 op.cit. (ref. 7) p. 53
11. WEBB, A., and WISTOW, G., 1982 'The personal social services: expediency incrementalism of systematic social planning?', in Walker A (ed.), *Public Expenditure and Social Policy: An Examination of Social Spending and Priorities*, Heinemann
12. FERLIE, E. and JUDGE, K., 1981 'Retrenchment and rationality in the personal social services', *Policy and Politics*, 9(3) pp. 313–14
13. SOCIAL SERVICES COMMITTEE, 1982 *The 1982 White Paper: Public Expenditure on the Social Services*, Second Report, Session 1981–2, HC 306. HMSO
14. TREASURY, 1979 *The Government's Expenditure Plans 1980/1*, Cmnd 7746. HMSO
15. WEBB, A. and WISTOW, G., 1982 op. cit. (ref. 11) p. 144
16. SOCIAL SERVICES COMMITTEE, 1984 *Public Expenditure on the Social Services*, Fourth Report, Session 1983–4, HC 395. HMSO, p. xiii
17. 1983 'Fruits of labour', *Social Work Today*, vol. 14, no. 23

18. BEBBINGTON, A. C., 1979 'Changes in the provision of social services to the elderly in the community over fourteen years', *Social Policy and Administration*, vol. 13, no. 2 pp. 11–123

19. WEBB, A. and WISTOW, G. op. cit. (ref. 11)

20. DHSS, 1981 *Report of a Study Group on Community Care.* Department of Health and Social Security, p. 115

21. Ibid. pp. 7–8

22. DHSS, 1980 *Mental Handicap: Progress, Problems and Priorities.* Department of Health and Social Security, para. 2.43

23. DHSS, 1981 *Care in the Community: A Consultative Document on Moving Resources for Care in England.* Department of Health and Social Security, p. 2

24. WISTOW, G., 1983 'Joint finance and community care: Have the incentives worked?' *Public Money,* vol. 3, no. 2 pp. 33–7

25. BEBBINGTON, A. C., 1981 'Appendix' in Goldberg, E. M. and Hatch, S. (eds), *A New Look at the Personal Social Services.* Policy Studies Institute, pp. 113–15

26. WEBB, A. and WISTOW, G., 1983 'Public expenditure and policy implementation: the case of community care', *Public Administration,* vol. 6l, no. 1, pp. 21–44

27. JOHNSON, M., DI GREGARIO, S. and HARRISON, B., 1981 *Ageing, Needs and Nutrition.* Policy Studies Institute; DAVIES, L. 1982 *Three Score Years . . . . and Then?* Heinemann; BOOTH, T. A., BARRITT, S., BERRY, S., MARTIN, D. N. and MELOTTE, C., 1983 'Dependency in residential homes for the elderly', *Social Policy and Administration,* vol.17, no. 1, pp. 46–62; *see also* DAVIES, B. and FERLIE, E. 1984 'Efficiency – improving innovations in social care: Social Services Departments and the elderly', *Policy and Politics,* vol. 10, no. 2, pp. 181–204

28. BOOTH *et al.,* op. cit. (ref. 27), p. 60

29. PLANK, D., 1977 *Caring for the Elderly,* GLC Research Memorandum RM 512. Greater London Council

30. WADE, B., SAWYER, S. and BELL, J., 1983 *Dependency With Dignity.* Bedford Square Press

31. Ibid.

32. BOOTH *et al.,* op. cit. (ref. 27), p. 60

33. HEDLEY, R. and NORMAN, A., 1982 *Home Help: Key Issues in Service Provision.* Centre for Policy on Ageing, p. 18

34. DAVIES, L., op. cit. (ref. 27).

35. HILL, M., 1981 'The policy – implementation distinction: a quest for rational control?', in Barrett, S. and Fudge, C. (eds), *Policy and Action.* Methuen

36. HEDLEY, R. and NORMAN, A., op. cit, (ref. 33)
37. GOLDBERG, E. M. and CONNELLEY, N., 1982 *The Effectiveness of Social Care for the Elderly,* Heinemann
38. WADE *et al.* op. cit. (ref. 30); MACDONALD, E., 1980 *Changing Patterns of Care, Report on Services for the Elderly in Scotland.* Scottish Home and Health Department, HMSO
39. CHALLIS, D. and DAVIES, B., 1980 'A new approach to community care for the elderly', *British Journal of Social Work,* vol. 10, no. 1, pp. 1–18

Chapter nine

SOCIAL WORK: SEEBOHM, BARCLAY AND OTHER MIXED BLESSINGS

PROFESSIONALISATION: A CASE OF THE CURATE'S EGG

A major, at times the dominant, strand in the history of British social work has been the search for professional status and that professional *sang froid* displayed by doctors, lawyers and even some of the more newly arrived professions. The search has involved the exploration of many by-ways and potential routes. Three of the most significant were the investment in the psychodynamic model of casework; the development of generic training and a more united professional front; and the Seebohm Report. The last of these, of course, resulted in the creation of Social Services Departments which embraced only a proportion of all social workers, but it is to social work in the SSDs that we will most clearly confine our attention in this chapter. It was through the SSDs that social work seemed to gain a real power base and it is in the SSDs that social work has subsequently encountered its greatest conundrums and setbacks. But each of the routes to professional status – not just one of them – has proved to be a mixed blessing.

Indeed, the end-product of the struggle for professional standing – as with the curate's egg – has only been 'good in parts'. And even that may be an unduly positive picture. The quest within social work for a satisfying self-image remains the longest running show in town and the British public is singularly disinclined to be a respectful audience, let alone to applaud the production. None of this need matter if social work could be shown to be doing a job about which society is equivocal – if not dismissively embarrassed – but doing it well. The sting, of course, is in the tail of that sentence. Limited public approval partly reflects a belief that social work does not work; it is a belief which has been partly supported, rather than firmly contradicted, by systematic evaluative research.[1]

The purpose of this chapter is a strictly limited one. It is to trace some of the key issues and questions underlying the dilemma posed at the very beginning of this book: that of the relationship – ideal and actual – of social work to the personal social services. Consequently, there would be little point in wallowing in the criticisms which have been levelled at social work; there would be even less point in undertaking a detailed exegesis of social work texts and writings. The need, for our purpose, is to step back somewhat from the philosophical disputes and topical issues in order to establish a basic framework for understanding the problem. We do not pretend that such a framework will yield easy solutions or blueprints for the future. The story of the personal social services already includes many half-baked solutions to insufficiently formulated problems and we do not want to add to that legacy. Our starting point is merely that social work is obviously central to, but not obviously synonymous with, the personal social services. That implies that the role of social work in the personal social services needs to be treated as a problem if it is to be understood. It also implies that some, perhaps many, of the dilemmas facing social workers – especially in SSDs – may arise from the past failure to establish an unambiguous and appropriate role for social work in the personal social services.

SOCIAL WORK AND THE PERSONAL SOCIAL SERVICES: SOME BASIC MODELS

The unification of the social work profession was treated in the 1950s and 1960s as a problem of professional training and identity[2] and as a problem of service structure. Less attention was paid to roles and tasks. Generic training and generic practice in unified SSDs was an enticing goal, but it papered over the uncomfortable fact that the different branches of specialist social work which had developed in the post-war years involved a variety of different roles for 'social workers' and differing role relationships with other workers. In the medical and psychiatric fields social workers worked in an often uncertain alliance with medical professionals in delivering individual or team-based casework help to clients. They had only limited direct control over client access to other services, but the assessment of need and the negotiation of access to external services was an important part of their role – especially in the hospital setting. Mental welfare officers and welfare officers were much less well established as independent professional workers. Managing access and entry to specific services and institutions was a dominant feature of their role. In child care, by way of contrast, field social workers had a much more direct control over access to child care services (particularly residential care, fostering and adoption) as well as carrying out the other roles noted above. Their relationship with other professions – including the medical professions – was indirect at best. They also worked in a close but ambiguous relationship with residential child care workers, who were not necessarily full professional colleagues but who were not aides or subordinates managed by field social workers. Aides and subordinate workers were employed in comparatively small numbers in some authorities (e.g., Family Aides), but not in all.

The SSD inheritance was therefore a curiously mixed one. It included several 'models' of field social work derived from the pre-existing specialisms onto which had been grafted newer ideas about group work and community work. It also included a rapidly growing body of workers of other kinds (e.g., residential, day and domiciliary workers, occupational therapists, social work aides) who needed to be related to social workers in some way. But how?

There were several possible routes open in the late 1960s and early 1970s. Many subsequent problems have been exacerbated by the failure to be clear about these possibilities and about the working relationships which they implied.

The choices available at the time can usefully be reduced to three basic approaches:

1. to treat social work as all-encompassing and to place social workers in a clear position of professional dominance akin to that traditionally held by doctors in the medical field;
2. to treat social work as one, central, but specific set of scarce skills and to see the personal social services as some form of 'teamwork' involving a variety of more nearly co-equal workers deploying a variety of skills;
3. to discard social work as a label altogether and to analyse needs, tasks, roles and skills from scratch with the possible end result being an entirely new division of labour, new professional identities and new training programmes.

Social work as all encompassing

This approach would involve a declaration that the personal social services are merely social work writ large and that social work embraces the central 'diagnostic' and treatment skills. The corollary is that *all* clients, virtually without exception, would have to be assessed by social workers before gaining access to specific services or help –

which might be highly specialised ⅃ and that social workers would retain control over the 'treatment plan' for all clients within the agency no matter which service they received. Many questions would remain; some of the central ones would be: who is and is not a social worker? how is assessment/diagnosis to be handled? and how do non-social work staff relate to social workers? Residential, as well as field, workers might be unequivocally seen as social workers, for example, and given the same basic training. A system of generalist 'diagnosis' and specialist treatment might be established (e.g., based on intake teams plus specialists), or 'diagnosis' might be seen as inseparable from 'treatment' – which implies a much larger cadre of generic workers and fewer specialists. The approach taken to diagnosis and referral would determine many working relationships, but the dominance of professional social work would itself permit only two basic patterns: other workers would be co-equal professionals to whom clients could be transferred, or professionally subordinate workers whose contribution would ultimately be orchestrated and monitored by the social worker. To take a specific example, an old person would be assessed, *by a social worker,* as needing home help and periodic short-term residential care and these services would be *either* staffed by co-equal professionals *or* by staff who could unequivocally be called to account by social workers (possibly via their own line managers) if the service delivered fell short of that deemed to be necessary.

Social work as a specific set of skills

This approach implies that the personal social services are more than social work writ large even though social work skills are a central – and scarce – resource. The primary question becomes: which bits of the personal social services enterprise require or are most likely to benefit from the attention of social workers? The answers might be sought to client group (e.g., are social workers really necessary to, or willing to serve in, the care of the elderly?); by mode of working or intervention (e.g., are casework, group work, residential social work, community work and planning all part of the essential social work role?); by tasks and the skills involved in specific tasks (e.g., are assessment, service allocation/rationing, treatment planning, case review and monitoring, counselling and advocacy all social-work tasks?); or by the degree of risk/benefit to the client involved in different situations (e.g., are admission to care, the preparation of reports for courts of law and legal purposes, too sensitive to be handled by non-social work staff?).

The question would remain: how should social workers relate to other personal social services workers? The central implication of this view of social work as especially relevant to 'bits and pieces' of the personal social services enterprise is that social workers do not necessarily have to be the key or continuity worker on every case. Some types of case might be seen to need a social worker for diagnosis and continuity, but others may be handled entirely, or primarily, by other co-equal professionals, by subordinate or para-professional workers, or even by independent 'sub agencies' within the SSD. The essential need is to ensure that all resources – including social work resources – are deployed at the right times and points. Consequently, it is possible in this approach, for example, to envisage less well-trained staff as the front-line workers in many instances. They would undertake initial diagnostic and assessment tasks and provide case continuity as key workers. The most crucial skill in this model is that of knowing when, how and to whom to refer for more specialist assessment, advice, and service.

Discarding social work as a label

Given the mixed antecedents of social work as a profession and the uncertain success with which social workers have traditionally carried out some tasks, this might have been the most intellectually attractive approach to have taken in the late 1960s. It would have involved the – at least temporary – abandonment of the term social work, along with all the inherited presumptions about the roles and training appropriate to social work. The starting point would have involved a break with history rather than an imposition of an unwieldly professional inheritance on the developing personal social services. The central questions would have been: what are the key needs, problems, tasks and roles which fall to the personal social services? which of them cannot feasibly be carried out with any real success and should be avoided or undertaken purely as a low-cost holding operation? what skills are required to carry out the others successfully? which of these skills can one hope to combine in workers with given attributes and types of training? and how can the scarcer skills be most effectively deployed? The answers may have re-invented social work as we know it and assigned it one of the roles noted above. But the answers might equally have produced an altogether different approach to staffing.

In practice the SSDs embrace an uneasy mix of these different approaches to the social work role. The last was never considered as a realistic possibility (the nearest approximation to it were the calls for a major shift towards community work, welfare rights advocacy and radical forms of social work). The history of the pressure for reform and the extent to which social work interests have been allowed to make much of the running in policy discussion have pushed the first to the fore. Despite the fact that England and Wales did not follow Scotland in creating *Social Work* Departments, the SSDs have been widely assumed to be social work writ large and therefore to pivot on the social work role. However, the inheritance from the pre-existing services combined with the great pressure for improved community care services for the elderly and handicapped (who were the least popular clients with social workers and whose care was least dependent upon the social work profession) ensured from the outset that the outcome would be complex.

The result in many SSDs has been – in effect – the creation of two or more semi-independent organisations under one departmental umbrella. Area teams of social workers have been the undisputed hub around which work with families and children and some other client groups has revolved, but particular facilities (e.g., homes, day centres) and other groups of staff (e.g., residential, day and domiciliary workers) have served as the basis for one or more additional and developing empires – often managed from headquarters. These 'semi-independent organisations' are characterised by different interests, different patterns of training (or lack of it), different organisational structures and different systems of management, accountability and discretion. Consequently, the SSDs have not generally developed in practice as social work writ large even though that is how social workers – and many others – tend to see them. Moreover, the key questions about the role of social work, the role relationships between social workers and other workers, and the effective and efficient development of appropriate skills to meet real needs have largely been left unresolved.

CRITICISMS AND PARADOXES

We will return to these issues of task and role later in the chapter. First, however, we need to explore further the uncertain standing of social work (and of the personal social services). To do so involves examining some of the central criticisms which have been levelled at both. While it is important not to become bogged down in them, some of the key themes developed by the critics provide important insights into our concern with the role of social work in the personal social services. Indeed, some of the most vehement criticisms suggest that neither social work nor the personal social services have any good reason for continuing in their present form.[3] The overall impression to be gained from the critics, however, is that the accusations and arguments are frequently paradoxical rather than an unambiguous foundation for further action and change. This does not imply that they have no force or validity. Indeed, paradoxical arguments can be especially revealing precisely because they pinpoint key conflicts of aim, interpretation, and of interest. Let us, therefore, examine a few of the more interesting assertions about the nature, status and impact of social work. It must be emphasised that they are our own distillation rather than a simple reiteration of individual writer's views.

Professionally arrogant, yet pusillanimous

One of the earliest and most respected of critics of social work was Barbara Wootton.[4] The force of her charges remains, not least because they were levelled by a socially aware and concerned radical who felt compelled to take up the cudgels. Her most damaging charge was that of professional arrogance. In her Orwellian phrase – 'Daddy knows best' – the image was that of social workers and the state colluding to adopt an overweening attitude to people in need of help. The argument was not so much that social work was often ineffective but that social work imposed its own conceptions of problems and needs on clients. The failure to heed the authentic feelings and voice of the client was a fundamental charge indeed to level at social work.[5] It is a charge which has echoed through three decades of criticism of all kinds: disinterested, scholarly, journalistic and just plain scurrilous.

To it, however, has been attached an equally powerful, yet apparently contradictory, image of social workers as pusillanimous: indecisive, unsure of themselves and 'wet' in all manners of ways. These twin pillars of criticism were most spectacularly conjoined, without attempt at reconciliation, by Brewer and Lait.[6] The pusillanimity of social work was highlighted for them by the approach to the non-accidental injury of children. They could see no evidence of effective prevention other than when children were removed from home – an action from which social workers nonetheless shrank because of their unfounded faith in the blood-tie between parents and their children. The authors' almost obsessive antagonism towards social work undermined the credibility of many of the serious criticisms put forward. In the particular instance of non-accidental injury, for example, no mention was made of any of the preventive work undertaken by specialist teams (by voluntary organisations as well as the statutory services). Nonetheless, the belief that social work is characterised both by professional arrogance and a certain paralysis of indecision has to be taken seriously; it is one summary of apparently widespread public attitudes.

Social work works best for those who least need it

Although the evidence is less clear-cut than some critics of social work would have us believe, evaluative research has undoubtedly called the effectiveness of social work into question. The most positive and reassuring findings concern the provision of the more practical forms of help: work with the less professionally attractive client groups such as the elderly; and relatively short-term, clearly focused interventions.[7] Moreover, the research message seems to favour a concentration of real effort on the middling needy rather than on clients who face the most devastating problems. Put differently, and in jargon which was apparently acceptable to the authors because it has its origins in military medicine, Brewer and Lait saw a case for the *triage strategy* (i.e., mitigate pain at minimal effort for the most hard pressed – if this is possible; move the least needy on as quickly as possibly; and allocate most resources to those whose problems are likely to be significantly modified by the skills and services to hand).

In one sense, none of the concern about the impact of social work should be surprising. Very similar doubts have emerged about the effectiveness of medicine and psychiatry. Spectacular results can be obtained in some branches of medicine, but they are matched by a steady stream of ineffective intervention and by some equally spectacular failures. Compared with other professions, however, the cardinal problem for social work is that it has failed to achieve that hegemony and mystique which the old professions have enjoyed and which has enabled them to weather doubts about their effectiveness. Moreover, its failure has made the very attempt appear presumptuous and has provided a fertile culture within which the anti-professional bacillus can multiply. Perhaps social work's loss will eventually prove to be the consumers' gain; a general reduction in the level of professional arrogance would be no bad thing.

A wider and more generally sceptical view of the helping professions is therefore a useful antidote to the cry: social work doesn't work. But once rhetoric is put aside the real questions emerge and have to be given due weight: what kinds of interventions work, in what sense, with which problems, and in what contexts and circumstances? To continue to explore these questions systematically is the only way of deciding whether particular forms of social work, as presently practised, have a role to play in the future. The findings to date certainly suggest that the role which was traditionally favoured by social workers – that of providing long-term casework support – is a blunt instrument and that many of the most needy clients are particularly unlikely to benefit from it at any reasonable level of expenditure.

A circumscribed palliative

The onslaught on traditional social work practice, especially psycho-dynamically oriented casework, brewed and bubbled steadily through-out the Seebohm years. It provided the foundation for a radical critique in which the very understanding of the problems facing clients was the core of the issue.[8] The psychodynamic model inevitably pointed towards defective relationships and personal adjustments as key factors. The radical critique began by shifting the focus to specific social causes of a more structural kind: poverty; bad housing; schooling as a source of tension and as an organised imposition of failure. As we noted in Chapter 4, this view of social causality underpinned much of the legislation of the mid and late 1960s. It also underpinned the call for community work, community action, welfare rights and advocacy work. If the notion of cause implied in the psychodynamic approach was even partly mistaken, the traditional model of casework was also partly redundant.

One product of this radical critique has been the move in some social work writing from the identification of specific social ills to the denunciation of the capitalist system as a whole.[9] Another product has been the development of a variety of new ways of working. However, the expansion of the social work repertoire has also been fostered by other changes – resulting in greater interest in groupwork, behaviour modification and a range of therapies and techniques. The net result merely emphasises the issues posed in the last section: one real need is to know the implications and outcomes of the different ways of working which are now on offer and how to enable appropriate and useful ones to co-exist as alternatives or complements.

Another need has been forced to the surface, at least in theory. Social work is in contact with people whose difficulties arise from many interacting sources: 'acts of God' (e.g., old age, disability, terminal illness); problems of socialization, learning and personal adjustment (e.g., inadequately developed parenting skills, bereave-ment); disrupted and damaging inter-personal relationships (e.g., divorce and desertion, child abuse); structural defects and the increasingly demanding requirements of a complex and changing society (e.g., low and insecure income, unemployment, the 'social redundancy' of the elderly). What the radical critique has underlined is that social work ought not merely to accept responsibility for the casualties of social change and the structural problems of an advancing but ailing socio-economic system.

Immediate help has to be provided wherever possible, but pressure for change and for alternatives to the defects of our society are also essential. Problems of structure and process should not simply be allowed to lie where they fall. However, it is equally clear that many social problems are common to all advanced complex societies – capitalist and non-capitalist alike. The social management of the labour force and coping with alienation are the lot, in part, of social work in our society – but they are problems which seem to be inherent in complex industrial societies. Similarly, social isolation in old age and disability have generally to be combated if they are to be avoided or reduced; they are not simply disposed of through structural change. The implication for social work in Britain is that it needs varied modes of operation suited to the variety of tasks confronting it. One mode which is crucial but which remains underdeveloped is that of analysing and effectively communicating the nature and origins of the problems with which society lumbers it, and the limits within which these problems have perforce to be tackled. Social work needs an effective analytical capacity and an effective political voice.

A failure of training, not a failure to train?

The goal of professionalisation was central to the social work upsurge of the 1960s and 1970s; a fully trained profession was central to that goal. Professional training became the cornerstone of professional recognition and the pressure for longer and more tightly packed training grew. Inevitably, the appropriateness of that training has been a prime target for the critics. The long-established dominance of the casework approach was a focal point of early criticism. At best it was seen to leave too little room for other approaches. At worst it was seen to result in trained incapacity: a blindness to problems and patterns of causation which did not fit into the dominant model.

The congruence of training and actual practice became a focus of more pragmatic attention in the post-Seebohm decade. The wide-ranging demands placed on social workers in SSDs, and the comparatively limited opportunities for systematic casework were highlighted by the seminal study undertaken by Goldberg and

Warburton.[10] The findings underlined the possibility of a significant gap between the expectations and skills derived from professional training and the tasks fulfilled by practising SSD social workers. The Stevenson/Parsloe study – also concluded in the mid-1970s – should have settled the query; they certainly set out to look for and understand any such gap.[11]

Some commentators were convinced that Stevenson and Parsloe's findings revealed such a gap and were depressing for social work. A more realistic view is that while it is difficult to be completely confident of findings based on the responses of social-work students and ex-students to questions on the value of their social-work training, the areas of most concern were concentrated in those fields of work about which students were least enthusiastic. The preparation for work with families and children was seen to be reasonably adequate, that for work with the mentally and physically handicapped and community groups was seen to be least adequate. Student judgements of adequacy probably reflected the historical preferences of the profession and the patterns of experience and inexperience of their teachers, but they underlined the need to train social workers, and to arouse their enthusiasm, for social care work. The only alternative would be the creation of a separate cadre of social care staff. Perhaps the most surprising finding in the light of recent history, however, was that less than a third of the respondents showed a preference for the more 'psychological' work orientation associated with the psychodynamic tradition and only 10 per cent identified with the more 'sociological' approach associated with the radical critique; the vast majority identified with an integrated approach which emphasised the wide range of problems which might impinge on clients.[12] If this is seen as evidence of quite rapid change in the image of social work acquired by social work students and an enthusiasm for the integrated approach to social work theory,[13] it emphasises the need for caution in interpretation. Fixed viewpoints are best not founded on shifting sands, especially as the rate of change in the social and political context of social work has been so substantial since the mid-1970s.

The appropriateness of contemporary training to practice was strongly questioned in one crucial respect which has undoubtedly grown in importance in recent years, however. The ability to work jointly with colleagues and to marshall diverse forms of help to meet differing needs did not emerge as a major skill well developed. Indeed, Parsloe cogently argued that the individualistic tradition of training might well inhibit a group/team approach to practice.[14] This perceived failure to promote flexibility and to foster an anticipation of future needs points to a general and therefore fundamental problem. The gap between the content of social work education and contemporary practice may not be as great as may be feared, but the educational process could still limit – rather than expand – the options available to practitioners in the future. The centrality to social work practice of individual responsibility for specific cases is but one example.

Social work and the SSDs: professional responsiveness or hidebound bureaucracy?

Social work appears to be almost inextricably bound up with the rigidities and insensitivities of 'bureaucracy' in the public mind. This may reflect public confusion over the nature and role of social work. People with income maintenance and housing problems, in particular, have frequent recourse to social workers even though their primary problems lie with other social agencies. The intricacies of professional and organisational boundaries and responsibilities are easily overlooked and clients may unfairly blame the often impotent social worker for the frustrations of bureaucracy, or blame local bureaucracies for the policies of central government. A dislike of bureaucratic behaviour may also stem in large measure from the large administrative units which swept away smaller-scale organisations in the early 1970s. But, in one sense, the origins of the problem are less important than the fact of its existence and that it strikes a chord with many social workers – especially those in SSDs. The growth of voluntary organisations has mirrored dissatisfactions with public bureaucracies among consumers and workers alike.

Viewed from this perspective, the creation of SSDs and the subsequent reform of local government in 1974 may have shackled social work to inappropriate structures rather than liberated and strengthened it by enhancing its status and power base. These demerits and merits of structural change certainly cohabit as uneasy bedfellows in SSDs, and the gains and losses have been unevenly distributed. The status, influence and power of *senior* staff have certainly been augmented, though a much more difficult political and economic context, and a more interventionist style among councillors, has recently offset these managerial gains in a number of authorities. The familiar story from the grass roots, however, has been of increased pressure of work and demand without similar compensations – even during the heyday of growth. There is an almost inevitable temptation within social work – as in other professions – to listen to the feelings and concerns of practitioners and by so doing to overlook the opinions of the consumer. In this matter of the stigmata of bureaucracy, however, there seems to be a measure of widespread agreement: harm and inconvenience is visited on worker and consumer alike.

Scale, bureaucracy and a tendency towards centralization have all made SSDs a much less congenial environment for social work than had originally been anticipated. We suggested in Chapter 6 that a determined and long-term commitment to decentralisation could reverse some of these defects; but other problems abound. One of the most central and most easily underestimated is the fact that public agencies necessarily operate within particular limits and constraints.

Because SSDs are a public service they cannot escape political control and public accountability; varying degrees of inflexibility, caution and hierarchical control are inevitable corollaries. At minimum, public authorities must make some attempt to establish and implement policies throughout the geographical area for which they are responsible. Consistency and equity alone imply an element of 'bureaucratic rigidity'. But social work, and the SSDs, are exposed to more detailed political control than is implied above and also to capricious, almost wholly negative, media scrutiny.

The protective layers of authoritative professionalism and public support which surround medicine, the police, and even education, are lacking. We have argued that the SSDs may represent the more generally acceptable balance between professional autonomy and political control; the other examples certainly suggest at times that professional arrogance can be dangerously institutionalised in some public services. Yet SSDs can hardly be said to be a good model of a politically controlled professional service. Neither the consumer interest nor the wider public interest has been well served by the sense of re-active defensiveness which has prevailed.

One potential solution would be to modify the style and content of public accountability rather than dilute it in the interests of professional autonomy. A system of public accountability which brings SSDs and social work to the attention of the public when things go badly wrong, but which fails to publicise achievements, is inherently damaging.

A *constructive* approach to public accountability is badly needed and – rightly or wrongly – the onus lies with social work as a profession and with the senior staff of SSDs. There is a need to identify and publicise positive outputs and effective service. There is a need to establish interest in, and understanding of, the full range of SSD work in the popular and national media. To say this is immediately to underline the inherent weakness of the legacy bequeathed to the SSDs, however. The Seebohm era did not in practice lead to a system of universal personal social services, based on SSDs, with which people from all social background could identify. The focus has remained on the needs of the poorer, more vulnerable and more socially marginal groups of the population. The sharp elbows of the middle classes may help gain resources; their respect and vocal support provide insulation against the more disruptive and negative forms of public accountability. The expansion of provision for the mentally handicapped provides a good and recent example of the value of services which are needed and welcomed across the social spectrum. This example also underlines the importance to social work as a public service profession of being identified in the public mind with things other than family and child care and social control.

To modify the style and content of public accountability could generate more flexibility in SSDs, but the inherent limits of public services remain. It is necessary to consider the whole range of tasks and needs facing personal social services and to examine which are best handled through public services and which might flourish more fully in non-statutory settings. Policy-making has been dominated and distorted not only by the failure to clarify the role of social work in the personal social services, but also by the unexamined assumption that the primary location for both should be the public services.

A particularly interesting example is provided by Holman's work. He sees his model of preventive 'Neighbourhood community social work' as an essentially non-statutory approach.[15] He advances a variety of explanations of why such work would be difficult to replicate in the statutory sector [Doc. 18]. Some of them refer to problems which ought in principle to be soluble, but which in practice are almost insurmountable. For example, clubs and activities for young people are a central part of his strategy but they are used as a social work tool. To achieve the same combination of goals and means in the statutory sector would entail a degree of collaboration, on a national scale, between Education and Social Services about which no one would be sanguine. He equally sees a minimum of statutory duties and a maximum of flexibility and freedom as essential to creativity.

In short, Holman identifies 'system characteristics' of statutory services (multiple goals, tasks and client groups; departmental boundaries based on functional divisions; statutory responsibilities and defensive accountability) as inimical to his model of neighbourhood social work. Although state provision is no longer as firmly and dominantly at the centre of thinking about social work and the personal social services as it was, this general issue of systems characteristics has not been faced. The mixed economy of welfare is a product of historical accident, assumptions about the role of the state arising from the early post-war decades, subsequent conflicts and shifts in ideology and policy, and ad hoc growth and expediency. At no time has there been a consistent attempt to match organisational forms and auspices (statutory/non-statutory) to tasks and functions.

However, Holman's example is also instructive in a different sense. Apart from certain characteristic features of public bureaucracies, Holman emphasises the values and objectives which characterise his own work. His basic aim is to help people resolve and forestall problems by a process of community development and community action rather than by working primarily with individuals, or by delivering services. He tends to assume that these aims and values cannot now be fully embraced by statutory social work and that the characteristics of statutory bureaucracies cannot be greatly changed. Although they were criticised at the time for not going far enough, these changes in goals, methods and forms of organisation *were* assumed to be possible by the authors of the Seebohm Report; the statutory services have changed much less than anticipated. Does that imply that the statutory sector is indeed a limiting base for social work, or does it imply a failure to will the radical reforms required? Moreover, highly critical accounts of some forms of non-statutory community work suggest that voluntary organisations are by no means always a good base from which to practise.

What is to be made of the diverse discontents within and criticisms of social work? One possible conclusion, as we have just noted, is that SSDs are the wrong place to practise social work.[16] This may well be true for a large slice of the social work enterprise, but it is difficult to see how most of the existing care functions of social work within SSDs could be transformed for the better by moving them into the non-statutory sector. A major expansion of voluntary sector social work would be more likely to *complement* the present work of the SSDs. A more fundamental conclusion, therefore, would be that the present role of social work is simply not viable – especially in the statutory services.

THE VIABILITY OF SOCIAL WORK

There are two quite different senses in which the social work task can be seen as non-viable. The first implies a deep seated and irreconcilable conflict of interests and expectations; the second implies a theoretically remediable and potentially temporary misalignment of tasks, roles and skills. The second extends the argument of the previous section into a somewhat different dimension. But let us consider the two in turn.

The argument in the first case is simply that 'society' and the social work profession are straining after quite different objectives and serving different interests. From this point of view, the task allocated to the personal social services and to social work is primarily that of exercising social control and providing a service of last resort – at 'manageable' cost. The objective is that of allowing decent citizens to sleep safely at night with easy consciences. Both tasks are essentially non-viable, however, if the resources and changes which are really required to resolve the problems are 'intolerable' when viewed from the standpoint of policy-makers with dominant interests. Yet even workers of last resort have to be motivated and they may therefore collude in loading themselves with unrealistic visions of what can be achieved. While this picture may be most obviously valid in hard times, its importance is that it offers a more general insight into problems of coping with the victims of competitive, grossly unequal and rapidly changing industrial societies: the price of doing a good job is always likely to be unacceptably high compared with the costs of simply containing some of the damage – at least from the perspective of the paymasters. The price is measured in material resources, of course, but it is also measured in terms of values and interests.

That this conflict can be lessened in economically good times is indisputable: needs are likely to be fewer in number and resources are likely to be more plentiful. The viablity of social work can therefore be seen to be a function – at least in part – of effective government. But to say that is to assume that good times are merely a matter of the political will and ideological bent of government; it is to ignore the possibility of continued long-term economic decline. Long-term economic decline inevitably provokes a scramble for protection or partial insulation from its consequences; whether the personal social services, their staff and their clients can avoid a continuing tightening of constraints then depends upon whether they can deflect the costs of decline elsewhere. To achieve this requires a substantial redistribution of income towards groups which lack status and power, and that is difficult for any government to achieve in good times, let alone in economically oppressive times. The only escape routes from this depressing scenario, therefore, are the reversal of economic decline itself or the transformation of the goals and values which tend to characterise industrial societies beset by the urge to maintain or improve growth, productivity and international competitiveness. But the message is clear either way. Social work can only partially escape the context created by wider forces, at best; economic and political change can substantially increase or reduce the viability of the social work task.

Not all the problems of discharging the social-work task can be laid at the door of economic, social and political change and conflict, however. Social work in SSDs often verges on the brink of non-viability because of a failure within public policy and the profession. There has been no concerted attempt to examine the congruency, or otherwise, of several key factors: the tasks which fall to the personal social services and the SSDs in particular; the nature of the social-work role; the preferences and role expectations of social workers themselves; and the skills needed and actually developed by social workers. Social work was grafted into the SSDs as if this operation was self-evidently straightforward. The fact that it was not, and is not, is reflected in the long saga of trials and errors with variants of generic and specialist working, intake teams, large area teams, small area teams, 'patch' teams, and centralised and decentralised management of service production and allocation (e.g., day, domiciliary and residential care services). Some of the issues reverberating through these different approaches relate to problems of organisation and management, but underlying them is the issue of tasks, roles and skills.

TASK, ROLES AND SKILLS

The initial failure to assess the compatability of tasks, roles and skills was Seebohm's. The committee responded to the historic search for professional unity by offering support to the idea of generic social work practice – albeit without developing the theme in detail. What this obscured was the very real possibility that the different client groups and services which were being organisationally united might continue to present different challenges to social workers. Moreover, they would inevitably call forth different patterns of service from SSDs and involve staff other than social workers. This in turn would inevitably raise questions about access to services for different client groups: would access have to be negotiated through social workers or would some services be directly accessible? It would also raise questions about the organisational structure appropriate to SSDs: should there be separate and parallel lines of accountability for social work and for day, domiciliary and residential care, or should the full range of SSD activities be brought together under a united management structure? Staffed by social workers?

It is always easy to be wise in retrospect and to see problems in a different light with the benefit of hindsight. Judgements about the Seebohm Report must be tempered with this realisation; it is difficult to say the same for criticisms of the report of the Barclay Committee,[17] however. The problems of achieving a good match between tasks, role and skills was far more apparent by the beginning of the 1980s. The tasks of the SSDs were clearer and changes in the social work role had begun to be identified. Barclay provided, albeit in a difficult climate, an opportunity to reassess the Seebohm inheritance and to set social work and the personal social services on a sounder footing. That it failed is not primarily a comment upon the conclusions it reached. The essential failure was one of scope of analysis, and of judgement.

Although the Barclay conclusions were seen by some as an unsatisfactory compromise, the advocacy of community social work represented a real attempt to return to some of the earlier Seebohm ideals and update or rescue them [doc. 19]. It acknowledged the inflexibility of overly hierarchical and centralised structures, the need for greater accessibility and the necessity of responding to the growth of social care as a primary function of SSDs. But this step forward was fatally flawed. The impression conveyed was of a limited, naive and unresolved debate. The report itself gave the appearance of a systematic elevation of consensus and readability over analysis. As an approach it can only be recommended, if at all, when the issues are clear and the way forward is unambiguous. But the Committee was created precisely because such certainty was lacking and it ought not to have made such inadequate use of the available evidence on tasks, roles and skills. Indeed, the battle of the academic titans waged in minority statements appended to the report and in the public arena thereafter was in practice a necessary but related attempt to stake out the issues clearly.[18] Expressed as minority statements, these arguments inevitably emerged as polarised alternatives (traditional casework versus generic, patch-based teamwork designed to mobilise 'community resources') rather than as two means of expressing different understandings of the social-work task in SSDs.

It is easy to overplay the argument, but Pinker's trenchant defence of casework practice and of specialisation, and his scepticism about 'the community' as a resource, partly reflected the casework traditions of child care and of psychiatric and medical social work. It also reflected the significant extent to which work with some clients involves statutory responsibilities, the exercise of social control and the management of access to statutory services. The advocacy of 'patch' by Brown, Hadley and White reflected the enormous growth in the importance of social care and the recognition which had gradually been accorded to a wide range of community resources, including informal networks of kin, friends and neighbours. The dispute highlighted the inescapable fact that for the most part SSDs are still best understood as multi-function, multi-client, and multi-skill agencies which have not yet developed a fully coherent way of working. Yet the committee located much of its discussion of social work quite firmly within the context provided by SSDs without first examining their nature and operation in detail or considering broader changes taking place in the whole field of the personal social services.

Barclay contemplated the future of social work when it should have studied the personal social services as a whole. The social work tail wagged the personal social services dog yet again. But Barclay also comtemplated the future of social work as if it could be wholly divorced from its political and ideological environment. As Jordan has underlined consistently and to such good effect, neither social work nor reförsm designed to change the role, method and organisational context of social work can usefully be discussed in a political vacuum.[19]

REFERENCES

1. FISCHER, J., 1973 'Is casework effective?' *Social Work*, vol.8, no. 1, pp. 5–20; and FISCHER, J., 'Does anything work?' *Journal of Social Service Research*, vol. 1, no. 3, pp. 215–43; MEYER, H. *et al.*, 1965 *Girls at Vocational High*, Russel Sage; REID, W. and SHYNE, A., 1969 *Brief and Extended Casework*, New York, Columbia University Press. GOLDBERG, E. M. *et al.*, 1970 *Helping the Aged*, Allen and Unwin; MALLEN, E. J., DUMPSON, J. R., 1972 *Evaluation of Social Intervention*, Jossey-Boss; DAVIES, M., 1974 'The current status of social work research', *British Journal of Social Work*, **4**, pp. 281–303; BERG, I. *et al.*, 1978 'The effect of two randomly allocated court procedures on truancy', *British Journal of Criminology*, **18** (3) pp. 232–44; GOLDBERG, E. M. and CONNELLY, W., 1982 *The Effectiveness of Social Care for the Elderly*, Hienemann.

2. DONNISON, D. V., 1975 *Social Policy and Administration Revisited*. Allen & Unwin, ch.11; HALL, P. 1976 *Reforming the Welfare*, Heinemann

3. BREWER, C. and LAIT, J., 1980 *Can Social Work Survive?*. Temple Smith

4. WOOTTON, B., 1959 'Daddy knows best', *Twentieth Century*,

Winter; WOOTTON, B., 1980 *Social Science and Social Pathology*. Allen & Unwin

5. MAYER, J. E. and TIMMS, N., 1970 *The Client Speaks*. Routledge and Kegan Paul; SAINSBURY, E., 1975 *Social Work with Families*. Routledge and Kegan Paul; GOLDBERG, E. M. *et al*. op. cit. (ref. 1); ROBINSON, T., 1978 *In Worlds Apart*. Bedford Square Press

6. BREWER, C. and LAIT, J., op. cit. (ref.3)

7. *See* works cited in ref. 1

8. SINFIELD, A., 1970 'Which way for social work?', In Townsend, P. *et al.*, *The Fifth Social Service*. Fabian Society; BAILEY, R. and BRAKE, M. (eds), 1975 *Radical Social Work*. Arnold

9 CORRIGAN, P. and LEONARD, P., 1978 *Social Work Practice under Capitalism*. Macmillan; SIMPKIN, M. 1979 *Trapped Within Welfare: Surviving Social Work*. Macmillan; BOLGER, S., CORRIGAN, P.,DOCKING, J. and FROST, N., 1981 *Towards Socialist Welfare Work*. Macmillan

10. GOLDBERG, E. M. and WARBURTON, R. W., 1979 *Ends and Means in Social Work*. Allen and Unwin

11. PARSLOE, P., 1981 *Social Services Area Teams*. Allen & Unwin

12. Ibid.

13. GOLDSTEIN, H. 1973 *Social Work Practice: A unitary Approach* Columbia University, South Carolina Press; SPECHT, G. and VICKERY, A., 1977 *Integrating Social Work Methods*. Allen & Unwin; PINCUS, A. and MINAHAN, A., 1973 *Social Work Practice: Model and Method*. Peacock, Illinois

14. PARSLOE, P., op. cit. (ref. 11)

15. HOLMAN, R., 1983 'Prevention in the neighbourhood: community social work on a council estate', In Bean, P. and MacPherson, S., 1983 *Approaches to Welfare*. Routledge and Kegan Paul

16. RIGBY, A., 1982 'I started hiding under the table', *Community Care*, Sept., pp. 20–1

17. BARCLAY, P. M., 1982 *Social Workers: their role and tasks*. Bedford Square Press

18. The two dissenting statements appended to the Barclay Report were: PINKER, R. A., 'An Alternative View, Appendix A; BROWN, P.,HADLEY, R. and WHITE, K. J., 'A case for neighbourhood based social work and social services', Appendix B

19. JORDAN, B., 1979 *Helping in Social Work*. Routledge and Kegan Paul; JORDAN, B. and PARTON, N. (eds), 1983 *The Political Dimensions of Social Work*. Blackwell; JORDAN, B., 1984 *Invitation to Social Work*. Blackwell

Part four
TOWARDS A NEW COHERENCE

Chapter ten
SOCIAL WORK, SOCIAL CARE AND SOCIAL PLANNING:
TOWARDS A NEW COHERENCE?

The record of the personal social services since Seebohm has attracted little approbation. One explanation of this fact has a timeless quality: it is comforting to abuse the messenger when the message is unacceptable. The staff of the personal social services are the night soil workers – or social hygenists – of the twentieth century. They are asked to cope with and to conceal from view the unacceptable problems, tensions and social disasters of a complex society undergoing long-term, relative decline. They offend the susceptibilities of polite society when they allow these problems to emerge into the light of day, but they risk failing their immediate clients – and offend against higher canons of political truth – when they simply apply panaceas without pointing to the extent and depth of social ills. A service of last resort, in particular, will always tend to be politically and professionally vulnerable; and the personal social services largely remain a service of last resort.

Beyond this inherent dilemma, however, there are other – more remediable – defects and shortcomings. Few, if any, elements of the organisation, management, service delivery and staffing of these services emerge unscathed from an assessment of their effectiveness. The failure to meet need adequately, the inflexibility of much of what is provided, the inappropriateness of the skills of service providers for the tasks they are required to perform, the failure to engage with or develop local communities, the failure to subject service delivery to searching scrutiny of efficiency and cost-effectiveness, the fact that clients may be harmed as much as helped through some forms of social service intervention, all these criticisms may readily be laid at the door of the personal social services – and especially the local authority social services departments. But these are not criticisms which are unique to social work or to the personal social services; they are a common critical theme throughout discussions of social policy, the role of the state, and the work of large-scale social services.

212

Simply to record such defects is also to present a partial picture. It neglects the degree of responsibility for these defects which must be borne by central governments: increasing and often unrealistic demands have been placed on the personal social services, the inappropriateness of applying a social work poultice to problems of structure and social change has been conveniently ignored, and the resources needed to tackle an increasingly impossible array of tasks have been constrained. Moreover, and on the positive side, much has been achieved since pre-Seebohm days: services have been greatly expanded; management is becoming more skilled; and there are a number of flourishing experiments designed to create flexible service structures which can be responsive to the individuality of clients and their needs. Yet the overall climate is often one of uncertainty and some disillusionment. There is a sense of services under siege – if not at breaking point – which extends from front-line field staff to management teams. We should not underestimate or dismiss the strength of commitment to client interests and needs which is to be found throughout the personal social services. But while the service ethic is by no means dead, its hold on life may be becoming more fragile as many staff, quite understandably, separate out the pursuit of their own interests from those of their clients.

The metaphor of services under siege is no less applicable to the relationships between central government and the personal social services. Ministers have quite explicitly gone onto the offensive: raising fundamental questions about the functions of social services departments, challenging them to adopt a new focus through the enabling role, and attacking their ineffective management of resources. If some of these developments are specific responses to the policies of the Thatcher governments, the underlying tensions pre-date 1979. As John Cypher, the former General Secretary of BASW has noted, the tenth anniversary in 1978 of the Seebohm Report

> passed without much celebration ... the social work journals gave little or no coverage of the event in the summer of 1978. BASW did not mark the anniversary in any way, and perhaps this signifies that social workers collectively feel there is little about that product of the report, the Social Services Department, which they wish to celebrate. With more than a little irony, the 1978 BASW Annual General Meeting resolved that 'the present organisational structure of social services departments is harmful to the practice of social work.' The resolution urged that consideration be given to 'alternative structures more compatible with the nature of social work.'[1]

The further, and in some respects more fundamental, irony is that it was the professional social work lobby which, more than any other single group, was responsible for the establishment and shape of the personal social services as we know them today. Not only did social work 'capture' the Seebohm Committee itself and determine the overall thrust of the Report, it was also responsible for mounting an effective and successful campaign to secure the implementation of the Committee's recommendations when delay seemed probable.[2] Thus, by 1971, social work seemed to have realised its most fundamental objective of establishing an organisational base in which it – and not medicine – was the dominant influence. The new Social Services Departments were to be the citadel within which the emerging profession would consolidate the position it had achieved in child care and complete the colonisation of the former welfare services. As we have argued, this very dominance of statutory social work interests and perspectives during the late 1960s and early 1970s gave rise to many subsequent problems. The social services departments were shaped by the existing interests, skills and preferences of social workers rather than by the needs and tasks facing them. The historically less prestigious social care services were largely kept at arm's length in separate departmental boxes from field social work. Organisational rigidities grew up around historical distinctions within social work and between professional and sub-professional workers. As the social care services have grown in importance and thrown off much of their inherited disadvantage, they have – ominously for the flexibility of service – become powerful empires in their own right.

During the 1970s the sense of direction and purpose which gave birth to the new SSDs began to evaporate under the weight of the range and numbers of problems which came knocking on Seebohm's 'one door'. Social workers continued to question their purposes, their role, their methods and – as Cypher reminds us – even their position within the structures they had been so influential in creating. By the mid-1970s the generic/specialist debate had been reopened, interest in the unitary approach was growing and the first experiments with highly localised 'patch' teamwork were about to begin.[3] The certainties which carried social work triumphantly through the Seebohm era had been tempered in the cold light of experience and replaced by the search for new roles which was chronicled in the Barclay Report.

In all of this, the influence of perceived shortcomings was probably as great as the sheer volume of demand. The growth of evaluative research questioning the efficacy of social work practice, and even whether interventions by social workers were a benign influence on clients, together with the day-to-day experience of the intractability of many client problems, all served to undermine professional self-confidence and prompt much soul-searching. The succession of child abuse scandals was an even more dramatic blow to the self-esteem of the profession and, no less importantly, to its public standing. Rightly or wrongly, social work continues to live in the shadow of Maria Colwell and her sad counterparts, at least in the public and political domain. This, in itself, is a revealing reflection of the failure of social work to establish a broadly based acceptance of its competence and authority. The contrast with established perceptions of medicine is striking. Social workers are publicly pilloried for contributing towards the avoidable deaths of clients. Doctors 'lose' patients not through negligence or incompetence, but after an unremitting struggle against the inevitable.

THE RISE OF SOCIAL CARE

Given this background, it is perhaps unsurprising that the social care tradition has assumed relatively greater prominence. Compared with the confused and unflattering popular image of field social work, the social care services have appeared as providers of direct practical support to individuals in need. While social work has reeled under the combined weight of a bad press and an insupportable workload of often insoluble problems, the bricks and mortar of the rapidly expanding residential and day services have provided tangible and public indicators of their achievement. If relatively little is known about what actually happens behind their architect-designed walls, we may be comforted by the thought that something concrete is nonetheless being provided for those whose needs are the result of accidents of birth and life, or derive from the slow run-down of the biological clock. Domiciliary services – the third arm of social care – similarly deal with the more publicly accepted client groups, most particularly the elderly. Providing practical assistance which makes it possible for individuals to remain in their own homes, their purpose seems beyond reproach and their only deficiency the inadequacy of the resources at their disposal. By contrast, the problems of those clients to whom the majority of social work time is allocated (families and children) can too often appear to be self inflicted.

The above undoubtedly draws too strong a contrast between social work and social care, even perhaps from the perspective of the averagely informed layman. Nonetheless, it is doubtful whether the shortcomings and failures of social care have intruded upon the public consciousness to the extent that those of social work have done.

Indeed, it is only relatively recently that day and domiciliary services have begun to be evaluated on a widespread and systematic basis.[4] While it is true that the critical analysis of residential care predates the creation of the personal social services,[5] it had received relatively little public attention in recent years until concern began to grow about the rapid growth of private care. Yet, as we indicated in Chapter 8, there is ample room for scepticism about the allocation and management of statutory social care services. Our particular concern in that chapter was with the extent of the match between need and resources. There are, however, other and in some ways more fundamental questions about these services, centring particularly upon their purpose and their impact on client well-being.

For example, and as we have argued elsewhere,[6] it is by no means clear what the purpose of the meals service actually is. How far is it to provide nutrition, 'surveillance' or social contact? Does it, in practice, *reinforce* social isolation and disguise the need to support and create opportunities for elderly people to remain active and provide for themselves? Johnson's study of the meals service provides some evidence that this may be the case: his findings suggested that 'the pervading need of the population served was not for a hot meal off an unchosen menu at a day and time they were not consulted about, but for aid with shopping.[7] Carpenter[8] also stressed that the provision of meals services was frequently an inappropriate response to need. More fundamentally, he calculated that SSDs need to face the possibility that they are *creating* dependency by overprotecting the elderly. He concluded that, unless more sophisticated needs assessments were conducted, social services run the risk of 'creating an overall level of dependence that is as frustrating for the elderly as it is expensive for the local authority'. The provision of hostel accommodation for mentally handicapped people capable of living more indpendent lives[9] is another example of overprotection which creates or reinforces dependency. This is most graphically illustrated in the case of young people and adults admitted to residential care after having been brought up in the community. In effect the routine of institutional life rapidly deskills them for life in the community, leaving them with too few choices to make or opportunities to develop self-help skills as basic as handling money or preparing snacks. Much residential care for the elderly is similarly restrictive: a recent study concluded – yet again – that the main experience of residents in old people's homes (and patients in geriatric wards) was 'doing nothing ... except sitting in a chair staring into the space ahead'.[10] Considerable efforts have been made by some authorities to introduce group living and opportunities for self care within their residential homes. Even so, they often recognise that they are seeking to give back to their residents a degree of independence and autonomy which should never have been taken away from them.[11] Nor does day care necessarily offer a more therapeutic and rehabilitive environment. While residents of old people's homes spent 62 per cent of their time 'doing nothing', the equivalent proportion in day centres was still as high as 51 per cent.

Great care is needed at this point. It would be quite inappropriate to force a tyranny of activity and engagement upon the elderly (or anyone else), but it is equally inappropriate simply to replace the disengagement and social isolation of people who are in residential care – or who are neglected in the community – with alternative patterns of disengagement, isolation and enhanced dependence on social services. As with domiciliary services, residential and day care do suffer from such defects. Poor assessment procedures and an unduly limited range of services can lead to needs being defined *in terms of services* rather than to needs being met *by services*. Moreover, while many are receiving too little support (especially hard-pressed carers), others receive too much. Both the limited repertoire of services available and the operational philosophies (or lack of them) under which they are delivered can result in social care being a disabling rather than an enabling force in the lives of too many people.

THE RISE AND FALL OF SOCIAL PLANNING

What of the record of social planning, the third of our principal themes? In the present climate it is easy to forget that planning was once blessed with political sex appeal. In the naively optimistic world of the 1960s, planning was considered a potent, indeed essential, instrument of social change. This perspective reflected changing views about the causality of social problems. Given the switch in emphasis from explanations based on individual pathology, planning at the societal level was complementary to – and ideally provided a macro environment for – a more radical community work approach to social work at the neighbourhood level.

Seebohm explicitly envisaged that the new SSDs would be agents of social planning and social change. One expression of this view was the suggestion that they should have 'responsibilities extending well beyond those of existing local authority departments'. At least three separate elements can be detected in this description of the Department's role. One was the over-riding necessity to extend the service base they would be inheriting from their predecessor departments. As we have noted, the extent of unmet need was a major motive for establishing a unified administrative base for the personal social services which would be sufficiently powerful to attract a more substantial flow of resources into them.

Seebohm did not favour an *ad hoc* extension of existing activities however. Rather, a planned matching of resources to the differing needs and problems of local environments was advocated. Yet in the mid to late 1960s few data were available on the scale and nature of social need. Thus, the second element in the extended role envisaged for SSDs involved going out into local communities to search out needs and gain a greater understanding of social problems. The way forward was to create strong departmental research capacities; the Committee argued that it could not 'emphasise too strongly the part which research must play in the creation and maintenance of an effective family service. Social planning is an illusion without adequate facts; and the adequacy of services mere speculation without evaluation.'[12] In emphasising the importance of planning, research and evaluation, Seebohm recognised the need to go beyond producing 'more of the same'. This approach had much in common with emerging ideas about corporate planning in local government. In both cases there was a concern that resources should be systematically allocated to meet known needs and to secure explicit objectives rather than unthinkingly 'thrown at' presumed problems. In other words, planning was to encompass the broader process of policy-making and not be limited to a narrow programming of resources.[13]

Just as Seebohm wanted service growth to be based on needs identified in the community, so it wanted the community to have a role in defining its needs and in shaping services to meet them. Thus the third element in its extended role for the new departments highlighted the importance of participation in the planning and review process. As such, it reflected the emphasis on participative planning then rapidly becoming part of the conventional wisdom in the physical planning world.[14] Later, Algie[15] was to take up this theme and advocate particular structures and processes to promote participative planning within and through the new SSDs.

We may summarise our discussion thus far by noting that Seebohm not only recognised the essential role of planning in making good the known inadequacies in service provision but also urged that it should serve a number of wider purposes. Thus it should: contribute towards a greater understanding of the nature of problems in local communities; relate service growth to identified needs and objectives; and promote effectiveness through the regular review and evaluation of established services. But it was not to be a purely technocratic activity: strong emphasis was laid on the importance of community involvement and the consumer viewpoint. Given these objectives, what has been the record of social planning in the personal social services? In particular, how far has it been a creative process by which purposes have been clarified and adjusted to changing community needs?

In the early 1970s, it seemed as if planning would indeed occupy a key position in the internal workings of the new departments and in their relationships with other local authority departments, other statutory and voluntary agencies, and with central government. One of the first major initiatives to be taken by central government in the personal social services field was the introduction in 1973 of the ten year planning system with its resource assumption of 10 per cent growth a year (see Ch. 8). Meanwhile, the Bains Report of 1972 had ushered in the heyday of local authority corporate planning.[16] It provided the basis for the new management structures and, less certainly, the management processes which underpinned the re-organisation of local government in 1974. In theory, at least, this move towards corporate planning was congruent with the development of planning within the social services departments. Seebohm had envisaged a bottom-up planning process which was broadly consistent with that envisaged by the advocates of corporate planning. Indeed, the leading proponent of corporate planning had spoken enthusiastically of the Seebohm approach suggesting that

> it could lead to a new emphasis on social planning in local government – a counterpoise to the emphasis on physical planning in planning departments and financial planning in treasurers' departments ... in the term ... In the short term it is an attempt to place a little less emphasis on the management of existing activities and a little more on the planning and review of those activities.[17]

Compared with such optimism the reality has been a disappointment – at best. There are a number of explanations for the failure of social planning in the 1970s, but in the case of the personal social services the DHSS must bear a substantial element of the blame. The processes and purposes of the DHSS ten-year planning system strongly contradicted those outlined in Seebohm and in the corporate planning literature. Instead of a bottom–up, needs-based approach the call for ten-year plans introduced a rather primitive and insensitive top–down mechanism through which DHSS sought to shape local developments while gaining an upward flow of information on such developments. The key to the whole exercise was the promulgation of a series of 'norms' for individual services – expressed as guideline levels of per capita provision (for example, 25 residential care places for the elderly per 1,000 population aged 65 and over). By requesting social services authorities to submit 'plans' based on such guidelines, the DHSS enabled many of them to transform planning into a mechanistic process of multiplying local population data by the planning guidelines and accommodating the results within the resource assumption which the department had already laid down.

The damaging effects of the DHSS approach on the planning methods adopted in many SSDs were reinforced by the narrow scope of the DHSS initiative. The ten-year plans – no less than the subsequent priorities documents of the mid-1970s – were focused on the interface of the personal social services with the NHS. From the very beginning, DHSS had considered the rapid development of social services to be an essential precondition for the implementation of national priorities for the NHS. To that extent, therefore, the Department was less concerned with – and perhaps less aware of – the links between SSDs and other local government services. This was further illustrated by the joint planning and joint finance initiatives of the mid-1970s which were seen to characterise the personal social services as mere 'adjuncts of the NHS'.[18] The neglect of the corporate dimension was also emphasised in local government responses to the 1976 priorities document. As DHSS acknowledged, 'local authorities generally criticised the document for taking a mainly health service perspective and because it did not adequately recognise the corporate element of local authority planning, and the links with housing, education, employment and the courts'.[19]

Some SSDs sought to develop a more inspiring approach to planning than that required for DHSS purposes, but they were swimming against the tide. The lead given by DHSS permitted an uncreative and unreflective process of resource programming rather than encouraging problem analysis and community involvement in need identification. Nor did it encourage sustained questioning of the purposes and achievements of SSD services or an examination of alternatives. Far from forcing SSDs to think broadly about the mixed economy of welfare and about different ways of understanding and meeting need, the growth of planning in the early 1970s locked many of them firmly into a preoccupation with the limited range of services which they themselves provided. Planning blinkered their vision rather than opening their eyes to new possibilities. It was a distortion of the inheritance which Seebohm had intended to confer on them;

breaking free has absorbed much of the energy of the more innovative authorities ever since.

To be fair to DHSS, however, it is questionable whether a bottom-up planning model could have survived a period of exceptionally rapid growth such as that which the personal social services enjoyed in the early 1970s. The great strength of a simple, norm-based, approach to planning was that it enabled services to be expanded at a rapid rate. Double-digit increases in real resources left little time for searching out needs and clarifying service objectives. Programming growth almost inevitably became an end in itself. There was a real sense in which local departments were chasing their tails to spend sums of new money on a scale and at a pace which revealed their inexperience and limited expertise. And all this took place in a climate of extreme management instability. Not only had it been necessary to establish new management structures and processes in 1971, but many departments had to go through a similarly disruptive experience only three years later when local government was reorganised. In such an environment, the planning guidelines did have the virtue of simplifying the process of service development and enabling a major expansion of provision to take place, albeit in a manner which was considerably less responsive to community-based need than Seebohm had anticipated.

Once this pattern of development was established, the mould was set. For the most part, policy planning had been driven out by project programming. Review and evaluation procedures have not become an established feature of policy-making in most departments. Apart from an early and brief flurry of needs identification in the wake of the Chronically Sick and Disabled Persons Act of 1970, most researchers in SSDs have found themselves providing routine management information services. They also became an early target for cuts in 1979/81 though there has subsequently been some upturn in their numbers. Indeed, while the present political climate is generally inimical to planning, a renewed emphasis on cost-effectiveness and efficiency is creating a demand for some forms of service monitoring and evaluation.

We have argued that the broader sense of planning as policy-making – developing services in relation to need and a clear sense of their intended purpose so far as individual and community well-being is concerned – was lost sight of in the scramble to programme the very large amounts of growth allocated to the personal social services in the first half of the 1970s. How did this experience affect the other element of Seebohm's view of planning: that it should not be a narrow technocratic process but one embracing an extensive range of interests in local communities? The experience of the community development projects and of local authority corporate planning has been seen by some observers as conclusive evidence of the technocratic approach. Thus planning has been criticised as the inappropriate importation of a business methodology which concentrated power in the hands of small central planning units from which community interests, not least elected members, were systematically excluded. Corporate planning became local corporatism.[20]

While corporate planning did not necessarily exclude the possibility of a more broadly based participative style, either in theory or in practice, there is little doubt that community interests have rarely been involved on anything other than a token basis. The record of social services planning is little different from that across local government as a whole. Much of the very substantial expansion of services which took place in the 1970s was capital-or buildings-led. As a result, planning tended to revolve around the imperatives and timetables of the capital programme. The rapid rate of capital growth pre-determined, in its turn, the use of new revenue monies: a considerable proportion of the revenue growth available each year was already 'spoken for' in the form of the spending needed to open and run newly completed capital projects. To a considerable extent social services planning became a highly specialised form of capital programming. As a consequence, responsibility for planning tended to be concentrated in the hands of relatively small numbers of people and especially small coteries of officers handling the capital programme. The norms based approach of DHSS simply reinforced this tendency for planning to be technocratic, centralised and remote from service delivery staff as well as from the communities they served.

Significantly, there is evidence that when the wider community interest is able – or allowed – to intrude, services are more likely to be planned on the basis of needs rather than norms.[21] Generally speaking, however, the isolation of planning processes from the wider department and public which Webb and Falk[22] discovered in their study of the first round of ten-year planning has remained the established pattern for most SSDs. In this respect, as well, therefore, the Seebohm ideal was still-born and it is only recently that a minority of authorities has begun to treat seriously the need for a consumer input. The apparently 'out of character' support for the voluntary sector which has been developed in a number of radical left-wing authorities is one product of attempts to develop a more pluralistic system in which 'user' needs are articulated alongside professional viewpoints (*see,* e.g., Hatch and Mocroft's[23] account of voluntary/ statutory relationships in Islington).

A WAY FORWARD?

We began this chapter by briefly recapitulating some of the main criticisms made against the personal social services in this and other studies of their work. Our overview of social work, social care and social planning since 1971 does little to challenge the view that serious shortcomings are to be found in their operation. A further weakness, which has remained largely implicit in our discussion thus far, is the tendency for social care and social work services to be administered as largely separate, specialist empires in many departments. Where a functional model of organisation has been adopted, responsibility for fieldwork, residential, domiciliary and day care services rarely comes together at any point below that of the senior management group. While managerial responsibility for fieldwork has been widely decentralised, most of the remaining arms of SSDs are usually managed directly from headquarters. Social planning has failed to serve as an integrating mechanism because it was first shunted into the programming siding and then all but abandoned. As a result there has been a failure to develop coherent models of practice which span all service functions. If social workers have too often been seen merely as dispensers of sympathy or agents of social control, this is not simply due to limited skills or the absence of alternatives; they have been unable to influence the allocation of resources. The semi-autonomous management of social care services means that allocation processes are jealously guarded and based on administrative procedures rather than on rounded assessments of need. The result, as we noted in Chapter 8, is a lack of fit between need and resources.

Is there a way forward? Can the three primary elements of the personal social services be combined so that they are mutually reinforcing and a means of making available better quality services designed to promote individual and community well-being? The keynote ideas on which to base change are 'flexibility and responsiveness', 'decentralisation' and 'cost-effectiveness'. The new conventional wisdom is that the strengthening of voluntary action and informal care will simultaneously promote a number of the desired objectives. It is an assumption which underpins the two most commonly advanced models of change: the 'community social work' and the 'contracting out/welfare pluralism' models. What differentiates these two models is the way they define and combine social work, social care and social planning. Do either of these models take us any further forward?

The community social work model

Community social work appears to address many of the problems and weaknesses which we have identified. The Barclay Report explicitly advocated its adoption as a necessary means for developing 'a close working partnership with citizens focussing more closely on the community and its strengths'.[24] In its discussion of 'what social workers are needed to do', the Report argued that 'social services departments need to discover and bring into play the potential self-help, volunteer help, community organisations, voluntary, and private facilities that exist'.[25] Thus a primary role for community social work was defined in terms of creating and mobilising resources at the community level. However, a second dimension to the role involves the identification of need among individuals as well as across communities. The emphasis in this case must be on identifying needs as early as possible and tailoring specific interventions to meet them. Individualised help is the name of the game.

While the community social work approach has a resource mobilisation element and implies the interweaving of informal and formal provision, it also involves substantial diagnostic and assessment tasks. Thus it implies face-to-face working with 'clients' as well as working with communities. This is important: the traditional emphasis in social work training has been on client-centred casework and the orientation of many would-be social workers remains that of working with individual clients through personal relationships. Darvill and Munday argue that, in their experience, applicants for social work training courses 'rarely refer to a desire to marshall an array of community resources as their preferred method of helping'.[26] They also refer to Baldock and Prior's findings to illustrate practising social workers' perceptions of what social work 'really is':

> extensive face-to-face dialogue between worker and client is the essential core component of social work practice. All our respondents felt that engaging in direct and regular talk with clients was what counted first and foremost as 'doing' social work, for example taking precedence over acting as an advocate in dealing with other agencies or mobilising community resources.[27]

Evidence such as this has been cited in the past to indicate the gulf between presently prevailing values and attitudes in social work and those underpinning community social work. That gulf remains. However, it is a mistake to polarise community social work and client-centred casework. If, as Barclay argued, there is a need for a new attitude of mind which sees other citizens as partners in the provision of social care, it is a ludicrous over-reaction to think that this would imply the end of casework as we know it or the end of close and intimate working with individuals. Skilled counselling remains a valid and necessary task. Equally, a major weakness of service delivery has been the failure to tailor formal services to the unique needs of individuals, a task which necessarily includes seeing them in the context of both family and neighbourhood support 'systems' and the interpersonal *relationships* on which such systems are founded.

Community social work ought not to be seen either as an alternative to, or as necessarily excluding, more traditional face-to-face inter-ventions with individuals. It is, however, an approach in which the repertoire of interventions must explicitly extend beyond one-to-one counselling and casework. Community social work is an irrelevance if it does not encompass major elements of both social planning and social care. The specific purpose must be to integrate within a social work role both a bottom–up needs-based approach to planning and an individualised service packaging approach to social care. But one consequence of combining these tasks and roles is to question whether they could, or should, be carried out by a single worker or even profession. If this consideration implies some kind of team working, it also raises the question of whether what is needed is a team wholly composed of social workers, or even a team led by social workers. The skills we have outlined are currently possessed at least in part by a range of social services personnel: specialist caseworkers, community workers, home help organisers, occupational therapists, senior resi-dential and day care staff, research and development officers, and 'management'.

In effect, therefore, while Barclay brought together community work, social care and decentralised social planning in a new model of social work, the term 'community social work' is misleading. What Barclay was really talking about was the need to find a different and more localised basis for the development and delivery of the personal social services as a whole. Barclay's description of its approach as a model for social work reflected both the traditional hegemony of the social work profession and also the limitations of its own terms of reference, which were defined in terms of the role and tasks and social workers. A more radical, across-the-board look at objectives, values, tasks, skills and occupational boundaries in the personal social services as a whole seems to have been precluded from the outset.

The major contemporary issue for the personal social services is to find an understanding of tasks, skills and organisational structures which permits a more flexible and effective response to the individuality of human need and the fraught social, economic and political context in which it exists and has to be met. It is necessary to engage with and develop community resources to the full; but it is also necessary to develop and commit formal services alongside such informal and voluntary resources. The harnessing of community resources and formal services is a task for the personal social services as a whole and not just for front-line social work teams.

The welfare pluralist/enabling model

Mr Fowler has advanced two arguments for developing the 'enabling role' of SSDs: cost-effectiveness must be prompted; and the mixed economy of welfare is the reality which must be made to work – the state has not, cannot and should not monopolise the personal social services.[28] Taken in isolation, neither argument can be gainsaid. But both arguments, and the idea of welfare pluralism supported by the local statutory services, have to be placed in a wider context.

The essential feature of that wider context is that, rather than emphasise the necessity for SSDs to adopt an 'enabling' role towards non-statutory provision, *the personal social services as a whole must be firmly charged with the task of enabling*. Their *raison d'être* must be seen to be that of enabling individual, group and communal growth and development to take place. The role of the SSDs can then be allowed to fit into place rather than act as a distracting obsession. Of course, such a reorientation is altogether more fundamental than that presently envisaged by ministers. We spell out its key features and requirements at the end of this chapter. But let us first note some of the attractions of adopting this wider view of enabling as the essential role of the personal social services and of allying it with a belief in the thoroughly pluralist model of welfare which has come to the fore in the past decade.

If one pushes aside fixed visions and special pleading (e.g., for substantial growth in any one sector), there are great advantages to be gained from a welfare pluralist/enabling model. The ideal advanced is that of a set of flexible, innovative, decentralised and participative services designed to support individuals, groups and communities in the exploration of their own problems and solutions. It implies an end to professional arrogance and to the separation of helper and helped by barriers of social distance and hierarchy. Class differences have always been a major feature of such social distance, but the welfare state has also harboured a tendency to lack faith in the ability of ordinary people to think and act for themselves.

The welfare pluralist/enabling ideal is also attractive in that it offers an alternative to 'curative intervention' as the hallmark of the professional. The personal social services have suffered as a result of importing this canon of professional respectability from medicine; it has still not been finally replaced by the touchstone of enabling individual and group or collective development. This new touchstone is appropriate to the change, control and care functions of the personal social services alike. Neither change nor control should be pursued as ends in themselves but as ways of creating possibilities for further individual and group development. The same is true in the case of social maintenance activities. As we have indicated, the problem is to sustain people's functioning or allow it to deteriorate; yet social maintenance activities must not be wholly routinised, nor must they induce unnecessary dependence. The opportunity for personal development and for the retention of personal dignity is essential and it means that even the most mundane caring tasks should be performed with this wider objective in view.

No development will yield all the benefits which we have associated with the welfare pluralist/enabling model. Nonetheless, changes in the statutory and non-statutory sectors which recognise the complementary roles of each in underpinning informal care and in enabling individual, group and community development offer the brightest hope to which we can presently aspire. No one version of this model is authoritative. Indeed, the commitment to diversity and decentralisation makes a single blueprint inappropriate. The core ideas have received support across the political spectrum and some of the most active developments have been in firmly socialist local authorities which might have resisted any significant role for non-statutory organisations and groups in the past. However, the fact that basic features of this approach have wide political appeal makes it all the more important to be clear about the wider environment in which it needs to be pursued. To sacrifice real progress to the demands of ideology or expendiency will be to risk rejection of the model itself and loss of the hard-won experience and gains of the post-Seebohm years. Unfortunately, the present economic and political environment makes such an outcome all too likely.

CONCLUSION

We have tried to reflect upon two of the approaches to the restructuring of the personal social services which have been particularly dominant in recent years. The debate continues. At the time of writing, it is not known how – or if – the ideas contained in Norman Fowler's Buxton speech will find more concrete form in specific government proposals for change. However, another, more fundamental, debate ought to be conducted before either DHSS ministers or individual departments introduce reforms to the basic structure and organisations of the personal social services. Indeed, without this discussion, very little real change may be achieved at the level where it matters most, that of the 'consumer'. We refer to the need for clarity about the fundamental values on which the personal social services should be based. In short, as George Woodcock bluntly demanded of the trade-union movement: 'What are we here for, brothers?' What underlying purposes and objectives should govern the relationship between personal social services, individuals and their communities?

These questions find echoes, sometimes powerful ones, in the community social work and welfare pluralism debates. Indeed, for some of their protagoinsts, such considerations were the starting point for their belief that reforms were necessary in the way we organise and deliver personal social services. Yet they have tended to become submerged as the debates have moved on to the nuts and bolts of change and as they have become polarised into 'community social work versus casework' and 'public versus private welfare'. The questions we have posed should, however, be at the forefront of discussion about the future. Unless we are clear about underlying values and the interests to be served, unless those values are reflected in philosophies of care and unless service structures are built on those philosophies, we are unlikely to root out many of the weaknesses which have emerged in the decade and a half since the SSDs first opened their doors. There is a real danger that the rhetoric of organisational change will obscure a reality in which business is conducted much as before.

As we have seen, Seebohm advocated, *inter alia*: partnership with, and the development of, local communities; the interweaving of formal and informal care; and a real degree of consumer participation. In addition it referred throughout its report to 'Social Service Departments' rather than Social Services Departments. In so doing, it sought to emphasise a philosophical notion of service giving rather than a technical process of service production. Yet none of these approaches has been universally developed since 1971 and, in some respects at least, SSDs have operated little differently from their predecessors. If genuine improvements are to be achieved from the present round of proposals and counter-proposals for reform, and the personal social services are to strengthen and develop their enabling role, several related changes are essential.

First, need must be brought back to the centre of the stage. By this we mean that the *primary* purpose of the personal social services should be neither to 'save' money, nor to make it; the *raison d'être* should be to ensure that the needs of individuals, families and communities are met. Second, such a commitment to need must be set against the undeniable scarcity of resources, but within a wider espousal of social justice as a primary political objective. Third, the operational philosophies of all services – whether public, voluntary or private – must be appraised. The objectives to be pursued and the outcomes which are desired should be clarified wherever possible so that a sense of direction can be maintained and effectiveness can be assessed. These are such obvious and basic statements that the reasons for making them should be explained.

The central role which need should play in policy-making and in service delivery has been challenged or actively undermined in a variety of ways. Principal among them has been the imperatives of resource constraint and cost-containment. There is nothing inappropriate about attacks on 'waste' and inefficiency if they are properly motivated, conceived and executed. Indeed, we have argued that cost-effectiveness must be a major preoccupation for the future and that it should not be presented as a defensive or merely pragmatic response.[29] There can never be any virtue in using scarce resources unproductively and the pursuit of cost-effectiveness is therefore essential to social justice. It is a moral imperative. Yet this perspective is very different from the preoccupation of recent years during which the emphasis has been on containing overall expenditure even to the detriment of long-term cost-effectiveness. Moreover, and even more damaging in some respects, the language of value for money has begun to resemble a threadbare cloak of respectability for cuts. The reaction which is invited is one of defending all existing uses of public money – especially in local authorities – even if of dubious benefit to those most in need. One moral imperative cannot thrive in a moral vacuum.

Unless services are managed within an overriding but broad philosophy of service to individuals and communities, resource decisions will be the master, not the servant, of social policy. However, to place need, as one element of a wider view of social justice, genuinely at the centre of the stage would be to outlaw knee-jerk reactions – of both the cutting and protectionist kind – from the discussion of public expenditure. It would also outlaw the pretence, which threatens the very foundations of the welfare pluralist/enabling model – that voluntarism can be self-financing.

Substantial support for voluntary organisations will always be required from the public purse and a large proportion of that support can only be channelled via local authorities, given their present responsibilities and role in local service systems. Yet local authorities cannot be expected to engage with non-statutory services and accept substantial measures of financial responsibility for them if they in turn are subject to unpredictable resource pressures which bear little relationship to the activities being urged upon them. A policy of supporting and enabling the non-statutory sector depends for its success upon a clear strategy for statutory provision and for public expenditure. The state need not be the sole provider of service, but its proper role as both provider and as a funding source must be recognised in both theory and practice.

SSDs are being asked to change their role and style while being denigrated and forced on the defensive. Public expenditure cuts are but a sympton of the problem. In Jordan's terms, SSDs are being used as a buffer between the state and its hard-pressed citizenry, not as a means of mediation.[30] Moreover, a profoundly anti-statist philosophy conveys the message that state services are both unacceptable and incapable of overcoming their defects. The most enthusiastic and opportunistic advocates of voluntary (as well as private) provision have added to this chorus of criticism. Yet the SSDs are being asked to become enablers!

Moreover, attitudes towards state provision are but one factor in a wider withdrawal of the state: social justice, equity and redistribution towards large numbers of the disadvantaged have disappeared from the agenda. Whether this is seen as a short-term expedient in support of an incentive-led model of economic growth, as a permanent redistribution towards the most successful members of a revitalised economy, or as a redivision of the remaining spoils in a declining economy is irrelevant. Unless social justice and a more positive attitude towards the role of the state are powerfully reinstated the results will be similar in each case. The function of the personal social services will become increasingly impossible and increasingly bound up with the maintenance of order in a deeply divided society; the call for reform and responsive change within the services will be dwarfed by these wider forces.

Privatisation has provided one of the most potent symbols of the demise of need as a central concept, of social justice as a goal and of state provision as a means of proceeding. We have argued (Ch. 5) that underlying forces and processes of change must be distinguished with care, but that the growth of the private sector has been powerful and has had a major impact on some parts of the personal social services cannot be denied. However, in one sense who provides care is ultimately less important that its quality and its 'fit' in relation to need; the eating not the recipe, must be the proof of the pudding. But is the profit-motive compatible with meeting the needs of vulnerable people? Juxtaposing two ideas may help to put the question in its proper perspective: first, profit *maximisation* implies subordinating *all* other considerations and it cannot therefore be compatible with meeting need. Second, 'making a living out of needy people' has to be made compatible with serving them and their interests whether services are statutory, voluntary or private. The only escape from this dilemma would be for all help to be provided by volunteers, but they too may require rewards which conflict with the clients' interests. The real issue, therefore, is to create systems which encourage or require the people who profit in material terms from them to work in the best interests of clients – whether they be individuals or communities. A traditional response in the public and voluntary sectors is to project the right kind of values in training programmes and in operational policies. But are those values sufficiently explicit or widely agreed?

What values should underpin our interventions on behalf of the clients or consumers of the personal social services? In short, what should the personal social services be aiming to achieve? One irony of the growth of private residential care is that the attempt to regulate it has helped to refocus thought about standards – and therefore about objectives. It has also prompted a degree of caution about casting out motes and throwing stones: there is much in the public social care services, as well as in social work, which gives cause for legitimate concern. While the grosser forms of abuse and exploitation sometimes found in the private sector and in NHS long-stay institutions have surfaced less often in local authority (and voluntary) services, we can scarcely argue that much of the care routinely offered is what we would wish for ourselves or our families. Inactivity, benign neglect and the creation or reinforcement of dependency are too often the norm.

Parsimony in providing services used largely by poor and 'lower class' people has been a limiting tradition in many instances, but it is not the only problem. An even more fundamental limitation is that the personal social services have tended to accord too much attention to the *production of services,* and too little to the *provision of service:* to the elaboration of what good practice could and should look like. Too much time – and too many resources – have been invested in buildings and too little in staff and the way they work. However, more concern is now being devoted to good practice and departments are increasingly seeking to develop explicit operational philosophies. An unusually well-developed example of this trend is the value statement drawn up by Derbyshire Social Services Department as the basis for the development and management of the full range of the Department's services [doc. 21]. This statement reflects the principles of normalisation[31] which are increasingly influencing both the health and personal social services. The King's Fund 'Ordinary Life' project for mentally handicapped people has been particularly important in disseminating this approach.[32] It argues the need for, and seeks to provide, an explicit statement of service philosophy to act as a framework for service planning and a reference point for operational practice. The *All Wales Strategy* for mentally handicapped people[33] provides a clear example of this approach and the principles on which it is based:

> The provision of new services should be directed and proposals assessed in pursuit of the following principles and objectives. It should be emphasised that these general principles apply to all mentally handicapped people, however severe their handicaps.
>
> (i) Mentally handicapped people should have a right to normal patterns of life within the community ...
>
> (ii) Mentally handicapped people should have a right to be treated as individuals.
>
> (iii) Mentally handicapped people require additional help from the communities in which they live and from professional services if they are to develop their maximum potential as individuals ...

In practice, some of these principles are less clear-cut than they seem. For example, normal life in the community has many different patterns and there is always a danger of imposing our own views of 'normality' and 'ordinariness' upon people unaccustomed or unable to participate fully in decision-making processes about their own future. Such doubts apply not only to provisions for mentally handicapped people but across all the client groups for which the personal social services are responsible and to which the normalisation philosophy is increasingly being seen to be of relevance. Nonetheless, the emphasis on the rights of 'clients' to be provided with individualised services in ways which respect their dignity, encourage their growth and enable them to live as fully as possible within local communities provides a basis for developing better quality services. Interestingly, it has much in common with Sainsbury's definition of the personal social services which we quoted on the first page of this book. The best practice already recognises and builds on such principles. The need is to explore and debate them more widely. It is widely accepted that effective joint working across agency boundaries depends on shared values and a shared vision. A similarly shared foundation is necessary for achieving greater coherence between social work, social care and social planning within the personal social services. It is the absence of that common vision of what is to be achieved which accounts for many of the weaknesses and inadequacies of what is on offer today.

REFERENCES

1. CYPHER, J. (ed.), 1979 *Seebohm Across Three Decades*. British Association of Social Workers, p. 1
2. THOMAS, N., 1973 'The Seebohm Committee on personal social services', in Chapman, R. A. (ed.) *The Role of Commissions in Policy Making*. Allen & Unwin; COOPER, J., 1983 *The Creation of the British Social Services 1962-1974*. Heinemann
3. SPECHT, H. and VICKERY, A. 1977 *Integrating Social Work Methods*. Allen & Unwin; CURRIE, R. and PARROTT, B., 1981 *A Unitary Approach to Social Work – Application in Practice*. British Association of Social Workers; HADLEY, R. and McGRATH, M., 1979 'Patch based social services', *Community Care*, 11 Oct., pp. 16–18
4. GOLDBERG, E. M. and CONNELLY, N., 1982 *The Effectiveness of Social Care for the Elderly*. Heinemann
5. TOWNSEND, P., 1962 *The Last Refuge*. Routledge and Kegan Paul
6. WEBB, A. and WISTOW, G., 1982 *Whither State Welfare*. Royal Institute of Public Administration, p. 19
7. JOHNSON, M.,DI GREGORIO, S. and HARRISON, B., 1981 *Ageing, Needs and Nutrition*. Policy Studies Institute
8. CARPENTER, M., 1983 *Help Me to Help Myself*. Department of Social Policy, Cranfield Institute of Technology
9. DEVELOPMENT TEAM FOR THE MENTALLY HANDICAPPED, 1982 *Third Report 1979-1981*. DHSS, para. 43
10. RODWELL, G., 1982 'Busy doing nothing', *Community Care*, 2 Sept. pp. 16–18

11. BILTON, K., 1978 'Origins, progress and future', in Cypher, J. op. cit (ref. 1), p. 21

12. SEEBOHM, F., 1968 *Report of the Committee on Local Authority and Allied Personal Social Services*, Cmnd 3703. HMSO, para. 473

13. WEBB, A., and WISTOW, G., 1986 *Planning, Need and Scarcity.* Allen & Unwin

14. SKEFFINGTON REPORT, 1968 *People and Planning.* HMSO

15. ALGIE, J., 1975 *Social Values, Objectives and Action.* Kogan Page

16. BAINS, M., 1972 *Report of the Study Group on Local Authority Management and Structures.* HMSO

17. STEWART, J. D., 1974 *The Responsive Authority* Charles Knight, pp. 33–4

18. HARBERT, W., 1977 'Moving into overall care', *Health and Social Services Journal*, 29 April, p. 745

19. DHSS, 1977 *The Way Forward: Priorities in the Health and Social Services.* HMSO, p. 28

20. COCKBURN, C., 1977 *The Local State.* Pluto

21. GLENNSTER, H., KORMAN, N. and MARSTEN-WILSON, F., 1983 *Planning for Priority Groups.* Martin Robertson; WHITTINGHAM, P., 1984 *Joint Planning in a London Borough.* Seminar paper to Centre for Research in Social Policy, University of Loughborough (mimeo)

22. WEBB, A. and FALK, N., 1974 'Planning the social services: the local authority ten year plans', *Policy and Politics*, vol. 3, no. 2, pp. 33–54

23. HATCH, S. and MOCROFT, I., 1983 *Components of Welfare.* Bedford Square Press

24. BARCLAY, P. M. 1982 *Report of Working Party on Social Workers, their Role and Tasks.* Bedford Square Press

25. Ibid. p. 198

26. DARVILL, G. and MUNDAY, B., 1984 *Volunteers in the Personal Social Services* Tavistock, p. 24

27. BALDOCK, J. and PRIOR, D., 1981 'The roots of professional practice', *Community Care*, 19 March, pp. 17–18, quoted in Davill and Munday, op. cit. (ref. 26), p. 25

28. FOWLER, N., 1984 *Speech to Local Authority Social Services Conference*

29. WEBB, A., and WISTOW, G., 1986 *Planning, Need and Scarcity.* Allen & Unwin

30. JORDAN, B., 1983 'The politics of "care": social workers and schools', in Jordan, B. and Parton, N., *The Political Dimensions of Social Work.* Blackwell

31. WOLFENSBERGER, W., 1972 *The Principle of Normalisation in Human Service*. Toronto: National Institute on Mental Retardation

32. KING'S FUND, 1980 *An Ordinary Life, Project Paper no. 24*. King's Fund Centre

33. *WELSH OFFICE, 1983 All Wales Strategy for the Development of Services for Mentally Handicapped People*. Welsh Office, pp. 1–2

Part five
DOCUMENTS

THE PERSONAL SOCIAL SERVICES: DEFINITION AND ROLE

Personal social services are those concerned with needs and difficulties which inhibit the individual's maximum social functioning, his freedom to develop his personality and to achieve his aspirations through relationships with others; needs which have traditionally been dealt with by personal or family action ('The state's principal duty is to assist the family in carrying out its proper functions', Ingleby Committee 1960); needs for which we usually ascribe some individual responsibility; and needs which call for a high level of adaptability in the helping process, rather than a uniformity of provision. If one thinks of them in terms of doing justice to others, the personal social services are concerned with the kind of justice which treats different people differently rather than the kind which treats people equally. Resources are tailored to individual or group differences rather than to the similarities between people. The personal social services seek a balance, therefore, between highlighting the shared needs of particular groups (for example, children deprived of a normal home life, the elderly) and emphasizing the individual needs and rights of one particular member of any group (this particular child, or this particular old person).

Personal social services are usually associated with the practice of social work. In Scotland, for example, the local authority personal social services are organized through departments of social work. But it is inappropriate to link personal service and social work too closely: some personal services, like the home help services, are highly individualized but are not staffed by social workers; while, on the other hand, social workers are increasingly concerned with levels of activity, such as working with neighbourhood groups, where the concept of individualization is of uncertain application.

The personal social services are concerned with the individualization of services, and with adjusting the use of certain resources by individuals, families or groups, according to an assessment of their differential needs. Although these services form only a small sector of the total range of social services they are the services most associated in the public mind with philanthropy and welfare. Both words need some consideration bearing in mind what has already been said about the social services in more general terms and about their dual concern with both the needs of citizens and the maintenance and development of social functioning, with both benevolence and control. Statutory personal social services may indeed represent philanthropic intervention, but it is philanthropy tempered by an awarenesss of the risks to society as a whole if individual and group distress and alienation go unchecked. The services are not *simply* ways of supporting people whose personal resources have broken down or have proved to be inadequate in the face of distress; they are also part of a wider programme geared to the maintenance of our present social life. They fulfil their part by emphasis on differential rights and responsibilities and on certain qualities and values in social relationships.

Similarly, the word 'welfare' in this context includes not only the attempt to offer partial compensation for physical, material or emotional handicap, but also an element of social protection. The statutory care of a child deprived of a normal home life is partly (some would argue, essentially) for his own personal benefit, but partly also to ensure if possible that he should grow up as a good (i.e. responsible, well adjusted and productive) citizen. These two functions are not, of course, necessarily incompatible; the quality of a service may be judged by the degree of compatibility it achieves. A probation officer's responsibility for an offender similarly contains these two components. Carrier and Kendall (1973)[1] have drawn attention to the possible tension between these elements of service by questioning whose definitions of social reality are actually embodied in social welfare legislation: legislation is not formulated in direct relationship to the realities experienced by the citizens whom it is intended to help; it is rather the outcome of political, administrative and professional opinions, and from these emerge a definition of what is 'best' for those in need. This is not intended to imply an attack on the personal social services or the legislation they implement: it is hard to see how legislation could embody the multiplicity of different 'realities' which lie within the experiences of service recipients. It is, however, significant how little research has been undertaken in this country to discover how the users of service feel about the personal relevance of the services they receive ... In personal social services, therefore – as in the broader range of social provision – the concept of welfare has to be seen in terms of economic, political and cultural imperatives as well as of individual needs.

---

1. Carrier, J. & Kendall, I. 1973 'Social policy and social change', *Journal of Social Policy*, 2 (3)

From: Sainsbury, E. 1977 *The Personal Social Services*. Pitman, p. 2.

Document two
THE STRUCTURE OF LOCAL GOVERNMENT

In England the number and size of the new social services departments altered shortly after their creation, when local government (excluding London) was recognised in 1974, following the report of the Royal Commission on Local Government (Cmnd 4040, 1969). The reorganisation instituted a two-tier system of local government by county and district councils and substantially reduced the number of local authorities. Two different types of 'top-tier' authority were created – county councils and metropolitan authorities. Much of England is covered by thirty-nine county councils with responsibility for the major local authority services such as education, police and fire services, libraries and the personal social services. The county councils vary in size from Hampshire, with the largest population of some 1,450,000, to Northumberland, with a population of 290,000, which apart from the atypical Isle of Wight is the smallest in terms of population, although not geographical area.

As a second tier, below the county councils, 296 district councils were created with responsibility for matters such as environmental health, the maintenance of minor roads, and housing, which is the most important of their functions. Thus, in the counties, responsibility for the provision of social services is separated from responsibility for local authority housing.

The second type of local government unit created in 1974 were the metropolitan counties, six in mumber, which covered the major conurbations in England: West Midlands, Merseyside, Greater Manchester, Tyne and Wear, South Yorkshire and West Yorkshire. These authorities serve populations ranging from over 2½ million in Greater Manchester, the largest, to some 1,200,000 in the smallest, Tyne and Wear. The metropolitan counties are responsible for matters such as strategic planning, transport, and the construction and maintenance of major roads.[1] There is also a second tier of district councils in the metropolitan counties but these, known as metropolitan districts, have much more extensive responsibilities than district councils in the counties. Metropolitan districts are responsible for services such as education, libraries and the personal social services, as well as the functions (such as housing) exercised by lower-tier district councils in the shires. The number of metropolitan districts varies between the metropolitan counties, from ten in Greater Manchester to only four in South Yorkshire. Again the size of population served varies widely, the smallest being only some 174,000 while Birmingham, the largest, has a population of over 1 million which is larger than most of the county councils.

Local government in London had been reformed earlier, in 1963, when the Greater London Council was created and thirty-three boroughs were given responsibility for providing many of the major services including the personal social services.

Thus, in a country as small as England, three types of local government unit have responsibility for providing personal social services through a social services department – 39 county councils, 36 metropolitan districts and 33 London boroughs – a total of 108 departments.

In Wales, where local government reorganisation took place at the same time as it did in England, there are no metropolitan counties. Otherwise the structure is similar to the county councils and district councils found in England and thus social services departments are found in the eight county councils into which Wales is now divided for administrative purposes ...

Local government was also reorganised in Scotland in the 1970's, consequent upon the report of the Royal Commission on Local Government in Scotland (Cmnd 4190, 1969) which recommended a two-tier structure comprising nine regional councils (plus the Western Isles, Shetland and Orkney) and some fifty district councils. Following the Local Government (Scotland) Act, the new authorities took over their responsibilities in May 1975 – a year later than reorganisation in England. The Scottish regions vary widely in geographical size and population served ...

---

1. The abolition of the Greater London Council and the six metropolitan counties in 1986 will not have an immediate and direct effect on the statutory services provided by the lower tier authorities, but it could adversely affect some or all of the voluntary organisations which have been receiving financial support from these county authorities.

From: Hallett, C., 1982 *The Personal Social Services in Local Government.* Allen & Unwin, p. 3

SCOTLAND: THE LEGISLATIVE FRAMEWORK

The Scottish legislation was a Social Work and not a Social Services Act. Importance was and is attached to this title as conferring professional recognition and characterising the nature of the service to be provided to the community. It was intended that social work services should be seen as comparable with education and health services and that each should be descriptive of its main profession. 'We are rather ahead of the English', said Bruce Millan in the Second Reading debate. This was partly because the Home Office and the Department of Health could not agree in Whitehall.

The Scottish legislation was intended by the Scottish Office to be directional and enabling, and to that extent it contained an overt philosophical element by placing a duty on the local authorities (later Regional Authorities) to promote social welfare under the authority of Section 12. This section was the distinguishing characteristic of Scottish thinking, foreshadowed in Judith Hart's speech, and later legislated for in Scotland and Northern Ireland but not in England and Wales. The section not only re-enacted the power first taken in the Children and Young Persons Act 1963 to give assistance in kind and exceptionally in cash to assist children to remain in the community, but it extended this power to all age groups so that no one was left out. Assistance in kind, or in exceptional circumstances constituting an emergency in cash, could be given to adults. In political philosophy this power had more kinship with the prevailing commitment to Third World initiatives in facilitating local enterprise and endeavour than with the giving of individual grants as an aim in themselves. This power was in no way intended to create an alternative discretionary system to social security or to provide for the administrative or professional casualties of other systems; rather it was to reflect a new attitude to the meeting of social need in the particular circumstances of Scotland. Individuals living in remote or isolated circumstances might, it was argued, more easily and effectively be helped in kind or, in an emergency, in cash and be helped less expensively through the pump-priming of local community initiatives than through the highly organised services more commonly available in densely populated urban areas. To this extent Section 12 can be interpreted as a pragmatic response to the particular circumstances of Scotland and its practical advantages were argued in Parliament. But alternatively Section 12 can be seen as important in defining legislative purpose, in creating the atmosphere, attitude and intent behind implementation. This feature of the Scottish legislation proved to be controversial. It was seen either as the 'one door' on which the troubled citizens could knock or as an open sesame to resources that did not exist. It proved to be by far the most difficult clause to negotiate with the Treasury in Whitehall because it seemed so open-ended. The Secretary of State of Scotland in proposing the Second Reading of the Bill in the House of Commons on 6 May 1968 said, 'The main thing I would emphasize here is that once the Bill is in operation it will not be necessary for the ordinary person to admit that he is in any way inadequate before feeling able to approach the local authority for help. Just as we have largely got rid of the stigma which used to attach to seeking financial help from public agencies, so it is time that we removed any stigma from the seeking of other kinds of help.'

Later the equivalent of the Scottish Section 12 seemed an attractive proposition to social workers when the legislation for England and Wales was being prepared. By then it had become even more unpopular in Whitehall. For the first two years of its operation in Scotland there was apprehension about the outcome of apparently giving a cheque book to social workers. It became manifest, however, that the power was generally being used with discrimination and only in the limited circumstances to cover the emergencies for which it was legislatively intended. The total annual expenditure quickly became minimal, allowing for inflation, although the ability to make a payment could be crucial to an individual. Nevertheless Section 12 remains an imaginative attempt to diversify the act of helping and to give purpose to legislation. The operation of Section 12 has not revived administrative untidiness in almsgiving which so exercised the minds of the COS in London in an earlier age. So far the Scottish experience does not justify such a fear. The small expenditure gives no indication of the great amount of work involved in processing applications for financial aid, particularly during the earlier years when the power was a new and much publicised one and swallowed up too much social work and administrative time at the teething stage.

From: Cooper, J., 1983 *The Creation of the British Personal Social Services.* Heinemann, p. 50–2

THE INHERITANCE: A 'MIXED ECONOMY OF WELFARE'

As industrialisation and urbanisation gathered pace in the nineteenth century, the persistent action of those who saw the need for social reform and social welfare provision found one expression in the growth of voluntary agencies.[1] Throughout this period the strength of the voluntary movement increased.[1] Despite the implementation of social policies designed to provide some measure of statutory provision for social welfare, the voluntary movement was not made redundant. Rather, it played an important complementary role in this development, evidenced not least by the establishment of a financial relationship between the statutory and voluntary sectors.[2] A changing, but surprisingly resilient, 'mixed economy' was created in the social welfare field. Voluntary agencies operated as alternative and as complementary sources of provision alongside the developing statutory services, while also pioneering some new areas of work.

This 'mixed economy of welfare' underwent its most celebrated transformation during and immediately after the second world war with the consolidation of the 'Welfare State'. It was suggested both at the time and retrospectively that this expansionist phase of state social policy would herald the declining importance not only of voluntary organisations but also of the volunteer.[3] Clearly this did not occur; both the voluntary agencies and the volunteer continued to be of considerable importance. However, marked changes occurred in the health services where the voluntary hospitals were incorporated within a national, statutory service; as in the education and income maintenance fields, the voluntary sector had ceased to be one of the main pillars supporting the super-structure. The highly expensive business of providing basic services had passed to the state.

This was not so in the case of the 'welfare services', or what we now call the personal social services. Voluntary agencies continued to provide residential care for the elderly, the handicapped, the mentally ill, and for the children – not least within the penal system as it affected juveniles. Voluntary agencies were also a main, and in some cases the only, source of advisory, domiciliary, social work and support services. The 'mixed economy' had gradually undergone a major change in the wider field of social policy, but it remained highly pertinent in the personal social services. Voluntary agencies provided much of the basic service, filled gaps in statutory services arising from deficiencies in the powers conferred by legislation, and provided community based services for many of the stigmatised groups of clients such as alcoholics.

It may reasonably have been predicted that this state of affairs would have changed even in the personal social services. Although it has taken a long time to create the basis for a comprehensive set of publicly provided 'welfare services', the legislative gaps have been repaired and the public resources committed to the services have increased steadily since the early 1960s. The Seebohm Report did for the statutory personal social services what post-war legislation did for the health, education and income maintenance services: it focused attention, concern, energy and, indirectly, resources on an untidy, ad hoc and under-financed group of services. But unlike the other major social services, the role of voluntary agencies has not changed dramatically. Voluntary approved schools have been brought into the local authority system of community homes, and financial contributions from the statutory services have become increasingly important to voluntary agencies. Nevertheless, by and large the 'mixed economy' has been accepted at worst as necessary and at best as positively desirable ...

... there remains a source of uncertainty about the relationship between statutory and voluntary organisations. A subsidiary, but important, part of the historical drive towards statutory social services represented a deliberate move away from voluntary provision not least within the Labour Party. Faith was invested in statutory services as a means of guaranteeing provision that was comprehensive and universal, professional and impartial, and subject to democratic control. The immediate post-war implementation of social policies marked an attempt decisively to move away from social policies that were partial in scope, socially divisive in action, and socially controlling by intent. Voluntary organisations were regarded with not a little suspicion in the process.[4] They have been treated as useful in practice, but peripheral in theory ...

Voluntary organisations now vary greatly and, to a degree, have always varied, in respect to their role and forms of governance. Roles vary from the pure service-to-clients function, through that of information giving and advocacy, to that of political pressure group. Forms of governance vary from the self-perpetuating clique dominating a hierarchical organisation which excludes the client from policy-making, to the client-based mutual support groups in which methods of organisation and policy-making vary considerably. The development of self-help agencies, many community-based, has been one expression of a broader disenchantment with some government policies, with the apparent remoteness of large scale bureaucracies and representative democracy, and with centralised planning and decision-making ...

This flowering of 'the voluntary sector' has two major consequences for policy-making. For the theorist, and all policy-makers have theories whether conscious or not, the voluntary organisation cannot now be dismissed merely as a threatening alternative to state services, redolent of the 'charity' and

Social work, social care, and social planning

intentional stigma which characterised earlier periods and unsubtle attempts at social control. Some voluntary agencies have acted as a powerful bulwark of the ideal of state social provision by highlighting deficiencies in the statutory services. But hereby hangs a complication; for the very organisation that may be criticised as diverting pressure from the state services by providing alternative services, may equally be treated with suspicion when defending the state services by criticising them. But within this area of confusion there are clear signs that having created basic state services and stretched them to their limits within existing resources, there is now an opportunity to re-examine and redefine the respective roles of statutory and voluntary organisations.

---

1. The number of charitable trusts along increased from 9,154 in 1880, to 22,607 in 1900. See M. Rooff, 1950 *Voluntary Societies and Social Policy*. Routledge and Kegan Paul, p. 14
2. This was made possible by Lloyd George's budget in 1914, although it was not implemented until after the war in 1919. See Rooff (1950). p. 23
3. R. H. S. Crossman, 1973 'The Role of the Volunteer in the Modern Social Services', Sidney Ball Memorial Lecture, Oxford, reprinted in Halsey, A. (ed). 1976 *Traditions of Social Policy*. Basil Blackwell
4. Ibid.

From: Webb, A., Day, L. and Weller, D., 1976 *Voluntary Social Services Manpower Resources*. Personal Social Services Council, pp. 5–8

Document five
DIMENSIONS OF TENDING

... I believe that there are four dimensions (of tending) in particular which need to be recognised and carefully explored. I will call them:

(a) duration;
(b) intensity;
(c) complexity, and
(d) prognosis.

Let me say a bit about each so that their significance can be appreciated.

It is very important to consider what resources are available for various *durations* of tending. We know, that rather different kinds of foster parents offer their services for long and short-term placements.[1] We also know that what are thought at first to be short-term foster care arrangements often become protracted and involve people in caring for a child for longer than they intended. With a view to better planning, an important study is currently being conducted by the National Children's Bureau in order to determine whether it is possible to assess more accurately at admission to care how long a child is likely to stay. As far as I know there is no parallel study which seeks to assess, say, how long an elderly person who becomes bedridden at 75 is likely to require tending. The potential commitment could be for ten or fifteen years. In the case of certain major handicaps it could be a lifetime. Why is this issue of duration so important?

First, because tending beyond the superficial level is likely to establish close relationships, affection, and a sense of obligation. These are not easily abandoned. And if, as I have suggested, additional help is liable to be reduced as dependence increases, it then becomes harder still for those who carry on to stop tending. Hence, people may become trapped in tending roles with no acceptable means of escape. How long the commitment is likely to last is, I contend, an important consideration for most of us when, and if, we contemplate helping. We may have it in mind to move house, to re-enter the labour force, to separate or divorce, or have more children. In short, there may be impending changes in our circumstances, or we may hope that there will be, or we may simply wish to keep our options open.

In circumstances where it is not clear how long a commitment will last, therefore, people may be understandably cautious in embarking upon it. It struck me when I re-read Titmuss' *The Gift Relationship*[2] that the willingness of many people to donate blood freely may have something to do with the very obvious limits to the duration and frequency of their contribution. Perhaps too, the fact that blood can be given anywhere in the country helps; people do not have to stay put in order to go on donating. In addition, of course, it may be the very anonymity of the act, which Titmuss found so commendable, that increases people's willingness to give. There are no relationships to complicate matters. Likewise requests for people to take a deprived child into their homes 'for Christmas' have been known to produce more offers than a general advertisement for foster parents. Seasonal goodwill only partly explains the differences; I think that the clear limits to the duration of the commitment are also influential . . .

In this respect there is an important difference between formal and informal help. Being employed to tend establishes a role, part of which comprises the notion of fixed duration – the shift or the hours of work – and, together with this, an element of organisational succession. When you leave, it is not your responsibility to see that a replacement is available. The informal caretaker's role contains no such clear set of assumptions, but they may be deliberately introduced in schemes such as the Kent Community Care project.[3]

In my view, therefore, those who wish to foster informal tending activities must be better able to judge the likely duration of different classes of tending episodes if they are to take appropriate action. Then, in the interests of all concerned, they should be as honest as possible in conveying this information to those people and groups whose help they seek to enlist.

How long tending lasts is not the only important variable. Another is the notion of its *intensity*. At one extreme there are highly dependent people who need constant attention. We acknowledge this in the social security field by paying constant attendance allowances. At the other end of the scale help may be needed only with very specific tasks say, once a week. The intensity of the care required is difficult to measure but it is not impossible. There are, for instance, 'activity of daily living scales'[4] which can be applied.

In institutional settings the demands of intensive tending are acknowledged by improved staffing ratios and, more generally, through the division of labour and the shift system. It is much harder to adopt such measures in the case of the bedridden old person or the severely handicapped person at home. There are rarely enough people. In these circumstances, being on call for 24 hours a day to feed, wash, lift and comfort, becomes a very demanding commitment. It is likely to limit or interrupt a whole range of other activities – employment, leisure or education. Or, because of the all-consuming nature of the task, other family members may feel deprived and resentful. We need to know what degree of intensity of care people are willing to provide – or should be expected to provide – and, related to my last point, for how long. Providing intensive care for a month is a very different proposition from doing it for a year as is doing it single-handed rather than as a member of a team, and these may be important features in the initial success of several experimental schemes for involving volunteers.[5]

The third element in my simple classification of tending introduces the idea of *complexity*. It is similar to intensity but not exactly the same. In short, it asks us to consider how far special skill is required. Superficially, it may seem a straightforward matter to make such an assessment. You actually do need to know how to lift someone in and out of a bath, and precise diets make catering more complicated. Behaviour may present perplexing problems, for example, how to cope with confusion or anger. Relationships with and around dependent people can also become complicated, even when the physical tasks are simple.

Looked at more closely other things may conspire to increase the complexity of the tending task. First, there is the context of the care. Visiting an elderly dependent person in order to look after them in their own home may be simpler than taking them into your home – when all kinds of new stresses and strains within the family may arise and have to be managed. Likewise, we know that some of the key problems that foster mothers face cluster around the new and complicated relationships which the presence of a foster child brings to the family as a whole.[6]

A second, potentially complex element in tending concerns its relationship with treatment. Care and treatment have for long been regarded as separate activities. Professional and occupational groupings are arranged in ways which reflect the division. Of course, those who offer treatment care about the people they help, but they do not often tend them. Indeed, those who counsel, treat or teach are frequently at pains to maintain a separate identity from those who tend. The distinction prevails despite the evidence of everyday experience and research findings, both of which suggest that no such sharp line of demarcation can be convincingly maintained. Successful treatment depends upon the quality of the associated tending. That has been demonstrated in the case of nursing, and there are other examples. Differences in outcomes are not found to be primarily the result of different forms of treatment but of different forms of tending. It is plain that good tending is a vital part of successful treatment but, and this is the important point, under some circumstances tending may be the treatment. That is, it is the means of recovery, adaption, development or a sense of wellbeing – a sense of being cherished and loved. Tending may well be an essentially simple activity but, especially in cases of great need, it may entail complicated and demanding relationships that have to be nurtured with considerable sensitivity and skill.

So, three of the categories in my suggested classification of the dimensions of tending are: its duration, its intensity and its complexity. The fourth and last element is its *prognosis*. Quite simply I mean by this whether more or less care is expected to be required as time passes, on whichever axis it be measured. There are profound differences between the old and the young in this respect. Progressive deterioration must be expected in the case of the old. In the case of the young a steady reduction in the need for tending is usually expected as they grow older and develop, although that is unlikely to be the case with those who are severely physically or mentally handicapped. Indeed, the fact that the normal expectations are not realised may create very special difficulties for people who look after them.

It is crucial to include the idea of prognosis in an analysis of tending. There are several reasons, One is because, at certain periods, the changes that occur are no longer ones of degree but of kind, and then different systems or arrangements for tending may be called for. Admission to a hospital or to a nursing home may become necessary; new resources have to be found, or a shift to substantial independence facilitated. The need for tending is rarely a static condition.

Another reason why it is necessary to consider prognosis if we are to entertain a realistic view of the potentialities for community tending is because different people who offer help may have different attitudes towards the course that that dependency is taking. Some may, not unnaturally, wish to see rewarding progress as a result of their tending – improvement, growth or recovery. Others may be willing to comfort and support an increasingly senile old person, or to tend the dying. We ought not to assume that tending to the needs of people with such different prognoses is equally acceptable to everyone. If this is ignored in the early stages of involvement, later changes may see a widening gulf between the predispositions of the tender and the needs of the tended.

These, then, are four practical features of the tending situation: duration, intensity, complexity and prognoses. I believe that their use, or the use of concepts like them, may enable us to consider more systematically the possibility and scale of a community contribution to tending. If their dimensions can be estimated, and if they are combined together as a set of terms on one side of an equation, then they may allow the currently unknown values on the other side to be calculated: namely, who, and how many, will be willing to offer informal help and tending in specific circumstances.

---

1.   See Parker, R. A., 1966 *Decision in Child Care*. Allen & Unwin
2.   Titmuss, R. M., 1970 *The Gift Relationship*. Allen & Unwin
3.   See Challis, D. and Davies, B., 1980 'A new approach to community care for the elderly', *British Journal of Social Work*, vol. 10, no. 1, Spring
4.   See, for example, Moroney, R. M., 1976 *The Family and the State: Considerations for Social Policy*. Longman, Ch.3.
5.   See Challis, D. and Davies, B., 1980 'A new approach to community care for the elderly', *British Journal of Social Work*, vol.10 no. 1.
6.   See Parker, R. A. 1978, 'Foster care in context', *Adoption and Fostering*. no. 93, pp. 27–32.

From: R. A. Parker, 1981 'Tending and Social Policy' in E. M. Goldberg and S. Hatch, *A New Look at the Personal Social Services,* London, Policy Studies Institute, pp. 26–30.

Document six
PROCEDURE WITHIN THE SEEBOHM COMMITTEE

The procedure adopted by the chairman was to set aside about four months for general discussion by the committee, during which period it issued requests for evidence to be submitted by the end of April 1966. It is perhaps understandable, given the pressures for a speedy report, that only four months were allowed for the presentation of evidence but unrealistic considering the delegation and consultation procedures some interest groups had to follow. Small amounts of written evidence were still being received during the summer of 1967. By the beginning of May 1966, Seebohm, in consultation with some of the members, had decided that general discussion should give way to more detailed consideration of issues, and sub-groups of the committee were formed. These included groups of children, education and probation, training and manpower, housing and voluntary organizations, organizational problems, community relations, medical issues and, finally research.

In the language of current decision-making theory the committee's approach to its task was essentially 'incremental'.[1] It started from the problems arising within the existing services, the three main questions to which it addressed itself being as follows. What is wrong with the present local authority personal social services and can improvements be made? If improvements are needed how far are these dependent upon organizational change and changes in the distribution of responsibilities? If there is a case for altering the present organization and distribution of responsibilities, what new pattern should be recommended? A rationalist, as opposed to an incremental, stance would have entailed an attempt to clarify their objectives by defining an effective family service, outlining the pattern of services which could effect those objectives and describing the steps required to reach them. There is no indication that the committee even discussed the possibilities of a rationalist approach.

During the early meetings the members began to define the problems facing them. It is clear that even before any evidence was requested, a partial formulation of the problems had been made. The committee asked for evidence to be submitted under certain headings which were suggested as 'guides' to those wishing to contribute. Under the general heading 'The strength of the case for changes' they suggested sub-headings such as 'weaknesses in the present pattern of organisation . . . extent to which these weaknesses might be remedied by greater co-ordination, better training, more resources, other measures not involving radical reorganisation; radical reorganisation'.[2] This formulation of the problem was arrived at early in 1966. Fundamental debates about the essential nature of social work and the concept of an effective family service did not take place until much later. Papers on these topics were circulated within the committee in January and June 1967 respectively[3] but the substance of neither paper appeared in the final report.

Acknowledging that in its request for evidence it might have over-emphasized certain issues, the committee invited groups and individuals to modify the proposed framework if they wished, but nevertheless it perhaps underestimated the power of suggestion. Many of those submitting evidence utilized the suggested headings, especially those who were advocating radical changes. In the final report the underlying causes of weaknesses in the personal social services are classified as lack of resources, inadequate knowledge and divided responsibility.[4] Its formulation is very similar to the early definition which implied that there were problems regarding resources, training and co-ordination. Not surprisingly much of the evidence later confirmed this diagnosis.

---

1. See Lindblom, C., 1959 'The science of muddling through', *Public Administration Review*
2. Report of the Committee on Local Authority and Allied Personal Social Services, 1968, Cmnd 3703. HMSO (Chairman: Lord Seebohm), Appendix A, p. 241
3. Family Service Committee Paper 381 & 472
4. Seebohm Report, op. cit., p. 34

From: Hall, P. 1976 *Reforming the Welfare.* Heinemann

147. If improved services are to be provided, more resources are required. Although such items as accommodation and transport are needed, the principal resource of the personal social services is manpower. Hence, as we have already pointed out, a reformed organisation should, in part, be justified by its greater ability to increase the recruitment and training of appropriate staff and to deploy them better. We believe a unified department has this advantage. Being larger it will provide a better career structure. A wider range of work and experience will be available without the present necessity of moving between departments. Movement in quest of promotion or extended experience may thus be reduced and a greater benefit derived from the accumulation of local knowledge, which we have come to consider an important factor in providing good services. It is unreasonable to expect staff to deal for a whole of their working lives with the same kind of people with specified need. A unified department should enable such a change to be made without a major upheaval for staff and their families ...

150. We cannot be sure, of course, that a unified department will secure a relatively bigger budget, but for at least two reasons it seems justifiable to hope for this. First, within local councils a committee responsible for the whole range of the personal social services would rank as a major committee. Second, more generally, the greater simplicity and accessibility of a unified department is likely to expose many needs which have hitherto gone unrecognised or unmet. Such a clear demonstration that a more extensive and better service is required on many fronts may in itself exert the necessary pressure for increased public expenditure. Even without a relatively larger budget the financial resources of a social service department ought to be more flexible. For instance, an organisation with a total budget of £100,000 should be able to do more with it than the sum of the achievements of two separate organisations, each with £50,000.

151. However it is increasingly obvious that conventional resources alone are not enough to secure an effective family service. The goodwill and the direct assistance of the community are also needed. We still know comparatively little about how best these might be enlisted and encouraged; of what can or cannot be expected of mutual aid, 'community development',

Social work, social care, and social planning

voluntary services, or neighbourliness particularly in urban areas undergoing rapid social change. What is more certain, however, is that the opportunities for involving the community will not always arise in a form which fits into the present fragmented structure of the personal social services. In this respect, a unified department should be able to adopt a more experimental and exploratory attitude to the stimulation and use of the community's potential contribution to social aid. In particular, as we argue in chapter XVI, it can and should exercise a general responsibility for community development.

From: Report of the Committee on Local Authority and Allied Personal Social Services, 1968 *Cmnd 3703*. HMSO (Chairman: Lord Seebohm), pp. 46–7.

THE RESULTING AIMS OF THE NEW SERVICE

... It was because the Seebohm Committee did not properly establish needs
that it did not properly formulate the aims of the new service. If the reader
combs the report he will not find a full and unambiguous statement of the aims
of the service. This criticism should not be misunderstood. There are
numerous statements about the possible aims of the new service, but these are
mostly 'second-order' aims. Thus, amalgamation is said to give the service
more power to speak up for a rightful share of resources within local
administration and help to make the service more adequate (pp. 30, 32–33 and
46–47). It is said to break down artificial boundaries between services, reduce
divided responsibility and lead to better co-ordination and continuity (pp. 31,
34–35 and 44–45). It is said to allow the development of more emphasis on
preventive as compared with casualty services for social distress (pp. 136–141).
A number of specific aims are also expressed in the chapters on particular
services.

But perhaps the best general statement about aims is the first paragraph of
chapter 7 of the report: 'We are convinced that if local authorities are to
provide an effective family service they must assume wider responsibilities
than they have at present for the prevention, treatment and relief of social
problems. The evidence we have received, the visits we have undertaken, and
our own experience leave us in no doubt that the resources at present allocated
to these tasks are quite inadequate. Much more ought to be done, for example,
for the very old and the under fives, for physically and mentally handicapped
people in the community, for disturbed adolescents and for the neglected
flotsam and jetsam of society. Moreover, the ways in which existing resources
are organised and deployed are inefficient. Much more ought to be done in the
fields of prevention, community involvement, the guidance of voluntary
workers and in making fuller use of voluntary organisations. We believe that
the best way of achieving these ends is by setting up a unified social service
department which will include the present childrens and welfare services
together with some of the social service functions of health, education and
housing departments' (p. 44).

An impression is given of inchoate, multiple aims and loose reasoning. Is the
primary purpose to provide family services for those who lack a family or

whose family resources are meagre? If so, there would be profound implications for the organisation of residential homes and hostels for children, the elderly and the mentally and physically handicapped. Either the residential homes would all have to be run on a 'family' basis, which is an aim that would require detailed exposition or a policy of closing them down and integrating their occupants in different types of private households would have to be followed. There would be profound implications also for professional social work roles, staffing and training. The system would have to be recast to a very considerable extent.

In opening the debate on the second reading of the Bill in the House of Commons the Secretary of State for Social Services, Mr. Crossman, plainly felt the need for a statement of aims. He said 'The primary objective of the personal social services we can best describe as strengthening the capacity of the family to care for its members and to supply, as it were, the family's place where necessary; that is, to provide as far as may be social support or if necessary a home for people who cannot look after themselves or be adequately looked after in their family. This is not the only objective of the personal social services. They have an important role to play in community development, for example. But it has been the idea for forming a 'family' service that has inspired the call for a review of the organisation of the services with which the Bill is concerned' (*Hansard*, 26 February 1970, col.1407).

He did not attempt to spell out what this view would imply for the re-organisation of services. Had he attempted to do so, or had the Seebohm Committee done so beforehand, the recommendations would have taken a different form and there might not have been a friendly welcome to the Bill from all political quarters in Parliament.

For the really important issues have been ducked in securing a precarious consensus. What kind of family relationships should the State support, and in what circumstances? How far must residential institutions be abandoned in favour of true community care? Is professional independence and the opportunity for the expression of public dissent threatened by monolithic bureaucratic conformity? Is the social worker an agent of social control or an articulate representative of minority interest and views? Should community development include a network of information and legal services, a policy of racial integration and an extension of democracy by means of local pressure-groups and protest groups?

A POLICY FOR SEEBOHM DEPARTMENTS

A radical statement of objectives would have to start by revealing the extent of inequality of resources and of social isolation and separation. Community development could be seen in terms of the equalisation of resources, the reduction of isolation, family support and community integration. I will describe these briefly in turn.

Although national social services, such as social insurance, family allowances and taxation, would be primarily concerned with the redistribution of resources, local social services have a major part to play in equalising amenities, providing special kinds of housing, supplementing transport services for the elderly and disabled, supplying aids in the home for the handicapped, delivering meals, undertaking housing repairs and improvement, and restocking houses which have become denuded because of debts, drug addiction, alcoholism or a husband's desertion. The identification and mobilisation of resource needs would be a major part of the work of the social worker. The Seebohm department should take the initiative locally in equalising facilities between different sub-areas of the authority and identifying and meeting the special needs of particular communities. For this there must be an area resource plan.

Second, the reduction of isolation. One important means of achieving this is by organising routine visiting services. The Seebohm Committee lamentably failed to understand the importance of these, particularly as a means of prevention and developing comprehensive services. Once routine visiting and assessment is started many sceptics will finally become convinced of the need to expand services. A start could be made with services for people of advanced age, later extending to all the elderly and to the handicapped, including families with handicapped children. One valuable feature of such a service is that social workers would check systematically whether people were receiving the various local and national benefits for which they were eligible. Isolation can also be greatly reduced by means of day clubs and centres, group holidays and improved methods of communication (including telephones). By extension to ethnic groups the same principles can be applied.

Third, support for the family. We have to remind ourselves that any policy aimed at replacing the family is inconceivable in present or prospective conditions. The Seebohm Committee did not consider the evidence that exists of the functions played by the family, and its strengths and shortcomings as a means of obtaining insights into policy. Certainly the 'welfare' work of the family for children, the handicapped and the aged, dwarfs that of the officially established social services. And certainly family relationships help to keep people in touch with the feelings and problems of all age-groups, and also help them achieve a sense of individual identity and integrate them with a variety of social groups ...

The aim of supporting the family, however, merges into the fourth aim, that of community integration. Any local development of a policy of family support must lead to a policy of community as against institutional care. The Seebohm Committee equivocated between the two and did not call attention to the fact, for example, that nearly three times as much is spent by local authorities on residential institutions as on home help services for the elderly and disabled. It also failed to anticipate and resolve a possible conflict between the personnel from children's and welfare department. The aim of the former has been broadly to keep children with their parents in their own homes and when that cannot be done to place them in foster homes or residential units similar in structure and operation to the family household. I believe that this policy

Social work, social care, and social planning

should be applied consistently to handicapped adults and the elderly as well, and that the subjective and objective evidence so far collected supports it. Yet because in the past the local authority welfare department has lacked the means it has practised a rather different policy of swelling the number of small residential institutions.

From: P. Townsend (ed.), 1970 *The Fifth Social Service*. London, Fabian Society, pp. 14–17

Document nine
THE COMMUNITY

INTRODUCTION

474. At many points in this Report we have stressed that we see our proposals not simply in terms of organisation but as embodying a wider conception of social service, directed to the well-being of the whole of the community and not only of social casualties, and seeing the community it serves as the basis of its authority, resources and effectiveness. Such a conception spells, we hope, the death-knell of the Poor Law legacy and the socially divisive attitudes and practices which stemmed from it. Our ideas about the relation between the social services and the community, and our proposals on some of the implications of the relationship are set out in this chapter.

475. Our emphasis on the importance of the community does not stem from a belief that the small, closely knit rural community of the past could be reproduced in the urban society of today and of the future. Our interest in the community is not nostalgic in origin, but based on the practical grounds that the community is both the provider as well as the recipient of social services and that orientation to the community is vital if the services are to be directed to individuals, families and groups within the context of their social relations with others.

477. The feeling of identity which membership of a community bestows derives from the common values, attitudes and ways of behaving which the members share and which form the rules which guide social behaviour within it. Such rules are the basis of the strong social control over behaviour which is a characteristic of highly integrated and long-established communities. Powerful social control may, of course, stifle the individual and produce over-conformity but it has been suggested that the incidence of delinquency is likely to be highest either where little sense of community, and hence little social control, exists, or where in a situation of strong control the predominant community values are, in fact, potentially criminal. Such ideas point to the need for the personal social services to engage in the extremely difficult and complex task of encouraging and assisting the development of community identity and mutual aid, particularly in areas characterised by rapid population turnover, high delinquency, child deprivation and mental illness

and other indices of social pathology. Social work with individuals alone is bound to be of limited effect in an area where the community environment itself is a major impediment to healthy individual development.

478. If the services are to meet effectively the complex range of individual family and community problems, then effort devoted to investigating the needs of an area, and to the overall planning and co-ordination of services and resources, both statutory and voluntary, is clearly of the utmost importance. The staff of the social service department will need to see themselves not as a self-contained unit but as part of a network of services within the community. Thus effective co-ordination with other services and individuals and the mobilisation of community resources, especially volunteers, to meet need are as important aspects of the administration of the social service department – and demand as much skill – as its internal management ...

COMMUNITY DEVELOPMENT

480. There are many benefits to be gained for individuals and families from the sense of belonging to a community and of participating in its various common activities, and the development of this identity and activity is important in securing an effective family service. The term 'community development' is used primarily to denote work with neighbourhood groups. Community development in this country is seen as a process whereby local groups are assisted to clarify and express their needs and objectives and to take collective action to attempt to meet them. It emphasises the involvement of the people themselves in determining and meeting their own needs. The role of the community worker is that of a source of information and expertise, a stimulator, a catalyst and an encourager ...

482. A sense of community (and all that implies) may need to be promoted amongst people for whom it does not exist, whilst in recognisable communities effort may be needed to preserve and strengthen common identity and activity. Community identity can be encouraged indirectly by the creation and development of the appropriate social and physical environment and here the social service department should be involved in social planning, acting in concert with, for example, housing, planning and other departments of local and central government concerned with new towns, schemes for urban renewal and other developments which affect the community environment. Community identity may also be developed through organisations such as community centres, clubs, play centres and tenants' associations, where the social service departments could provide technical and professional help, information, stimulation and grant-aid.

483. A clear responsibility then should be placed upon the social service department for developing conditions favourable to community identity and activity. Just as we have argued that the family often needs assistance and

encouragement to perform many of its mutual aid and caring functions, so too the wider groups to which people belong need help in developing these attributes. We are not suggesting that 'welfare through community' is an alternative to the social services but that it is complementary and inextricably interwoven.

484. We realise that a general responsibility for community development is difficult and that the means to its achievement are only now coming to be understood but looking ahead we are convinced that this must become an essential part of the work of the social service department. Potentially, such action can, we believe, constitute a major contribution to the prevention of social distress and the promotion of physical and social environments in which people find it pleasant to live.

CITIZENS PARTICIPATION

491. Implicit in the idea of a community-oriented family service is a belief in the importance of the maximum participation of individuals and groups in the community in the planning, organisation and provision of the social services. This view rests not only upon the working out of democratic ideas at the local level, but relates to the identification of need, the exposure of defects in the services and the mobilisation of new resources. The consumer of the personal social services has limited choice among services and thus needs special opportunities to participate.

492. Above all, the development of citizens' participation should reduce the rigid distinction between the givers and the takers of social services and the stigma which being a client has often involved in the past. The whole community 'consumes' the social services, directly or indirectly, as well as paying for them through taxation, and consumers have an important contribution to make to the development of an effective family service ...

494. In general terms, we believe participation has all these potential advantages. However, it is important to distinguish between the various forms which it might take. It could be participation of an active nature, where people are engaged in providing services or help; it could be participation in the process of decision, particularly in planning; or there might be participation in the form of groups aiming to publicise particular needs or shortcomings in provision: for instance, the parents of severely handicapped children. There are many difficulties in developing participation. For instance, too few members of the community may be asked to do too much; the urge to participate may be weak and in any case ebb and flow; the participants may wish to pursue policies directly at variance with the ideas of the local authorities and there is certainly a difficult link to be forged between the concepts of popular participation and traditional representative democracy. The role of the social worker in this context is likely to give rise to problems of conflicting loyalties ...

THE ROLE OF VOLUNTEERS AND VOLUNTARY ORGANISATIONS

495. Linked with the idea of the importance of the participation of consumers of the social services is the question of the role of the volunteer and the voluntary organisation. Voluntary organisations pioneered social service reform in the past and we see them playing a major role in developing citizen participation in revealing new needs and exposing shortcomings in the services. In certain circumstances, voluntary organisations may act as direct agents of the local authority in providing particular services, though such arrangements can present problems both to the local authority, which may be led to neglect its own responsibilities and to the voluntary organisation which may be prevented from developing its critical and pioneer role. Voluntary organisations will have an important part to play in social development areas especially by considering the redistribution of their resources to those areas of greatest need.

498. It is not surprising that the reaction to the increased government responsibility for health, welfare and education is to assume that there is less need for voluntary service. This is not the case. With the continuing growth of the personal social services it will be more and more necessary for local authorities to enlist the services of large numbers of volunteers to complement the teams of professional workers, and the social service department must become a focal point to which those who wish to give voluntary help can offer their services. There is sometimes difficulty in obtaining an adequate supply of regular voluntary workers, not only to meet new demands but also to replace those who have served for many years. We have little doubt that there is a large untapped supply of such people who would willingly offer their services if the job were worthwhile, were clearly defined and shown to be relevant to present-day needs even though they might involve a very modest amount of time. Volunteers would be forthcoming if it were known that, without their continued help, many of the social services might find it impossible to do much more than help the known casualties, with little hope of extending preventive action. Volunteers have an important role to play in residential institutions, such as hospitals and old people's homes, though a different one from that of professionally trained residential care workers. The recent growth of young people's voluntary service movements is among the developments which show a new response to demonstrated need.

From: Report of the Committee on Local Authority and Allied Personal Social Services (Chairman: Lord Seebohm) 1968. Cmnd 3703. HMSO pp. 147–54.

Document ten
IDENTIFYING NEED

How should the Seebohm Committee have set about the job of defining policy objectives? There are a number of awkward alternatives. First, subjective opinions can be collected from both consumers and suppliers of services about the quality of existing services, how they might be improved in the future and what new services might be added. The comments of those with direct current experience of particular services can be illuminating but the comments of others may be largely meaningless. The opinions of individuals offer little guidance to the policy-maker unless they are founded on information and experience. Even then it is difficult to evaluate them without a knowledge of the social circumstances and situation of those expressing them. The same is true of subjective expressions of need. The individual may feel deprived even if others consider he has no cause to feel like this and even if there appear to be no objective criteria to justify his feeling. Equally, he may deny any need whatsoever and yet be destitute, ill or live in squalor. Subjective deprivation is subtle and hard to ascertain, because there are social rules and situations which govern whether or not and when it will be expressed, and yet this information is not superfluous. It is one bit of vital information in planning.

Second, there are conventional or social 'views' or definitions of needs and standards of service. These too can be identified and collected. There are social norms about the upbringing of children, the care of the ill and the handicapped and the help that should be given to families who are poor. These are often implicit in behaviour, organisation and opinion rather than consciously formulated, and have to be analysed out. Sometimes they form the basis of law and regulation. For example, Government and local authority regulations embody social views about decent standards of housing and the point at which houses or flats are treated as overcrowded. Different societies (and indeed different sections of any single society) may define these standards differently but in principle the social scientist can measure the extent to which they are or are not met. He can help a society to understand how practice may differ from precept. How many in the population fall below the poverty line? How many in the population fall below the poverty line as defined socially by public assistance scales? How many are living in conditions treated by society as unsanitary or overcrowded? How many are in need of hospital care, residential care, sheltered housing, rehabilitation special schooling, domiciliary service and so on, according to criteria implicit or explicit in laws and regulations and government policy statements? In examining social or normative definitions of need the social scientist can help to bring them into the open, reveal contradictions and loose ends and show the different functions played by law, regulation, policy and custom. He can even show the degrees of efficiency with which different standards are being met and therefore suggest what might be gained with alternative emphases in policy.

This gives a rough outline of a two-stage procedure or model that might be followed in planning. Certainly we would have a basis for comparing subjective with collectively acknowledged need, and policy aims with policy achievements. We could pursue the connections between the rise of subjective deprivation in particular groups and professions, change in society's definition of need and change in society's services and practices.

But this would be insufficient as a basis for planning. Social policy would be viewed too much from within, psychologically and institutionally. Services would be judged too much in terms of objectives already defined than of those which have yet to be defined, too much in terms of needs already recognised, subjectively and socially than of those which have still to be recognised. Standards and needs have to be judged also from some external standpoint. While ultimately it may be difficult to substantiate a true objectivity, nonetheless this goal is worth striving for. Need can be shown to exist, independent of the feelings engendered within a particular society and independent of those which are recognised by society's institutions. Just as there is subjective deprivation and socially acknowledged deprivation, so there is objective deprivation. A man may not feel deprived and he may not even meet society's rules defining someone who is deprived and yet may be shown to be deprived. He lacks what his fellows can be demonstrated to have and suffers in some tangible and measurable way as consequence.

This would complete a three part model for the analysis of social policy and the production of policy objectives. But how could need be defined objectively? How could standards be evolved, independent of those that have been developed historically and which society recognises? The interconnections between the concepts of inequality and deprivation provide the best answer. Inequality has two aspects. There is inequality of resources: individuals and families fall into horizontal strata according to their incomes, assets, fringe benefits received from employers, and benefits in kind received from the public social services. Through rigorous comparison between regions and communities as well as individuals and families the inequalities in the distribution of resources can be revealed in elaborate detail, including, for example, inequalities of space at home, working conditions and school facilities. There is also inequality of social integration: individuals, families and ethnic communities fall into vertical categories according to the degree of isolation or segregation from society ...

Complementing these two measures of inequality would be measures of deprivation. In descending the scale of income or of other resources, such as assets, there is a point at which the individual's or the family's participation in the ordinary activities, customs and pleasures of the community is likely to fall off more sharply than the reduction of income. His opportunities to share in the pursuits and meet the needs enjoined by the culture become grossly restricted. As a consequence he may be malnourished, inadequately housed, disadvantaged in schooling, unable to use public services like buses and trains, and restricted to impoverished sectors of the social services . . .

Such is a possible framework of thought and analysis. How did the Seebohm Committee proceed? First, subjective opinion. Through memoranda presented as evidence and through various consultations the committee learned the views of suppliers of services. The opinions of 'all those concerned with the services' were felt to be important but the opinions of those utilising the services were not collected. 'We were, regrettably, unable to sound consumer reaction to the services in any systematic fashion' (p.21). This decision was taken, the committee say, because a research programme would have delayed publication by a year or two. But the committee took 2½ years to report, and the Government took a further 20 months to react to the report. Much research of value could have been launched, even if some of it could not have reached fruition until the months following the publication of the report . . .

The implications of failing to find out consumer opinion run deep. Some far-reaching criticisms of professional activity may be either undetected or underestimated. Some needs which are felt by individuals or groups may be ignored. Most important, some of the rights of the consumer to a voice in planning and administration may be unrecognised . . .

From: Townsend, P., 1970 *The Fifth Social Service*. Fabian Society, pp. 8–11.

Document eleven
THE CONCEPT OF COMMUNITY CARE

COMMUNITY CARE: A DESCRIPTION OF SERVICES OR A POLICY OBJECTIVE?

2.2 Possibly the most important source of confusion over the term community care arises from switches between its use as a *description* of what services/resources are involved (e.g. community care is those services provided outside of institutions ...) and *statements of objectives* (e.g. community care for the mentally ill is minimising disruption of ordinary living ...). It may be useful to look at each of these separately.

2.3. Used *descriptively*, community care sometimes means those services provided by local authority social services departments rather than the NHS. This shorthand stems from the policy thrust, stressed particularly in the late 1960s and early 1970s, of shifting the main responsibility for some people, particularly some long-stay hospital patients, from the NHS to the PSS. However, it has always been recognised that this was something of an over-simplification since community health services – general practitioners, district nurses, health visitors and so on – are a core element of community care. They contribute to community-based packages of services, provided as alternatives to long-term hospital care, as well as dealing with about 90 per cent of illness presented without any recourse to in-patient services. Moreover, personal social services staff often exclude residential care when they use the term community care. Frequently, therefore, community care is used to mean all services/support provided outside of institutions, regardless of which agency (NHS, PSS or voluntary) provides them. But even this is not quite such a water-tight distinction as it may first appear – are hostels or group homes covered by the institutional umbrella or not? And what about community-based packages of care which in relation to the mentally ill might include short spells of acute psychiatric care in hospital or, in relation to elderly people, a short acute episode (e.g. a hip replacement) which may enable the elderly person to continue to live at home, possibly with continuing domiciliary support (e.g. from district nurses or meals on wheels). A further complicating dimension is a growing tendency to equate community care with support provided by individuals in a given community to its own most vulnerable members and to exclude formally provided services, whether from statutory agencies or the organised voluntary sector.

2.4 If, on the basis of paragraph 2.3 above, it would seem that on a descriptive level there is no one predominant concept, the problem is further complicated when we turn to community care defined in terms of its *objectives*. The range includes:

- to treat conditions which do not require in-patient services and to select for referral those cases requiring secondary care;
- to facilitate early discharge of acute in-patients;
- to provide back up for day surgery or out-patient treatment;
- to provide an alternative for some of those people currently cared for long-term in hospital or residential home;
- to enable an individual to remain in his own home wherever possible rather than have him cared for long-term in a hospital or residential home;
- to give support and/or relief to informal carers (family, friends and neighbours) so that they can cope with the stress of caring for a dependent person;
- the delivery of appropriate help, by the means which cause the least possible disruption to ordinary living, in order to relieve an individual, family or neighbourhood of the stresses and strains contributing to or arising in consequence of physical or emotional disorder;
- to provide the most cost-effective package of services given the needs and wishes of the person being helped;
- to integrate all the resources of a geographical area in order to support the individuals within it. These resources might include informal carers, NHS and personal social services and organised voluntary effort but also sheltered housing, the local social security office, the church, local clubs and so on.

It will be noted that the objectives, explicit or implicit in statements about community care, range from the very specific to all encompassing approaches to care giving. The client group in relation to which objectives are set is perhaps the most important variable. But the nature of the resources available and current practice patterns in a given locality also help fashion objectives. It therefore seems likely that the concept of community care will continue to elude a definitive statement and the aspects of the various definitions described above, either descriptive or in terms of objectives, will be given prominence at different times.

From: DHSS, 1981 *Report of a study group on Community Care*. DHSS, pp. 7–9.

COMMUNITY CARE – THE RELEVANT PREPOSITION?

Our interest in the community is not nostalgic in origin, but based on the practical grounds that the community is both the provider as well as the recipient of social services and that orientation to the community is vital if the services are to be directed to individuals, families and groups within the context of their social relations with others ... The staff of the social service department will need to see themselves not as a self-contained unit but as part of a network of services within the community.

The Seebohm report made it clear that it expected the social service department to take an active role in community development. 'A clear responsibility then should be placed upon the social service department for developing conditions favourable to community identity and activity.' The report goes on to say in the same paragraph (para. 483): 'We are not suggesting that 'welfare through community' is an alternative to the social services but that it is complementary and inextricable interwoven ... '

This study has tried to spell out some of the ways in which the social services might interweave themselves with the community so as to provide a more effective service. It has in fact gone a little further than the Seebohm Report suggested, in that it has sought to involve the hospital service in the process, which fell outside the terms of reference of the Seebohm Committee.

The simile of the interweaving of the informal helping and caring process active throughout society, and the contribution of the social services, is a sound one. It takes one beyond the stage of care *in* the community at home but living in isolation from those round about. It takes one beyond care *in* the community *in* institutions, even small ones, which have little involvement or share in the community. It takes one beyond care *by* the community, if by that one is suggesting that members of the community, untrained and unaided, should be left to get on with it. It takes one to the point where a partnership of the community at large and the social services is seen as essential by both. The caring done by families, friends, neighbours or large, more organized groups of people is seen, recognized and acknowledged. An attempt is made to see both particular needs, and the strengths and limitations of the informal resources available. The social services seek to interweave their help so as to use and strengthen the help already given, make good the limitations and meet the needs. It is not a question of the social services plugging the gaps but rather of their working with society to enable society to close the gaps.

From: Bayley, M., 1973 *Mental Handicap and Community Care*. Routledge and Kegan Paul, pp. 342–3.

A PLURALIST APPROACH TO WELFARE SERVICES

33. Bearing in mind the criticism of much of the present system and bearing in mind the constraints of the present, and likely demands of the future, we would argue that a pluralist approach to the provision of some, indeed many, welfare services can provide the most promising strategy for the future. We would not argue that services that are organised and provided by voluntary and community groups are necessarily more successful; though it is often easier to stop the supply of money from government to an unsuccessful programme run by a voluntary organisation than it is to halt a statutory-based programme. We would argue that a pluralist approach more readily lends itself to experiment and innovation. We would argue that a pluralist approach can enhance participation, allowing people a greater say in the decisions affecting their lives as well as opportunities to become involved in meaningful activities. Finally, such approaches are frequently more cost-effective than statutory-based programmes.

34. What are the essential elements of a pluralist approach? First, that the job of government is to encourage, regulate and fund welfare services but not to indulge in centralised, blueprint planning. Second, that maximum opportunities should be provided for citizen involvment in the design and the provision of services. Third, that a gradually increasing number of groups (both statutory and non-statutory) should have ready access to central and local goverment funds for the purposes of providing welfare services. In addition, more support should be given for innovative and experimental programmes, having regard to different geographical needs, greater emphasis should be placed on supporting informal caring and self-help and, where appropriate, services should be integrated in order to meet the needs of the community in a comprehensive manner and in order to maximise the support available from different quarters of the community.

35. The State would not wither away. Indeed its role in allocating resources, in acting as an arbiter between conflicting interests, in agreeing on mechanisms for co-operation and, in general, securing social justice would be greater than at present. Nor would the part played by those employed in the statutory services diminish, though it would certainly change. Much more emphasis would be placed on the need to stimulate and encourage the interest

of community groups and local voluntary organisations, on the need to galvanise resources, to support and sustain those actually providing the services.

36. In summary, a pluralist approach invites a wide and potentially limitless range of voluntary, community and statutory organisations to play their part in providing services. But the role of government, central and local, remains crucial; in part as the provider, or major provider, of funds, in part as the guardian of equity and justice, and in part as the provider of expert information, training and support ...

From: National Council for Voluntary Organisations, 1980 *Beyond the Welfare State?*. NCVO, pp. 7–9.

Document fourteen
THE STATE, THE VOLUNTARY SECTOR AND INFORMAL CARE

Turning to the concerns of this conference, it makes it all the more important that we use such resources as we have as effectively as possible. As a nation we are rich in human resources – in terms of skills, concern and compassion. The voluntary sector flourishes in Britain as in almost no other country in the world. When I speak to audiences of local authorities or other statutory services, I tell them that they can make their resources go very much further by working closely with the voluntary bodies and all sorts of community groups. Indeed, is it now becoming clear that over the last couple of decades we have tended to get the perspective wrong. There has been a tendency to believe that as the statutory services grow, as more and more services are provided by public authorities, so the community can safely entrust their cares and concerns for the elderly, the handicapped and others in need to townhall and Whitehall and need not themselves bother over much. I was a little saddened to see a letter in The Times last week from a distinguished prelate arguing precisely this fallacy. He argued that the nation's failure to afford the level of statutory services we might wish betokened a lack of Christian compassion on the part of the authorities. He simply could not be more wrong. His letter seemed to me to ... (say) ... that caring is the job of the State and not of the people. I am bound to say that I am not conscious of caring when I write out a cheque to the Commissioners of the Inland Revenue or the London Borough of Lambeth. Yet, is not that the logic of the Bishop of Coventry's message? ...

In all this, it does seem to me very important that we should put the responsibility for day to day help back where it firmly belongs – into the communities in which elderly people live. It is a simple fact that most care is already provided in informal ways – by families, by friends and neighbours and never comes in to the official statistics of voluntary work. I have often heard David Hobman say when people make facile remarks about uncaring families, that there are more old people being looked after in their homes by their families today than ever before in our past. The task of the voluntary sector is to channel people's goodwill and ability to care on a wider basis; and to help the statutory and other bodies to build up what I would call 'networks of help' to make sure that support is given when it is needed and in the best way. The statutory agencies have of course an important role as a back-up to this informal and formal voluntary effort, and of course they have to act as a long stop for the very special needs going beyond the range of voluntary services. But I do see it very much that way round. The primary responsibility rests on the community; the statutory services are there to provide a framework, a back-up and special help in particular circumstances. It really is not and cannot ever be the other way round – the statutory services as the central provider with a few volunteers here and there to back them up. That simply does not represent the reality and we delude ourselves if we think that that's what it could or should be.

From The Right Honourable Patrick Jenkin's speech to Age Concern, 7.2.1980

A BASIC VOCABULARY FOR THE ANALYSIS OF THE WORK AND ORGANIZATION OF SOCIAL SERVICES DEPARTMENTS

ORGANIZATION

An *organization* is a system of people who play complementary roles and observe common procedures and policies in pursuit of some common and specific aims.

According to most sociological commentators, an organization is distinguished from other forms of human groups – crowds, cliques, families, communities – by two features. The first is the formal and often explicit nature of the internal role structure. The second is the existence of specific or specifiable aims – though there may well be vigorous discussion as to what exactly these are at any moment of time. Other features of organization are the possibilities of establishing both common procedures and common policies to guide action.

SSDs are themselves organizations by this definition. They are part of the larger organization of local government, which exists within the context of a further organization – central government.

ACCOUNTABILITY

Accountability is an attribute of a role which indicates the likelihood of the occupant of the role to be subject to positive or negative sanctions according to assessments of his performance in the role.

The accountability inherent in a given executive role, and the range of functions to which it relates, can usefully be distinguished from the *sense of responsibility* which any particular occupant may feel, and which may spread well beyond the bounds of his particular executive role. People frequently feel some responsibility for all that goes on in their social environment. Again, social workers, for example often talk of responsibility to their clients'. This may be valid, but is different from their accountability, which is clearly to their employers.

MANAGERIAL ROLE

A *managerial role* arises where A is accountable for certain work and is assigned a subordinate B to assist him in this work. A is accountable for the work which B does for him.

A is accountable:

- for helping to select B;
- for inducting him into his role;
- for assigning work to him and allocating resources;
- for keeping himself informed about B's work, and helping him to deal with work problems;
- for appraising B's general performance and ability and in consequence keeping B informed of his assessments, arranging or providing training, or modifying his role.

A has authority:

- to veto the selection of B for the role;
- to make an official appraisal of B's performance and ability;
- to decide if B is unsuitable for performing any of the work for which A is accountable.

Clear examples of managerial roles in SSDs are provided by Directors themselves in relation to their immediate Assistants, or by Area Officers in relation to their own immediate staff.

MANAGERIAL HIERARCHY

A *managerial hierarchy* is a system of roles built upon successive layers of *managerial relationships*.

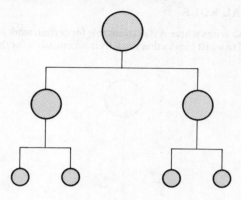

Managerial hierarchies can be contrasted with other institutionalized role systems, for example committees, coalitions of different interest groups (e.g. 'joint committees' of different authorities) or simply co-operatives or partnerships (e.g. general medical practices).

In general, the word 'hierarchy' can of course be applied to any set of characteristics which can be ordered. In organizations it can be applied to status or grade, or even to discernible increments in authority whether managerial or supervisory. A hierarchy of full managerial roles has the characteristic that the person at the top carries as clear and unlimited accountability as is possible for the work of all those beneath. For this reason it is a form which is frequently chosen or accepted by governing bodies for their subordinate executive systems where other circumstances allow it.

MANAGERIAL LEVELS AND GRADES

Grade is an attribute of an organizational role or position which indicates a particular level or range of pay and particular condition of employment.
Managerial Level (or Rank) is the level of any organizational role which is part of a managerial hierarchy.

It would seem that these concepts are easily separable, but they are regularly confused in practice. It is so often assumed in an unthinking way that differences in *grade* imply some particular relationship of organizational authority – that senior social workers automatically carry authority in respect of basic grade social workers, for example, or Assistant Directors in respect of (more lowly graded) Area Officers. This may or may bot be so. Since there is usually a need to employ more steps in a total grading structure than there is possible room for in terms of managerial levels, it is quite conceivable for managers to have subordinates at several different levels of grade, thus:

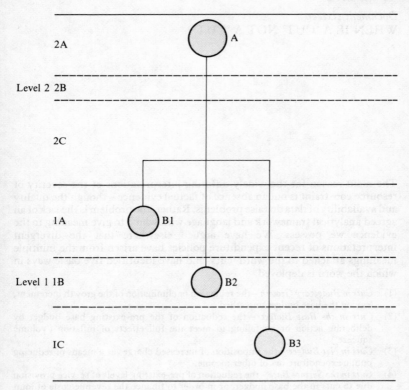

Here, two successive levels in a *managerial hierarchy* have been broken for convenience into three successive *grades* each.

From: Brunel Institute of Organization and Social Studies, 1974 *Social Services Department*. Heinemann, Appendix A.

Document sixteen
WHEN IS A 'CUT' NOT A 'CUT'?

The main reason for the widely differing interpretations of the severity of resource constraint is not an absence of factual evidence – though the quality and availability of data do raise problems. Rather, the problem is the lack of an agreed analytical framework and language with which to give meaning to the evidence we possess. We have argued elsewhere that the divergent interpretations of recent expenditure policies have arisen from the multiple meanings attached to the word 'cuts' and have identified five basic ways in which the word is deployed.

(1) *Cuts in Budgetary Growth* – the reduction or elimination of the growth increment, leaving the base budget unscathed.
(2) *Cuts in the Base Budget* – the reduction of the pre-existing base budget by deliberate action or by failing to meet the full effects of inflation ('volume squeeze').
(3) *Cuts in Net Budget* – the imposition of increased charges as a means of reducing public expenditure net of other income.
(4) *Cuts in the Service Base* – the reduction of pre-existing levels of service provision due to cuts in the base budget, or in order to finance the revenue costs of joint finance projects and capital projects coming on stream.
(5) *Cuts in Service Cover* – the failure to increase services to match growth in need.

The problem of making sense of a confused debate about expenditure policies is revealed by this simple taxonomy: central and local government protagonists have been talking about different things through the medium of a single, undifferentiated term – 'cuts'. Underlying this taxonomy – and confusion – are two basic dimensions of analysis. The first is the distinction between resource inputs and service outputs. Unless trends in inputs and outputs are clearly distinguished and movements in each are compared, we can only assume – perhaps erroneously – that we understand the relationship between the two which is effected through the production process. The need to study the relationships between input and output trends has, until recently, been obscured by public expenditure accounting conventions. Comparisons over time were possible because of the use of survey prices as a base for constant price series. However, White Paper data could be profoundly misleading as a proxy for changes in output. As we will demonstrate, they inadequately reflected detailed cost changes in comparatively small areas of provision such as PSS. And their very existence minimized the need for close examination of the relationship between input and output trends.

The recent move towards a cash basis for public expenditure accounting has at least emphasized the need to study this relationship. Expenditure series expressed in cash terms cannot be used to indicate changes in output and we must therefore make good the deficiency for ourselves as best we can. However, there is little merit in trying to chart absolute changes in outputs unless we go one step further and take account of the second dimension underlying our taxonomy. Just as inputs expressed in cash terms need to be assessed relative to price, so outputs need to be assessed relative to need and demand. Difficult as it undoubtedly is, discounting for inescapable changes in need and demand is necessary if we are to judge whether 'cuts' or 'growth' are 'real', or merely keeping pace with underlying changes in the required level of output. Our task, therefore, is to transform data on expenditure inputs expressed in absolute (cash) terms into information on changes in service outputs expressed relative to inescapable changes in need and demand.

Having distinguished trends in inputs and output, we can now re-unite them in order to create an analytical benchmark from which to assess 'cuts' and 'growth'. What we need is a definition of 'standstill' from which change can be identified. Our suggestion is that we adopt a *constant level of service output* as such a benchmark. We define this as a constant quantity of a given quality of service provision per head of the relevant population. This represents a 'standstill' relative to inescapable need or demand, not a crude standstill in absolute provision. Such a benchmark may not be politically, professionally or managerially desirable. It may seem too ambitious or too restrictive depending upon perspective and the rate of change in needs and in technology. However, it is unambiguous – in principle. Given a constant level of service output as a benchmark, we can clearly identify divergences from it as either 'cuts' or 'growth'. We can also ask questions about the implications of given changes in expenditure for outputs, or the implications of achieving particular changes in outputs for expenditure.

Perhaps the most difficult feature of our benchmark is allowing for need and demand. Our position is that changes in public expectations, in technological progress, or in treatment developments should not be included. These would constitute changes in the quality of service. The requirement is rather that a person's chance of gaining a given standard of service should not change as a result of inescapable shifts in need and demand. The most obvious source of such inescapable shifts is that of demographic change – which clearly varies by locality within an overall national picture. In addition, however, we would argue that socio-economically induced changes have to be taken into account. For example, a rising trend in criminal charges imposes inescapable demands on the services associated with law and order.

Taken together, demographic and socio-economic changes constitute the shifting 'need' pressures on systems of interlocking services. From the perspective of any one particular service within such a system, however, we must add a final and important factor: the change in 'demand' experienced by one service in a system of provision when the role of another constituent service changes. This has been of particular importance in the health and personal social services as government policies have consistently attempted to shift responsibility for some clients from the health services and onto local government.

Our benchmark is clearly a standstill in service coverage. It can be converted into expenditure by estimating the cost of maintaining coverage. There can be no ambiguity about whether we are talking about expenditure changes in 'real' terms or not. The pricing must take account of actual changes in the cost of producing the particular services in question: it is not enough to allow for generalised rates of inflation. Activity specific inflation must be estimated and local levels of inflation in particular services should be taken into account if significant variations exist nationally.

From: Webb, A. L. and Wistow, G. 1983 'Public expenditure and policy implementation: the case of community care', *Public Administration*, vol. 61, Spring, pp. 21–44

Document seventeen
CHANGES IN UNIT COSTS

Our data suggest that an annual growth of 2%, or even substantially more than 2%, has been insufficient to produce a constant level of service output. An explanation for this must be sought and an examination of changes in unit costs is the most obvious place to start. The impact of changes in unit costs is demonstrated in Table 5 below. This suggests, in bald terms, that by 1980/1 (compared with 1975/6) it cost, for example, a net additional 19% *in real terms* to produce an additional 2% in residential care places for the elderly – an increase of some 17% in net unit costs. By comparison, net unit costs for meals and home help had remained constant, while those for the residential care of mentally handicapped children has increased by 55.0%: a net expenditure increase of 91% purchasing an increase of only 31% in the number of places.

The lowest rates of growth in unit costs are to be found in the domiciliary and field services (especially meals services and home help). However, boarding out suffered a very large increase in unit costs – a rate of increase which appeared to match or exceed that of residential child care. Residential services generally evidence the most rapid increases in unit costs. Table 5 therefore demonstrates the importance of *differential rates of increase* in unit costs, with day care and field services increasing less quickly than residential care. However, it must be remembered that differential costs per case depend upon the particular package of services offered as an alternative to residential care and 'best buys' cannot therefore be deduced from these unit cost trends alone.

Two factors are important in explaining the differential pattern of unit cost increases: the impact of changes in charging policy on the one hand and of cost increases on the other. Surveys have found significant numbers of SSDs increasing charges for meals and home helps. The effect of such charging policies would be to limit increases in net unit costs. A similar effect might be observed in the case of residential care. Charges for the elderly are set in relation to social security benefit levels, thus net costs in this case are to some degree affected by the extent to which benefit upratings accurately reflect actual inflation rates: 'overpayments' and 'clawback' will respectively limit or exacerbate the consequence for net unit costs of other changes in the cost of providing a given level of service. That the costs of such provision are growing

Table 5   A comparison of trends in activities, expenditure and unit costs

Activity		Activity trends		Expenditure trends (November 1980 prices)		Unit cost trends (November 1980 prices)	
		No. of places/staff in 1975/6 (thousands)	1980/1 on 1975/6	Expenditure in 1975/6 (£m)	1980/1 on 1975/6	Unit costs in 1975/6 (£000s)	1980/1 on 1975/6
Residential:	Elderly	115.0 = 100	102	260.3 = 100	119	2261 = 100	117
	YPH	10.7 = 100	91	24.1 = 100	107	2263 = 100	117
	MI	4.0 = 100	110	7.2 = 100	158	1801 = 100	143
	MH adults	9.1 = 100	147	21.5 = 100	187	2357 = 100	127
	MH children	1.6 = 100	113	10.3 = 100	191	6658 = 100	155
	Children	38.0 = 100	85	227.5 = 100	111	5987 = 100	131
Day care:	Elderly	19.9 = 100	137	20.5 = 100	155	1029 = 100	113
	YPH	13.0 = 100	105	13.4 = 100	118	1029 = 100	113
	MI	5.5 = 100	144	5.6 = 100	164	1026 = 100	114
	MH	36.6 = 100	119	48.2 = 100	126	1316 = 100	106
Day nurseries		28.4 = 100	106	47.3 = 100	124	1664 = 100	117
Social workers (WTE)		20.4 = 100	113	168.0 = 100	133	8235 = 100	119
Home help (WTE)		42.5 = 100	110	177.3 = 100	109	4172 = 100	100
Boarding out		31.5 = 100	113	27.9 = 100	163	886 = 100	145
Meals (000s)		40.5 = 100	102	25.5 = 100	102	629 = 100	100

Source: Social Services Committee 1982, *Second Report*, Session 1981–2 Vol. 2, HC 306-11. HMSO, pp. 19 and 199.

is widely accepted: increases in the age and dependency of residents and the growth of short-stay provision have increased unit costs. Similar factors have also been seen to have affected the costs of residential provision for mentally handicapped children. At the same time, pay and conditions of service for residential staff have improved in recent years. More generally, it may be said that the growth of units costs in the PSS exemplifies the limited extent to which the caring services are able to absorb, through higher productivity, increases in labour costs derived in part from growing levels of dependency. Consequently, costs in this sector grow faster than those in the economy as a whole with the result that the real cost of maintaining a constant level of service production grows especially rapidly.

We have suggested that factors are at work which both contain and exacerbate the growth of net unit costs within the PSS. We are not able here to calculate their interaction with any degree of precision. Nonetheless, their impact is basically clear: virtually all types of PSS activity have experienced rates of escalation in net unit costs exceeding the level of inflation already allowed for in the constant price expenditure series. In other words, expenditure standstill, in real terms, would have been insufficient to maintain the absolute volume of services produced. Consequently a significant element, if not the whole, of the DHSS 2% growth allowance has been absorbed by increased unit costs rather than by the maintenance of a constant level of service outputs for growing numbers of clients. Yet the limited perspective imposed by the conventional expenditure white paper focus upon changes in 'real' levels of resource inputs, entirely obscures the inadequacy of such real expenditure growth in the face of the scale of increase in unit costs highlighted here.

From: Webb, A. L. and Wistow, G., 1983 'Public expenditure and policy implementation: the case of community care', *Public Administration,* vol. 61, Spring, pp. 34–6

Document eighteen
COMMUNITY SOCIAL WORK AND LOCAL AUTHORITIES

The ingredients of the project have now been identified as the use of local residents over a considerable time span with an emphasis on providing activities which allowed mixing and diversion combined with a flexibility which could draw upon other approaches. Of course, the personalities and skills of workers were also important but these attributes were allowed to develop because of the above features.

The next question is, can this community social work be run by local authority Social Service Departments? The query might be dismissed with the retort that they already do so. Thus in the late 1960s and early 1970s some SSDs (and previously the Children's Departments) began to experiment with Family Advice Centres. More recently they have devised 'patch systems'. A brief mention must be made of their nature.

Seven Family Advice Centres (FACs) have been studied in minute detail by Leissner, Herdman and Davies[1]. Their functions were to provide advice, guidance and assistance, usually in areas of high social need. The authors strongly advocate that local authorities should run the centres but admit that certain difficulties were encountered. For instance, some FACs appeared little different from traditional social work offices. The workers found it almost impossible to rid themselves of the roles they had executed as statutory officials. They were not adept at running playgroups, youth clubs or other community services. Further, the departments' administrators could not free them from the rules and regulations which other social workers had to observe. On the other hand, those centres which were detached from the main offices were successful in making services more accessible, in improving the image of social workers, and in stimulating some collective action in the neighbourhood.

Whatever their pros and cons, FACs have not multiplied. Indeed, even some of the seven have folded up. I regret this for any initiatives which break down the barriers between social workers and communities is to be welcomed. However, FACs are not the same as the neighbourhood project described in this essay. The former tended to be based on buildings, not homes, they were not usually available during evenings and weekends and they did not, to the same degree, revolve around clubs.

The 'patch system' is defined as teams 'functioning ... from a small geographical case and with community orientated methods of working'. Hadley and McGrath[2] go on to say that the teams are characterised by a readiness to use volunteers, informal methods, an emphasis on teamwork rather than administrative rigidity and an identification with localities with populations usually between 5,000 and 10,000, but occasionally up to 20,000.

Despite the similarities, considerable differences exist between SSD patch systems and the neighbourhood project which I have described. First, to state the obvious, the former are obliged to maintain certain statutory obligations. Second, the local authority team is responsible for the elderly, the chronically sick, the disabled and the mentally disordered in the community and are not confined to work with families. Third, the patch system does not necessarily entail workers living in and being a part of the neighbourhood. Fourth, the volunteer help may be drawn from outside the patch and hence there may not be the same emphasis on residents assuming responsibilities. The patch system, in my estimation, is a valuable attempt to make social services more accessible and more responsive to localities. But this cannot be equated with neighbourhood community social work as recounted in this essay.

So there is litte evidence that SSDs are already running such preventive projects on any scale. Even if convinced of their value, I now recognise some of the disadvantages SSDs would face if attempting to incorporate them into their set-ups. For instance, SSDs are obliged to concentrate on those children most 'at risk' and so might find it difficult to justify expenditure on clubs and activities which serve a whole neighbourhood. Of course, a local authority as a whole (in particular its Youth Department) can provide such clubs but in our project the focus is on a social work strategy whereby a minority of youngsters are mixed into activities which embrace a whole locality. Next, SSDs – because of their size and complex procedures – do find it difficult to free social workers from the constraints of bureaucracy.[3] I am convinced that the creativity, the liveliness and the commitment to initiate and maintain neighbourhood projects are more likely to occur where workers possess the minimum of statutory and administrative duties and the maximum freedom and flexibility. Perhaps these advantages are not unknown within SSDs but certainly they are rare. Not least, SSDs appear stretched to their limits and it is doubtful if many would tolerate their social workers confining themselves to very small localities. Moreover, there is no guarantee that the latter would want to live there. It follows that SSDs might be ill-placed to provide the facilities which promote diversion and mixing, the local concentration which stimulates resident involvement and the organisational freedom which allows flexibility.

If preventive projects of this nature are to be expanded, the most sensible form of progress is not for SSDs to run them but for local authorities to back voluntary bodies. Only statutory agencies have the resources to fund a large number of projects spread over the country in areas where children are most likely to be taken into care or to appear before courts. Yet voluntary organisations are the ones most likely to promote the ingredients which make for effective community social work. However, local authorities as a whole, not just their SSDs, would need to take the initiative. SSDs are not empowered to run clubs for the whole locality but councils are. Youth Departments are not empowered to engage in preventive work but councils are. Needless to say, the 1980s is hardly the moment to urge statutory bodies to increase their expenditure on new outlets. But the backing of community social work would be an investment. For a start, the local authority contribution would draw forth a contribution – in terms of finance and expertise – from the voluntary societies. In turn, they would then utilise the often neglected abilities of local residents. But, in the end, the question turns on how much local authorities are prepared to devote to projects which can prevent youngsters having to leave their families in order to enter public care. And the outcome should be measured not just in cash spent but in how much distress and unhappiness has been averted.

In 1962 I commenced my social work career as a child care officer in a local authority Children's Department (as they were often called). The following year, the Children and Young Person's Act seemed to signify the development of statutory preventive work. Looking back I realise that I – and others – made several arrogant assumptions, namely that

local authorities would achieve effective preventive work and that the contribution from voluntary sources was marginal;

within the local authorities, one department (the Children's Department) was the natural leader in this operation;

the main method of intervention was casework combined with a little practical relief;

the service would be dominated by trained social work professionals.

Twenty years later I find myself challenging all these assumptions. Without relieving statutory bodies of their obligations, I now look to voluntary societies being treated as partners. I advocate services which serve neighbourhoods rather than those which offer casework to a few selected deviants. Above all, I put my faith in projects which not only involve residents but which also give them responsibilities and powers.

---

1. Leissner, A., Herdman, K., and Davies, E., 1971 *Advice, Guidance and Assistance*. Longmans.
2. Hadley, R. and McGrath, M., 1979 'Patch based social services', *Community Care*, 11 October.
3. Twelvetrees, A. 1981 'Partners in time', *Social Work Today*, 28 July

From: Holman, R., 1983 'Prevention in the neighbourhood: community social work on a council estate', in Bean, P. and MacPherson, S., *Approaches to Welfare*. London: Routledge and Kegan Paul, pp. 192–5.

13.23 Community social work is concerned both with responding to the existing social care needs of individuals and families and with reducing the number of such problems which arise in the future. Its actual form will vary greatly from place to place and time to time, but its underlying rationale is more enduring.

13.24 It rests, as we have made clear, upon recognition that the majority of social care in England and Wales is provided, not by the statutory or voluntary social services agencies, but by individual citizens who are often linked into informal caring networks.

13.25 This recognition leads to a widening of the focus of social work attention. The individual or family with problems will of course remain the primary concern of social services agencies. The solution, easing or prevention of individual or family problems is and remains the reason for the existence of personal social services agencies. But the focus will be upon individuals in the communities or networks of which they are part. There has been a tendency for social workers to see their own clients in sharp focus against a somewhat hazy background in which other people were somewhat less than life-sized. Community social work demands that the people who form a client's environment are seen for what they are or may be – an essential component of the client's welfare.

13.26 Social workers have already moved from a focus upon individuals, or mothers and children, to seeing people as members of families. What community social work demands is that the circle of vision is extended to include those who form, or might form, a social network into which the client is meshed. Social workers have to be able to take account of a variety of different kinds of networks. These will vary in size and in the bonds which hold them together. There are many ways of describing these groupings but we have found it useful to consider the different ways in which social workers may need to view them. We think there may be three ways which are particularly important.

13.27 First, social workers need to stand, as it were, in their client's shoes and see the various people with whom that person is in touch. For example an elderly person in Haringey may have a personal network whose most important members are her neighbours on either side, with whom she talks, a son in Brighton who sees to her finances, a daughter in Enfield who comes over twice a week to do a bit of cleaning and who always brings a casserole with her, and a friend in Camden who comes over to play cards once a week. The example is of a fairly restricted network; many families are involved in much more complicated ones. None the less the aim in either case is the same: to see the people who make up the human contacts in a client's life whether they consist of five people or a hundred, whether they are local or more distant, based on relationships in leisure time or at work.

13.28 The second way social workers need to view networks is by focusing upon the actual or potential links which exist or could be fostered between people who live either in the same geographical area or in the same residential home or long-stay hospital or attend the same day centre. Staff in residential homes, day centres and hospitals need to understand and promote relationships between people who live or spend their days together, as well as between them and the people of the locality. This they often do already but it does not always receive the time and thought required.

13.29 Finally, social workers ought to keep in mind the communities of interest which develop between people who share similar interests, sometimes because they suffer from the same social problems. An example of a group who tend to be closely linked are parents of mentally handicapped children. The size of such groupings may vary. In this example they might be expected to consist of a hundred or more people who will certainly be spread across a wide geographical area.

13.30 These ways of viewing networks are not mutually exclusive. Each takes, as it were, a picture from a different angle. The first looks outwards from an individual or family, the second looks down on a neighbourhood or group who live or spend time together, and the third traces the links created by a shared interest or concern. Comparing the first with the other two viewpoints may suggest possibilities for enriching individual networks.

From: Barclay, P., 1982 *Social Workers: Their Roles and Tasks,* Report of the Barclay Committee. Bedford Square Press, pp. 205–6.

Our first need is to decide what is the essence of planning. Let us distinguish three types of decisions which together constitute any systematic approach to purposeful behaviour: decisions about what is to be achieved and by what means; decisions about how available resources are to be used; and decisions about how the day-to-day work of pursuing these ends is to be organised. Although they are only analytical distinctions and they do not form a single chain of practice, these types of decisions can usefully be labelled policy making (the choice of objectives and of a broad strategy), programming (the assignment of resources and priorities), and implementation (the execution of agreed programmes).

Planning can now be characterised thus: first, it is about constructing sets of *inter-dependent decisions* – in a *consistent way*; second, it entails a *time dimension* – a commitment to decisions through a period of time; and, third, it is about *any one* – or all – of the three types of decisions noted above. In short, planning can involve making commitments to sets of objectives, to the assignment of resources to particular uses, or to roles and schedules of work. This may seem very obvious and over-simplified, but it is distinctly pertinent to an understanding of the recent past. There was a choice: to plan or, alternatively, to proceed reactively and relatively unselfconsciously. Given the decision to plan, there was a further choice: to plan in one, two, or all three of the identified areas of decision making. The conventional wisdom of the early 1970s emphasized the importance of subjecting both policy making and programming to a single, rational and comprehensive approach. That at least was the ideal and, if planning is to be attempted at all, it has much to recommend it. Logically, and in practice, it would also have made sense to have brought implementation into the fold.

However, one of the most striking features of the DHSS approach to forward planning was the emphasis on just one of these areas of decision making – programming. The ten year plans – and, to only a slightly lesser extent, the LAPS exercise – were dominated by the commitment of *resources* through time. Policy objectives entered the picture indirectly, but implementation not at all ...

Social work, social care, and social planning

Planning is not merely about the preparation of forward plans for DHSS, but little else received close attention in the mid seventies. If we are to plan, we need to develop positive theories about what does happen and prescriptive theories about what should happen. The most fundamental justification for DHSS involvement in SSD thinking at the beginning of the 1970s was that remarkably little was known about who received what services and to what effect. The sad fact is that all the effort put into planning did little to diminish that well of ignorance. We still know surprisingly little about how home help, day care, meals services and field social work interact one with another and with people's own patterns of dealing with their problems. We still do not know whether, for example, a marginal shift of home help resources from the elderly to the mentally handicapped and mentally ill would be a cost-effective move. Nor do we have a systematic body of performance indicators with which comparatively to explore SSDs and with which to highlight potentially interesting examples of practice and resource use.

A national body of management data is certainly needed if we are to use inevitably scarce resources in an effective way, but the blanket approach to planning which involved the creation of a national data base did not produce the required data. Indeed, the processing of the national returns may well have absorbed the available manpower in DHSS and left no room for a more selective exploration of the actual use made of resources by local authorities. It is in this sense that the 1970s approach may be seen as particularly 'dirigiste'. The failure was not so much the imposition of a uniform plan on local authorities – many authorities used their discretion and followed their own notions of what was needed – the problem was rather the uniform and unselective management information which DHSS itself obtained, through which it was able to explore very few of the crucial questions.

From: Webb, A. L. and Wistow, G., 1986 *Planning, Need and Scarcity*. Allen & Unwin, pp. 109 and 111

Document twenty-one
A VALUE BASE FOR SERVICE DELIVERY AND DEVELOPMENT

DO WE NEED VALUES?

Social Services work is essentially practical. It is about *doing* for, to, with people who need help with their living. Often the doing must be done quickly: the battered child cannot wait for a measured analysis of his moral predicament. Often what ought to be done is prevented or circumscribed by legal, economic, social, political or expedient considerations. Yet in every conceivable social services intervention a choice must be made – even if the choice is to do nothing. Every choice raises the question of what *ought* to be done. Choice means putting our personal or corporate values into action.

Those individual choices embodying our values come together in the structures, processes and services through which we work. An Adult Training Centre is not just a tangible resource; it is also an expression of our estimation of mentally handicapped people (or an inherited estimation which we are not able or prepared to change). Nothing that we do escapes influence by our values.

It follows that if we are to account properly for our actions we should make explicit the values which underpin them. And if we are to act consistently together, then we should agree upon the framework of values which guide our main choices. Of course, values often have to be presented in general terms so that, even where we have common values, we need not agree on their application in every particular case. Nor do we have to share each value with equal conviction. But even where we differ in application or conviction, we would seek an agreed baseline.

DON'T WE HAVE A VALUE BASE ALREADY?

We probably do have a respectable but shaky foundation in the values, assumptions and standards of the wider society. We have values, usually implicit, derived from interpretations of professional good practice. We have a mixed bag of principles derived from other already established professions and from political, religious and other ideologies. This interesting mixture is on the whole too imprecise, and inconsistent to guide concerted and effective action.

Social work, social care, and social planning

IS THERE AN ALTERNATIVE?

Without writing a new text on philosophy in social work or rehashing the BASW document on ethics we can devise a framework comprising values, an account of the ways in which these values are distorted or unfulfilled in our society, the social services key task in overcoming this distortion and the guiding principles which derive from this task.

A framework of this kind can be accepted either as a philosophical or an ideological statement. For all practical purposes the distinction is probably academic. There is, however, a distinction which may become relevant for those who are asked to hold to these principles. If what follows is treated as a philosophical statement then it should stand up to rational examination of its validity and truth. Rational examination should clarify and develop it, or reveal its limitations. On the other hand, if it is treated as an ideology then it is not capable of support or justification from reason. Conversion, unmediated by rational persuasion, is what is required.

A FRAMEWORK OF PRINCIPLES

A Primary Value

We respect the value and dignity of every human being irrespective of origin, status, sex, age, belief or contribution to society.

(1) Every human being should have opportunities to sustain and enhance his/her value and dignity.
(2) Respect should be expressed in actively promoting those opportunities for human beings who have lost, forfeited or been deprived of them.

Key Task for Social Service Workers

Many adults and children lose, forfeit or are deprived of their value and dignity. The causes may range from the constitutional, through the personal and interpersonal, to those arising from the attitudes and structures of our society, or any combination of these. The consequences for the individuals are exclusion from the normal processes of ordinary life and existence as lesser human beings.

People who lose their value and dignity also lose access to approved means and opportunities for reclaiming their value. Their apparently valueless and undignified behaviour as lesser humans, or their unsuccessful use of disapproved means, provokes further devaluation from society.

The key task for social services workers is to break this vicious downward spiral by providing access to means and opportunities which restore personal value and dignity in ways which are used, approved and preferred by most people.

Principles

Services aiming to restore, sustain or enhance value and dignity for people who need our help should thus:

(1) be based on an assessment of what these people want and need, and what most people approve and prefer;

(2) be local so that people are not removed from their homes or community unless they so choose;

(3) support and supplement existing positive personal and social relationships;

(4) provide shelter based on ordinary domestic arrangements;

(5) be comprehensive so that the needs of people are met across a very wide area of their lives in co-ordinated and continuous ways;

(6) impose no restrictions beyond those compatible with each individual's readiness to grow in ability, independence and self-determination.

From: Derbyshire Social Services Department, n.d. A Value Base for Service Delivery and Development, Derbyshire County Council (Mimeo).

SELECT BIBLIOGRAPHY

ABRAMS, P., Dec. 1977 'Community care: some research problems and policies' *Policy and Politics*, 6.2

ABRAMS, P., 1978 *Neighbourhood Care and Social Policy*. Volunteer Centre

ABRAMS, P., 1981 *Action for Care*. Volunteer Centre

BAILEY, R. and BRAKE, M., 1975 (eds) *Radical Social Work*. Edward Arnold

BARCLAY, P., 1982 *Social Workers: Their Role and Tasks*, Report of a Working Party. Bedford Square Press

BARRETT, S. and FUDGE, C. (eds) *Policy and Action: essays on the implementation of public policy*. Methuen

BAYLEY, M., 1973 *Mental Handicap and Community Care*. Routledge and Kegan Paul

BAYLEY, M., 1977 *Community-Oriented Systems of Care*. Report to the Personal Social Services Council

BAYLEY, M., 1982 'Helping care to happen in the community', in Walker, A. (ed.), *Community Care*. Basil Blackwell and Martin Robertson

BEAN, P., MACPHERSON, S. (eds), 1983 *Approaches to Welfare*. Routledge and Kegan Paul

BEAN, P. (ed.), 1983 *Mental Illness, Changes and Trends*. John Wiley

BEBBINGTON, A. C. 1979 'Changes in the provision of social services to the elderly in the community over fourteen years', *Social Policy and Administration*, vol. 13, no. 2, pp. 11–123

BILLIS, D. *et al.*, 1980 *Organising Social Services Departments*. Heinemann

BILLIS, D., BROMLEY, G., HEY, A. and ROWBOTTOM, R., 1980 *Organising Social Services Departments*. Heinemann

BOLGER, S., CORRIGAN, P., DOCKING, J. and FROST, N., 1981 *Towards Socialist Welfare Work*. Macmillan

BOOTH, T. A., 1979 *Planning for Welfare: Social Policy and the Expenditure Process*. Basil Blackwell and Martin Robertson

BREWER, C. and LAIT, J., 1980 *Can Social Work Survive?* Temple Smith

CHALLIS, D. and DAVIES, B., 1980 'A new approach to community care for the elderly', *British Journal of Social Work*, vol. 10, no. 1, pp. 1–18

COLLINS, A. and PANCOAST, D. L., 1976 *Natural Helping Networks: A Strategy for Prevention*. National Association of Social Workers, Washington

COOPER, J., 1983 *The Creation of the British Personal Social Services 1962–74*. Heinemann

CORRIGAN, P. and LEONARD, P., 1978 *Critical Texts in Social Work and the Welfare State*. Macmillan Press

CORRIGAN, P. and LEONARD, P., 1978 *Social Work Practice Under Capitalism: A Marxist Approach*. Macmillan

REPORT OF A LABOUR PARTY STUDY GROUP (Chairman: Lord Longford), 1964 *Crime, a challenge to us all*

CURRIE, R. and PARROTT, B., 1981 *A Unitary Approach to Social Work – Application in Practice*. British Association of Social Workers

CYPHER, J. (ed.), 1979 *Seebohm Across Three Decades*. British Association of Social Workers

DARVILL, G. and MUNDAY, B., 1984 *Volunteers in the Personal Social Services*. Tavistock

DAVIES, B., 1980 *The Cost Effective Imperative: The Social Services and Volunteers*. The Volunteer Centre

DAVIES, B., and FERLIE, E., 1984 'Efficiency-improving innovations in social care: social services departments and the elderly', *Policy and Politics*, vol. 10, no. 2, pp. 181–204

DAVIES, L., 1982 *Three Score Years . . . and Then?* Heinemann

DAVIES, M., 1974 'The current status of social work research', *British Journal of Social Work*, 4, pp. 281–303

DHSS, 1972 *Local Authority Social Services Ten Year Plans 1973–1983*, Circular 35/72. Department of Health and Social Security

DHSS, 1976 *Priorities in the Health and Personal Social Services*. HMSO

DHSS, 1977 *The Way Forward: Priorities in the Health and Social Services*. HMSO

DHSS, 1978 *Social Services Teams: The Practitioner's View*. HMSO

DHSS, 1980 *Mental Handicap: Progress, Problems and Priorities*. Department of Health and Social Security

DHSS, 1981 *Care in the Community: A Consultative Document on Moving Resources for care in England*. Department of Health and Social Security

DHSS, 1981 *Care in the Community*. HMSO

DHSS, 1981 *Report of a Study Group on Community Care*. Department of Health and Social Security

DHSS, 1983 *The Social Work Service of DHSS: A Consultative Document*. HMSO

EQUAL OPPORTUNITIES COMMISSION, 1980 *The Experience of caring for Elderly and Handicapped Dependents*. A Survey Report

FERLIE, E., and JUDGE, K., 1981 'Retrenchment and rationality in the personal social services', *Policy and Politics*, **9**(3), pp. 313–14

FISCHER, J., 1973 'Is casework effective?', *Social Work*, vol. 8, no. 1, pp. 5–20

FISCHER, J., 1978 'Does anything work?' *Journal of Social Services Research*, vol. 1, no. 3, pp. 215–243

GLADSTONE, F., 1980 *Voluntary Action in a Changing World*. Bedford Square Press

GLENDINNING, C., 1983 *Unshared Care: Parents and their Disabled Children*. Routledge and Kegan Paul

GLENNERSTER, H., 1975 *Social Service Budgets and Social Policy*. Allen and Unwin

GLENNERSTER, H., KORMAN, N. and MARSLEN-WILSON, F., 1983 *Planning for Priority Groups*. Martin Robertson

GOLDBERG, E. M. and CONNELLY, N. (eds), 1981 *Evaluative Research in Social Care*. Heinemann

GOLDBERG, E. M. and HATCH, S. (eds), 1981 *A New Look at the Personal Social Services*, Policy Studies Institute

GOLDBERG, E. M. *et al.*, 1970 *Helping the Aged*. Allen and Unwin

GOLDBERG, E. M. and WABURTON, R. W., 1979 *Ends and means in Social Work*. Allen and Unwin

GOLDSTEIN, H., 1973 *Social Work Practice: A Unitary Approach*. Columbia University, South Carolina Press

GOODMAN, A. A., 1976 *Charity Law and Voluntary Organisation*. Bedford Square Press

HADLEY, R. and McGRATH, M. (eds), 1980 *Going Local: Neighbourhood Social Services*. Bedford Square Press

HADLEY, R., 1981 *Social Welfare and the Failure of the State*. George Allen and Unwin

HALL, A. S., 1974 *The Point of Entry: a study of client reception in the Social Services*. Allen and Unwin

HALL, P., 1976 *Reforming the Welfare*. Heinemann

HALLETT. C., 1982 *The Personal Social Services in Local Government*. George Allen and Unwin

HATCH, S., 1980 *Outside the State*. Croom Helm

HATCH, S. and MOCROFT, I., 1983 *Components of Welfare*. Bedford Square Press

HEDLEY, R., and NORMAN, A., 1982 *Home Help: Key Issues in Service Provision*. Centre for Policy on Ageing

HENDERSON, P., JONES, D., and THOMAS, D. N. (eds), 1980 *The Boundaries of Change in Community Work*, George Allen and Unwin

HERAUD, B., 1970 *Sociology and Social Work: Perspectives and Problems*. Pergamon Press

HUNT, A., 1978 *The Elderly at Home*. HMSO

JOHNSON, M., DI GREGARIO, S. and HARRISON, B., 1981 *Ageing, Needs and Nutrition*. Policy Studies Institute

JONES, G., (ed.) 1980 *New approaches to the Study of Central Local Government Relationships*. Gower (for the Social Sciences Research Council)

JONES, K., 1972 *A History of the Mental Health Services*. Routledge and Kegan Paul

JORDAN, B., 1979 *Helping in Social Work*. Routledge and Kegan Paul

JORDAN, B. and PARTON, N. (eds), 1983 *The Political Dimensions of Social Work*. Blackwell

JORDAN, B., 1984 *Invitation to Social Work*. Blackwell

JUDGE, K., 1978 *Rationing Social Services*. Heinemann

JUDGE, K., 1982 'The public purchase of social care: British confirmation of American experience', *Policy and Politics*, **10**(4), pp. 397–417

KING'S FUND, 1980 *An Ordinary Life*. Project Paper no. 24, King's Fund Centre

MACDONALD, E., 1980 *Changing Patterns of Care, Report on Services for the Elderly in Scotland*. Scottish Home and Health Department, HMSO

MALLEN, E. J. and DUMPSON, J. R., 1972 *Evaluation of Social Intervention*. Jossey-Boss

MAYER, J. E. and TIMMS, N., 1970 *The Client Speaks*. Routledge and Kegan Paul

MEYER, H. *et al.*, 1965 *Girls at Vocational High*. Ressell Sage

MITTLER, P., 1979 *People not Patients*. Methuen

MORONEY, R., 1976 *The Family and the State: Considerations for Social Policy.* Longman

NISSEL, M. and BONNERJEA, L., 1982 *Family Care of the Handicapped Elderly.* Policy Studies Institute

PACKMAN, J., 1981 *The Child's Generation: Child Care Policy in Britain.* Basil Blackwell, 2nd edn

PARSLOE, P., 1981 *Social Services Area Teams.* Allen and Unwin

PAYNE, M., 1979 *Power, Authority and Responsibility in Social Services.* Macmillan

PINCUS, A. and MINAHAN, A., 1973 *Social Work Practice: Model and Method.* Peacock, Illinois

PINKER, R. A., 1978 *Research Priorities in the Personal Social Services.* SSRC

PLANK, D., 1977 *Caring for the Elderly.* Greater London Council

REID, W. and SHYNE, A., 1969 *Brief and Extended Casework.* New York: Columbia University Research

REPORT OF THE COMMITTEE ON LOCAL AUTHORITY AND ALLIED PERSONAL SOCIAL SERVICES (Chairman: Lord Seebohm), 1968 Cmnd 3703. HMSO

REPORT OF THE COMMITTEE ON THE FUTURE OF VOLUNTARY ORGANISATIONS (Chairman: Lord Wolfenden), 1978 *The Future of Voluntary Organisations.* Croom Helm

REPORT OF THE KILBRANDON COMMITTEE, 1964 *Children and Young Persons in Scotland,* Cmnd 2306. Scottish Home and Health Department and Scottish Education Department

REPORT OF THE COMMITTEE (Chairman: P. Barclay), 1982 *Social Workers: Their Role and Task.* Bedford Square Press

RHODES, R. A. W., 1981 *Control and Power in Central-Local Government Relations.* Gower

RICHARDSON, A. and GOODMAN, M., 1982 *Self Help and Social Care: Mutual Aid Organisation in Practice.* Policy Studies Institute

ROBINSON, D. and HENRY, S., 1977 *Self Help and Health.* Martin Robertson

ROBINSON, F. and ABRAMS, P., 1977 *What We Know About The Neighbours.* Rowntree Research Unit

ROBINSON, T., 1978 *In Worlds Apart.* Bedford Square Press

ROSSITER, C. and WICKS, M., 1982 *Crisis or Challenge? Family Care, Social Policy and Elderly People.* Study Commission on the Family

ROWBOTTOM, R. W., 1973 'Organising social services: hierarchy or ... ?', *Public Administration,* vol. 15, Autumn, pp. 291–305

ROWBOTTOM, R., HEY,A. and BILLIS, D., 1974 *Social Services Departments: developing patterns of work and organisation.* Heinemann

SAINSBURY, E., 1975 *Social Work With Families.* Routledge and Kegan Paul

SAINSBURY, E., 1977 *The Personal Social Services.* Pitman

SIMPKIN, M., 1979 *Trapped Within Welfare: Surviving Social Work.* Macmillan

SOCIAL SERVICES ORGANISATION RESEARCH UNIT AND BRUNEL INSTITUTE OF ORGANISATION AND SOCIAL STUDIES (BIOSS), 1974 *Social Services Departments: Developing Patterns of Work and Organisation.* Heinemann

SPECHT, G. and VICKERY, A., 1977 *Integrating Social Work Methods.* Allen and Unwin

STEVENSON, O., 1978 *The Realities of a Caring Community.* Eleanor Rathbone Memorial Lecture

THE GOVERNMENT AND THE VOLUNTARY SECTOR: A CONSULTATIVE DOCUMENT, 1976. HMSO

THE VOLUNTEER CENTRE, 1976 *Creative Partnerships: A Study in Leicestershire of Voluntary Community Involvement.* The Volunteer Centre

THURZ, D., and VIGILANTE, J. L., 1975 and 1976 *Meeting Human Needs.* Sage, Vols 1 and 2

TINKER, A., 1981 *The Elderly in Modern Society.* Longman

TITMUS, R. M., 1976 *Commitment to Welfare.* Allen and Unwin, 2nd edn

TOPLISS, E., 1982 *Social Responses to Handicap.* Longman

TOWNSEND, P., 1970 *The Fifth Social Service.* Fabian Society

BOSANQUET, N. and TOWNSEND, P., (ed.), 1980 *Labour and Equality.* Heinemann

VICKERY, A. and SPECHT, H., (eds), 1977 *Integrating Social Work Methods.* Allen and Unwin

WADE, B., SAWYER, S. and BELL, J., 1983 *Dependency with Dignity.* Bedford Square Press

WALKER, A. (ed.), 1982 *Community Care.* Basil Blackwell and Martin Robertson

WALKER, A., (ed.), 1982 *Public Expenditure and Social Policy: An Examination of Social Spending and Priorities.* Heinemann

WARHAM, J., 1977 *An Open Case,* Routledge and Kegan Paul

WEBB, A. 1980 *Collective action and Welfare Pluralism.* Association of Researchers in Voluntary Action and Community Involvement (ARVAC)

WEBB, A. L. 1985 'Alternative futures for social policy and state welfare', in Berthoud, R. (ed.), *Challenges to Social Policy*. Gower

WEBB, A. L. and WISTOW, G., 1982 'The personal social services: incrementalism, expediency or systematic social planning?' in Walker, A. (ed.), *Public Expenditure and Social Policy*. Heinemann

WEBB, A. L. and WISTOW, G., 1982 *Whither State Welfare? Policy and Implementation in the Personal Social Services 1979–80*. Royal Institute of Public Administration

WEBB, A. L. and WISTOW, G., 1983 'Public expenditure and policy implementation: the case of community care', *Public Administration*, vol. 63, Spring, pp. 21–44

WEBB, A. L. and WISTOW, G., 1985 'Structuring local policy environments: central–local relations in the personal social services', in Ranson, S., *The Changing Relationship Between Central & Local Government*. Allen & Unwin

WEBB, A. L. and WISTOW, G., 1986 *Planning, Need and Scarcity: Essays on the Personal Social Services*. Allen and Unwin

WELSH OFFICE, 1983 *All Wales Strategy for the Development of Services for Mentally Handicapped People*. Welsh Office

WILDING, P., 1982 *Professional Power and Social Welfare*. Routledge and Kegan Paul

WISTOW, G., 1983 'Joint finance and community care: have the incentives worked?', *Public Money*, vol. 3, no. 2, pp. 33–7

WOLFENSBERGER, W., 1972 *The Principles of Normalisation in Human Services*. Toronto: National Institute on Mental Retardation

WOOTON, B., 1980 *Social Science and Social Pathology*. Allen and Unwin

YOUNG, K., (ed.), 1983 *National Interests and Local Government*. Heinemann

INDEX